IRELAND NOW

WILLIAM FLANAGAN

IRELAND NOW

Tales of Change from the Global Island

University of Notre Dame Press • Notre Dame, Indiana

Designed by Wendy McMillen
Set in 11.8 / 14 Fournier by Four Star Books
Printed on 60# Williamsburg Recycled Paper by Versa Press

Library of Congress Cataloging-in-Publication Data

Flanagan, William G.
   Ireland now : tales of change from the global island / William Flanagan.
     p. cm.
   Includes bibliographical references.
   ISBN-13: 978-0-268-02886-2 (pbk. : alk. paper)
   ISBN-10: 0-268-02886-9 (pbk. : alk. paper)
   1. Ireland—Economic conditions.   2. National characteristics, Irish.
3. Ireland—Social conditions.   4. Ireland—Social life and customs—
20th century.   5. Ireland—Social life and customs—21st century.   I. Title.
   DA925.F53   2007
   941.70824—dc22

                                 2007019491

Contents

Acknowledgments

Putting this book together has been a pleasure for me. For others, it involved a certain amount of effort—making contacts, reading drafts, opening their lives, and searching their thoughts. Readers will be able to recognize how indebted I am to many of those who appear on these pages. Others' contributions will not be as evident, but I know the value and will always be grateful for their work in reading, commenting, encouraging. Thank you, Cauvery Madhavan, Lorna Gleasure, and Khalid Sallabi, for your help in making contacts, as well as for your own stories. Thank you, Mary Katherine Freeston and Resmiye Oral, for your able assistance in research and recording, for putting people at ease in your presence. Thanks to Al Fisher, Josef Gugler, Robert Marrs, Rick Hills, Nukhet Yarbrough, Tim Flanagan, and Karen Wachsmuth for reading and commenting on parts of the draft. Thank you, Connie Birmingham, for slogging through the whole thing and liking it. Thanks to Beth Wright of Trio Bookworks for a great job of copyediting. And my thanks to the people at the University of Notre Dame Press: director Dr. Barbara J. Hanrahan, managing editor Rebecca R. DeBoer, and design manager Margaret A. Gloster. And I am especially grateful to all the people in the book for guiding us through the way a profoundly changed Ireland has looked and felt in their lives.

IRELAND NOW

Introduction

A man in bright green warm-ups made his way slowly along the main street of a small town in the west of Ireland. He wore a baseball cap with an Irish saying on the front of it, and he carried a polished blackthorn stick. He paused, then entered a shop that sold souvenirs and gifts. He poked around, waiting for the shopkeeper to be done with her few customers. When the place appeared to be otherwise empty, he approached the woman behind the counter as if he were going to ask for directions somewhere, as if he might be lost. He said in an American accent that he had spent the past week going up and down the coast, from one town to the next. Everywhere he stopped Pakistanis or Indians were running the shops and hotels. There were people with Eastern European accents. He thumped his stick on the floor and demanded, "What's become of Ireland?"

The traveler had come looking for something dear to him that had never existed in the place where he had come to look for it. The Irish place he was looking for lived in the once-a-year parade in New York or Boston (site of the first St. Patrick's Day celebration in the United States in 1737) or other American cities. He was appropriately turned out for such an occasion. The shopkeeper was no help to him. She said quietly that Ireland had become home to people from all over the world now, and she thought that they ought to be welcomed as long as they went to work and behaved themselves and that most of them were very good in that way. She was done saying her piece on that topic and so busily tidied up the already tidy sales counter, wishing she could please her customer and knowing that her answer would not. It didn't. He shook his head, the bill of his green baseball cap exaggerating the movement, the Irish saying swinging side to side, negating itself as he left the shop.

Maureen Dezell laments the orchestrated marketing of a particular version of American Irishness, the St. Patrick's Day–themed version: "Descendants of dreamers and tale-tellers in the land of money, myth, and Disney, the American Irish early on developed a capacity for romanticizing their heritage and sentimentalizing themselves" (2000, 18). Ireland in the United States became transformed in popular music and on the stage into the Emerald Isle, Mother Ireland, a place where in the twice-removed memory of immigrant descendants the sod had belonged to those who worked it—not to the landlords. During the Easter Rising in 1916, while Dublin was devastated and the rebellion's leaders were executed, "Americans were whistling and singing the popular 'Ireland Must be Heaven for My Mother Came From There'" (23–24). It is not that the green man was mistaken when he dressed himself that morning and set out to find his Ireland: that Ireland exists, in himself and millions of others who share a similar imagery of the homeland. His only mistake was to look for it in the country his predecessors came from, rather than looking for it in the country they had come to, where such an image of Ireland was pieced together and magnified and marketed over the years.

It is understandable that he assumed something like the American sense of Irish culture might be reflected in the Irish Republic. There are ten times as many Irish Americans as native island Irish, and the American cousins come to Ireland in droves, paying good money to get what they have come for—a lot of money. Nearly a million North Americans visit Ireland each year, and, according to the Minister for Arts, Sports, and Tourism, they tend to stay longer and spend more cash compared to other visitors (*Irish Times*, August 24, 2006). Understandably, the tourist board and well-developed tourist industry do try to serve up what they have come looking for. But it is becoming more and more difficult to prop up the imagery of the tired old sod: day-to-day Ireland is about business and economic expansion. It is the poster child of European Union prosperity. Old Ireland is drifting away, and the international enterprise zone that the country has become clashes with the bucolic and easygoing reputation that has characterized the place in the collective memory of its dispersed sons and daughters. Most of the people in the land of a thousand welcomes have just so much time for nostalgia and tourism's fancies these days, as they get on with trying to get ahead—or just trying to make ends meet.

The man walking the little town appeared to be in his sixties. He had spent a life as a proud Irishman in whatever region of the United States he called home, and he was obviously steeped in the culture he identified with back there. He was a perfectly authentic Irishman. He grew up in a place where millions of Irish immigrants over the course of two centuries have left their mark on town life, where their once-a-year March celebration of the shiny green legacy is a time when Irish immigrant descendants take to the streets to show the world that they remember and are proud of who they are, of their origins. When you come back to Ireland, of course you want to show that you're Irish; you put on the green, and you go to find the place that fits the expectations that you've brought with you. It is the familiar Ireland, your sense of place, the homeplace. People bring other Irelands, many, many others, not all in mummer's parade greens, all equally—none more—authentic. Authenticity, the dignified truth of who we are at the core of our being, is not open to question from outsiders. The experience of being Irish is steeped in centuries of Irish being, of history and culture, wherever it may have been lived. The green man who wondered what all these "foreigners" were doing living in the Ireland he had rented for his holidays tells us something valuable about the fragmented nature of what Ireland is in the minds of people for whom that meaning is an important part of who they are.

If not an American version of Ireland, the visitor might more appropriately have expected to find an Irish version of America in the land of his kinfolk. The reverse migration of U.S. capital investment to Ireland, especially since the early 1990s, means that American firms have materially reinforced the ties between the countries and the cultures. The effect of the United States buying up a good share of the Irish economy has indeed worked to make life more like that in the United States. Economic globalization generates a prosperity that makes the cosmopolitan lifestyle pretty much the same everywhere. In 2006, over six hundred U.S.-headquartered firms were operating in Ireland, representing a total investment of $73 billion. They directly employed 5 percent of

Irish workers while supporting an additional 250,000 jobs in Irish businesses (*Irish Times,* May 25, 2006). In the 1990s U.S. and other foreign companies played a major role in fueling Ireland's economic takeoff, drawn by tax incentives and a well-educated and employment-starved English-speaking workforce. The boom, in fact, led to the labor shortages that have attracted immigrants from all over the world—like the people the disappointed traveler had found in the shops and hotels. The 2006 Irish census found that the population of the Republic had topped four million for the first time since 1871; four hundred thousand of those counted were foreign nationals. The census forms were printed in eleven foreign languages, including Arabic, Chinese, Polish, and Latvian (*Irish Times,* July 19, 2006).

The economic expansion that has led to the new levels of prosperity and international-style consumerism has caused, among other things, an increase in serious inequalities within the population. Those who have been stuck in place in parts of the economy that have lagged behind the galloping growth sectors struggle to pay their bills. The upwardly mobile have begun to complain that the hustle involved in keeping up with the cost of living leaves them with no time to live the kinds of lives they were used to. As we will see in the chapters that follow, increases in personal wealth and consumerism are blamed for an increase in crime and (coupled with the effects of scandal) a serious decline in the prominence of the Roman Catholic Church in the lives of the people. The economic transformation has led to a precipitous decline in the number of farmers as young people refuse to stay on the farm. This is the world the green man stepped into.

In the 1970s I brought my own version of Ireland with me when I went to teach sociology in Cork. Since then, during my regular visits, I have watched and listened to the emergence of a New Ireland. I have been especially interested in the stories the Ireland Irish have told me about how their lives have recently been altered. In the late 90s I began to write the stories down. Then I went looking for more stories to add to those that appeared to have come looking for me. I became absorbed by the enterprise, and it drew me away from other things I was writing. As this book took shape around what I learned, I sought out particular people, my visits became more purposeful, the storytelling more focused on particular themes. At some point it occurred to me that the way this work evolved paralleled the way my own unlooked-for developing experience as an Irishman progressed.

I hadn't thought to look for a teaching job in Ireland, but faculty in my graduate program, who knew of the opening at University College Cork in 1976, thought that, given my family name, I would be well-suited for it. I was hired over the phone and found myself, without plan, re-emigrating "back" to Ireland after a span of a generation. I had not looked to do a book on social change in Ireland, but the work found me. The stories I had heard over the years were too valuable as accounts of cultural upheaval and personal change to be set aside for other work. Having become, by degrees, more Irish in some peculiar mixture of professional sociology and ethnic awareness, I became a part of my work and it a part of who I was. If I had any personal suitability for such a project, I think it was that the people who talked to me could see that I had an earnest interest in what they had to say about themselves. The interest was based on the gap of the generation that lay between my emigrant grandfather and myself, my growing need to fill in the blanks and bring myself up-to-date.

What we have in this book, for the most part, are a number of reflections on what the Ireland Irish think Ireland is and what it is becoming. We discover what they think is happening to the place that they live in as they tell us about how life has changed. It is in that sense largely a book based on stories. These are stories as they were told to me and as I heard them and organized them as a particular person of some mixture of Irish descent who was trying to work out some personal and global issues. So this is also in part my story—but not to worry: I try to keep my part in this small in comparison to the bulk of the stories given to me by those I have met.

Although I am a sociologist, this is not strictly speaking a work in social science. If a few principles from sociology creep in here and there, they may pass unnoticed except for those who are aware of them. This is an exercise in discovery, written for any reader who has an interest in Ireland, in the way the world is changing, and how we are all connected in surprising and interesting ways in this new global machine for generating wealth and leveling cultures. Since it is a work in storytelling, there has been no attempt to formally sample the population. The strategy was to find some interesting people in certain categories and hope that they would talk to me. Everybody did. Most were enthusiastic, though a few perhaps a little uncertain, when they discovered what I was up to and that their stories might appear in print. Some of the people in the book are identified by name, when there is no real purpose in obscuring their identity or where it would have been overly awkward or misleading to do so. Most of the central characters in the book were given the opportunity to read and comment on the sections that concerned their lives. On the other hand, people I met incidentally, whose words or ideas I have used, some of them written down before I had a formal plan to use them in a book, are given fictitious names and for the most part located only generally within their county or region. Sociologists and anthropologists extend this common courtesy to subjects in order to guard their privacy.

What I have produced here with enormous help from people who were willing to tell me their lives is a mosaic of what change feels like. The nature of the change is what we have come to call in everyday language "globalization." What that means here, simply, is the powerful focusing of economic resources according to a worldwide system of rational efficiency. The economic organization of the world into a single marketplace for raw materials, manufacture, labor, and sales is producing a cultural leveling, where regional cultures remain in evidence for the present, but where a single worldwide market is having an effect on regional or national cultures in the form of homogenizing tastes and lifestyle. It is expensive to keep up with these changes. Everywhere in the world some can while others cannot. Ireland has transitioned in just a decade from one of the poorest to one of the richest countries in Europe. The alteration in how people live, how they relate to each other, and what they value is profound.

THE IRISH: A PEOPLE

There are a number of ways to classify the Irish. We can choose to emphasize division or unity. Both choices are appropriate, depending on the situation. At times we can put the people who are identifiably Irish into two categories: those who were born and have lived their lives in Ireland, whom it might be appropriate to call "native Irish" or "island Irish," and those who are descended from previous generations of emigrated Irish, and we can call them the "scattered Irish" or "diaspora Irish." "Diaspora" is particularly descriptive, referring to a large number of people who, though they recognize a common origin, live scattered about and settled far from their homeland. The distinction between the Ireland Irish and diaspora or scattered Irish is often used in this book and, of course, represents a logical and an important classification.

However, the term "Irish" is deliberately intended, as it is used here in a book about global effects, to include all of the various categories of Irish—emigrants from, immigrants to, native islanders, and descendants—as if they could all fit into a single meaningful category. The intended implication is that, wherever they may live, the Irish are a single people with a single history. Some Irish remained at home on the island through all of the difficult times, and some went abroad. In the past and present those who were absent from the island continued to work their influences on local economies and on the national culture in many ways. For example, in chapter 4 we see the ways in which Irish emigrants helped to define Irish music "traditions" in the eighteenth and nineteenth centuries by introducing various musical instruments from abroad to the people at home (Ui Ógain 1995). If we are to understand the origins of island traditions today, it turns out that we need to acknowledge diaspora influence, in the past and now.

In addition to the influence of the Irish who traveled away, Ireland has been transformed by those who came to the island. A small nation, Ireland has been subject to the whims and tyranny of invader and colonizer for centuries. The descendants of many of those who came, stayed, dictated change, and uprooted natives are today and have long been part of the island Irish—that is, "natives." Already, in the early 1600s, a distinction was made between the "Old English" colonists and the arriving "New English" colonists taking part in the plantation scheme that granted large landholdings of one thousand to two thousand acres. Both the New English and King James considered the established Old English colonists "Irish," despite their protestations and pledges of loyalty to the Crown (de Paor 1986, 144). Today, the many recently arrived New Irish immigrants are making Ireland their home and are being made over by the experience. They and their children, of course, must be counted as Irish. Together, those who left, those who stayed, and those who have come to stay have made and are making Irish history, have made and are making Ireland.

An inclusive history of Ireland, an inclusive definition of the Irish, is as potentially empowering as it is necessary. As Ireland's linkage within the international economy gives the small nation a prominent place in the world, it is only natural that the diversity of its population increasingly reflect this standing. But a nation of four million is indeed a small place. Tim Pat Coogan has a provocative thought in this regard. He sees potential in drawing together the island Irish and the scattered Irish of the world into a body aware of itself. "The Irish worldwide are one of the globe's success stories, emerging from slum, swamp-draining, coal-mining, brawling, and boozing illiteracy, literally to the scents of the Rose Garden of the White House. . . . The only group which over-looks its potential is the Irish Government" (2003, xiv), although they are finally coming around. With up to forty-three million Americans giving their ethnic origin as "Irish" at census time, "that resource should be respected, and mobilized by Dublin" (2003, xiv). What a powerful lobby, what a force to affect policy and to promote common Irish inter-ests in the world, Coogan muses.

It may be that the combined Irish worldwide are a great poten-tial political and economic force, if ever they could be induced to pull together. But, at the very least, the complexity of the meaning of "the Irish," the diversity of the body, needs to be recognized. Setting aside the New Irish for the moment (our focus in chapter 7), we must acknowl-edge some differences between the native born and the Diaspora Irish, most of the latter having been away for generations. The generations-away Irish who return to Ireland as tourists often have only a vague knowledge of the political history of the place, a knowledge plastered over by sentiment or even colonial grudges that have become all but ir-relevant to younger people in many parts of the island today. Their com-mon forebears would have known keenly and personally the story of famine, eviction, and general hard times.

Emigrants could describe the regular seasons of hunger that they lived through each year where the rugged beauty of the western coast only signified a stepping-off place, the edge of a distance to be overcome in a passage to America. The old emigrant generations would have been able to tell those stories in the first person and could give the names of several dead of weakness, disease, and hunger. A million died of hunger and the diseases that followed in the wake of the mid-nineteenth-century famine. By 1848, with continuing crop failures, emigration swelled in the minds of a stricken people as the only means of survival, and, once underway, the exodus continued well into the next century. Between 1841 and 1925, 70,000 migrated to Canada, 370,00 to Australia, even more hundreds of thousands to the industrializing cities of Britain, and lesser numbers to South Africa, South America, and elsewhere. Four and three-quarter million came to the United States. Between 1861 and 1921, 84 percent of those leaving the twenty-six counties of what is now the Republic went to the United States (Bottigheimer 1982, 247 ff.).

The descendants of those driven out of Ireland by the harshness of their existence may have only a sketchy knowledge of the experience of those whose lives brought them to the new lands of England, Canada, Australia, or the United States. But no less than those who remained in Ireland, the descendants have in their tens of millions lived Irish history. They are the Irish who lived it elsewhere. Many of them may be able to recount only the most general events of the history of Ireland in the nineteenth and twentieth centuries, but that is not the question to put to them. If you want Irish history in the first person, ask them about their lives in the place that their predecessors brought them to—Boston, Montreal, New York, or Phoenix, for that matter—and you will have authoritative Irish histories. If they are not authorities on history that took place in Ireland, the same is true of some young scholars there.

Not long ago I spent a few days with a group of university students from Ulster who were studying for the year in the United States. They delighted in the tale told by one of them of the ignorance of the American Irish about Ireland. He said he dispelled the myth of leprechauns as little people, explaining instead that these are actually small tree-dwelling mammals, not unlike koala bears. A young American woman in his audience who had expressed a strong Irish identity went the rounds of her residence hall sharing her newfound knowledge with others. However, this same group of visiting students was a little surprised at the interest and knowledge that was shown in the United States regarding the sectarian violence in the North. Two of the students admitted that they had gone to the libraries of the U.S. colleges where they were studying to look up the background to the conflict so that they could answer the questions put to them. The island's political history, submerged beneath a general prosperity and this generation's personal concerns with preparing for lucrative careers back home, only became a relevant piece of identity for the students while visiting the United States. The web of meaning, the web that captures the full meaning of what it is to be Irish, is cast around the globe, and has been for a long time. If a young woman from America is looking for koala bear—like creatures up in trees somewhere in Ireland, we know native Irish students have been looking for Ireland in textbooks in the United States.

When early Irish immigrants came to the United States, they were confronted with ugly stereotypes of what Irish meant in the popular mind and equally ugly caricatures in the popular press (see, e.g., Soper 2005; Kenny 2006; or any of the caricatures produced by Thomas Nast for *Harper's Weekly*). Now that prosperity has come to Ireland and brought the attention of the world along with it, the Ireland Irish will have another mirror in which to view themselves, a new test of knowing and defining who they are. All of us interested in the nature and meaning of Ireland have a rapidly changing target to come to terms with. It is the same for those who were born there.

In certain neighborhoods in the Bronx Irish names predominate on the mailboxes of apartment buildings, and accents from every region of Ireland can be heard in the multiple Irish-themed pubs that line the avenues. These neighborhoods, peopled largely by recent Irish immigrants, were by fall 2004 experiencing a mass exodus. Irish nationals, living and working in the United States legally or illegally, were headed back to Ireland. The Irish economy was still enjoying something of the robustness of the late nineties, and the U.S. economy, where housing and health care costs were not matched even by New York's healthy trade union wages, was facing uncertain post-bubble times. The U.S. government, initiating generally more restrictive policies on illegal aliens, was making it tougher for those whose paperwork was not in order to stay and work in the country.

Meanwhile, the Bronx's Irish immigrants, along with those in Boston and Philadelphia, realized that friends and relatives visiting from Ireland, judging from their spending habits, were doing very well indeed. The writing was on the wall: it was time to go back and take advantage of conditions in the New Ireland. But going "back" might not be so simple. The personnel of various bureaus that counseled Irish immigrants, both in the United States and in Ireland, were concerned about the returnees. Those with skills in the building trades might do alright, but all would face a "rude awakening," they warned. Even those who had been gone for only a few years would find that the cost of living in Ireland had increased enormously. For those who did not have the kinds of skills currently in demand in the high technology economy, they would learn that immigrants from Asia, Africa, and Eastern Europe, with their reputation for working harder for lower wages, were filling service sector jobs. Some of the returning emigrants might hear themselves echoing the words of the man in the green sweats.

Ireland has become a creature of the world economy. It moves and feels just like any other spot on the globe that has been caught in the swift current of global economic change. As the current washes around and erodes the structures of Old Ireland, the place will become less and less like many of the images that people carry within them. What is Irish about Ireland—a certain quality of being that we think of and react to when we think of Ireland—is not inside Ireland but inside ourselves. If we go to Ireland to look for that quality, we may find some of it there, but we need to be prepared to find something else as well. This is as true for those who just stepped off the island a few years ago as it is for anyone else. As one emigrant advice officer said of the Bronx returnees, "They are not returning. They're emigrating to a different country" (Bernstein 2004). They will have interesting stories to tell about what that was like, and one day we can add them to the ones told here.

AN OVERVIEW OF THE BOOK

Chapters one and two frame the telling changes that have affected Ireland in the past decade, and the remaining chapters explore what people have to say about the shifting condition of their lives. Chapter 1 points to the clash between the lingering idea of Ireland and its unfolding realities. Chapter 2 provides a systematic overview of the dimensions of recent historical changes. It introduces the idea, attested to in the stories of native islanders that follow, that these changes come at a cost for some. Chapter 3 invites consideration of the idea that today the Irish who have remained in Ireland have finally emigrated: the fact that it is the world that has come *to them* is a minor detail in the story, just the most recent episode—when the last of the island Irish leave Old Ireland behind. As those on the edge of change, uncertain about its promise, watch the society they know slip away, they become "strangers at home."

Nothing endears Ireland to the other peoples of the world as much as its musical traditions, and in chapter 4 we see that now, since those traditions are performed on the world stage, they are adapted to the international marketplace. Distant listeners reach into the music of the past and bid for what they like and, in this way, change tradition. Nevertheless, the traditional music of Ireland has always been a mix of pieces from elsewhere in the world, and we see that "tradition," by its nature, involves change.

Chapter 5 is divided into two parts. The first focuses on the history of farming as a way of life. In examining the past we come to understand a time when farm, family, and community bound people together in a web of mutual obligation that gave meaning to how and why life was lived in just that way. In contrast, Part 2 reports on how farmers today are leaving the land in such numbers that this decade will end with only a small fraction of those who were on the land in 2000 remaining.

Chapter 6 traces decades in the life of a country priest, Father Pat Twohig, who is also a historian (an authority on Michael Collins), author, musician, head of a respected music school, and a conservative keeper of the Catholic faith. Life in the village of Churchtown, Church politics, and his curates have presented challenges over the years, but none so great as the charge of misconduct that confronted Father Pat in his eighties.

Chapter 7 explores how the island Irish have had to get used to a new story in a hurry—the story of immigration. We learn about a different perspective on keeping the faith in Ireland, as described by the outspoken soccer-playing Imam of the Galway Mosque and members of his Muslim community. Cautious hope regarding their future in Ireland is reflected in the words of two Indian families who have made Ireland their home.

Chapter 8 returns to the theme that Ireland is a set of attachments as much as it is a place. The people in this chapter express Ireland by saying what they get from it. They range from those who have gone there to look for themselves in a richly interpreted past to those who have gone there and simply found themselves at home.

CHAPTER 1

There Is No Map of Ireland

We live on stories. I always think of that phrase, "I am the way,

the truth and the light." You see, the truth comes second;

it's the way that matters. It's how you tell things. And that

is the oldest Irish tradition.

—Brendan Kennelly,
poet and professor of modern literature,
Trinity College (Hoge 2000)

The future caught up with Ireland just as people had become comfortable with the idea that Ireland was one spot —in a world of rapidly collapsing certainties —where things changed slowly. A person could experience time travel, going back across the years simply by crossing the Atlantic Ocean or the Irish Sea. Narrow winding roads that discouraged long journeys and preserved remoteness, an assured sense of personal safety in city and country, a no-need-to-rush attitude regarding either work or play, a modest standard of living matched to modest expectations about living standards, a relative disregard for fashion (except in Dublin and, maybe, Cork), the predominance of rural lifeways and values that fit hand in glove with the influence of religion on daily life—all of these appeared to change so little and so slowly that, from wherever in cosmopolitan Europe or North America you happened to be coming, you had the comforting impression that in Ireland things were many decades, perhaps the better part of a century, behind the times. It remained, literally, a sanctuary in a secular fractured world.

The landscape invited romantic myth making: crumbling stone castles and monasteries, lacey stone walls around tiny fields, abandoned cottages scattered over rocky or moss-covered hills. There are as well the much more ancient piles and circles of stones, forts and graves and altars from a remote past. The remains of strange creatures, human and otherwise, are pulled periodically from the bog. So many centuries protrude from the earth, centuries worth of life and cultures that were marginally apart from and marginally a part of what was happening on the nearby continent and beyond. Today even people who have some idea of the history and prehistory of the place can be seduced into fanciful speculations of what kind of past might have produced such artifacts—bits of evidence adaptable to the personal meanings of Ireland that different people carry within them. Today the imaginations of visitors to many of the more well-known sites and piles of stones are guided by a new race of little people, Disneyland-style theme-park imagineers, who create "narratives" of the more shockingly brutal details of history, making it suitable fare for self-guided touring for families on vacation.

Never very far from the stony remnants and interpretive exhibits are the artifacts of a different Ireland, a fantasy world rooted in the present rather than the past. These are elements that inspire a different kind of imagination, the kind of imagination that thrives in the global economy, an imagination that by the 1990s had discovered in Europe's island outpost a strategic bargain ripe for development. Since then, for visitor and citizen alike, Ireland has been changing so fast that there has been no time to loosen the grip on the symbols of the old Ireland, which are now overshadowed by signposts of what Ireland's future will look like. In the space of little more than a decade, Ireland has gone from being one of the poorest nations in Europe to one of the ten most affluent nations in the world, and the new wealth has fundamentally reworked the social and physical landscape. Experiencing the space in between the old and the new often produces a visual and mental blur, like having slipped into a fast-forward-and-backward mode of the time-travel plane, as it juxtaposes in rapid succession scenes of life, manners of speech, and moral communities from different centuries. These elements of past and future are not segregated from each other in everyday experience but interpenetrate one another in odd juxtapositions, give rise to blinking double-takes, and provide mutually reflective surfaces for the observer in which each facet appears curious, incongruous, distorted.

When a place changes so quickly, the changes are bound to raise difficult questions and conflicted answers about just what is its real and true nature. How much of what Ireland has been is being swept away, what elements remain in what modified form in what it is becoming, and what does it all mean for the way people live every day? Is it possible to tell the story of such a changed and changing place, a story that will hold together, capture its true character, be a useful guide for understanding? This book is based on the assumption that it is both possible and useful to tell some of the story, or rather some of the stories, of a place of rapid change as the place is changing. Moreover, it is vitally important to try to do so at the moment that change is altering people's lives so they can tell us what that is like. It is a perishable and priceless kind of knowledge that is gone when its day is done.

In time, historians will tell us what happened to Ireland during the present turn-of-the-century decades. They won't agree, and they will have endless academic arguments about the role of technology, the operation of the multinationals, the ill- or well-placed emphasis of government policies, timely interventions by the European Union, the costs and benefits of the displacement of religion and the Church, and so forth. Economists, political scientists, and sociologists will join the debate. In time, sorting through all the volumes and papers, future readers will have some answer to the question of what happened to Ireland at the end of the twentieth and the beginning of the twenty-first centuries. But something will be missing in these accounts. Interested parties in the future will wish they had some sense of what it was like to live through it—as an immigrant, a parish priest, a farmer, a pensioner, or a visitor on some sort of personal pilgrimage. I have tried, with the help of many of the good people of Ireland, to provide some answers to the question of what it is like to live through the rapid change Ireland is undergoing today. Their interpretations are ultimately true, not subject to later expert debate. They are the experts who are inside the experiences of which they speak.

Most of this book seeks a more intimate understanding of what Ireland was and is as a place of meanings and a meaningful place. This is an understanding that readers may cobble together from the personal accounts of people who are watching a coldly rational global economy stride through their small communities of intensely local sensibilities. Some tell stories that reflect the benefits of the modern Ireland that is being drawn closer to the center of the global economy. Others speak of how they themselves or people they care about are being displaced as everything seems turned upside down. Another important category of Irish people talk about the way that they themselves have been changed by coming to Ireland, as they participate in Ireland's makeover, as they are made over themselves.

The stories people tell of their lives add something vital to the overall picture of Ireland as an important base of corporate activity in the global economy: we are reminded that it remains, despite its aggregate commercial successes, nevertheless a small nation caught in an economic storm where individual fortunes are acutely vulnerable to shifts in the swirling global markets. As a center for technological innovation and thriving businesses, Ireland is a far different place from what it was a quarter of a century ago. The change has been as abrupt as it is dazzling. Yet the whole sweep of Ireland's recorded history is one of change. At times change has come in these sudden and convulsive bursts, interlayered with long periods of adaptation. Part of the paradox that Ireland represents is that the former, slowly changing version of twentieth-century Ireland, the Old Ireland still warm in memory, represents more than a century of ongoing adjustment to the traumatic changes introduced in the nineteenth and early twentieth centuries by natural disaster, colonialism, and the struggle for political independence. Ireland is peculiarly a place of comings and goings, an island on the fringes of different histories that have been played out across the world. This is one sense in which Ireland has a history larger than its geographic self. Of course, we could say the same thing about any nation's history, but here we are interested in the distinctive qualities of the events that have made Ireland and the Irish.

Wherever we find people who identify themselves in some way with an Irish past we find important elements of Irish history. The international movement of Irish people away from Ireland played an important role in shaping the whole of Irish experience. On the fractal island republic itself, conditions changed only very slowly during most of the twentieth century in part because the gross demographics—the number of people living there—remained virtually stagnant (Aalen 1963; Central Statistics Office Ireland 2003). As elsewhere in the world, people moved to the city during the 1900s, but the native Irish migrants moved to the cities of *other* countries, just as was the case for the waves of emigrants that left the Irish countryside for the world's cities in the previous century (Doyle 2006; Bottigheimer 1982, 249–52). Many of the cities of England (Busteed and Hodgson 1996; Walter 1985) and the United States

(Dolan 1972; Marston 1988) acquired concentrated Little Ireland enclaves early on, virtual Irish cities in exile, that sustained some of their ethnic character well into the twentieth century. Meanwhile, quaint old Ireland remained so because it emptied out, generation by generation, leaving behind those who felt trapped, on the one hand, and natives who were generally satisfied making the most of what opportunities they found there, on the other. Thanks to the fact that the place remained fairly marginal to the global economy, we have had, up until very recently, that apparent time-capsule Ireland. Farming mechanized, rural areas electrified, slate replaced thatch, university enrollments grew, cities and urban jobs did expand, but the world outside changed more rapidly, and Old Ireland still looked like Old Ireland from beyond. From the outside it might be imagined that Ireland remained what it had been when great grandmother left the place so many decades ago.

Now the world has moved to Ireland, and the country is in the midst of one of those periods of abrupt change that will be followed by a long historical wave of adjustment. There are a number of ways to describe what is happening. One can say the place is becoming less identifiably Irish as it becomes more internationalized or global in the ways that people live. It could be said that the fanciful Irelands of an imagined past must finally be undone by today's real Ireland, bearing ever less resemblance to those impressions. It would appear that the new realities must finally and certainly extinguish sentiment and fancy. In truth the matter is not so simple. Strong sentimental attachments to place are not so extinguishable, not subject to dismissal by others or by changes rooted in the present. Ireland as a *homeplace*, a place of meanings, is something much deeper than a set of objective social and economic conditions that exist at a particular point, even this particularly powerful point, in time. Ireland is a place of the overlapping and contested collective and personal imaginations of both the people who live there and the people who identify themselves in some measure with Ireland as a place of origins.

For the most part, the Ireland we are trying to understand here is Ireland as people experience it—which makes it not so much a place as it is a set of meanings, a personally meaningful place. In this sense there are as many Irelands as there are personal stories about the Irish and their attachments. Places such as this are not found on maps but inside people, in the personal connections they feel to the stories they tell about who they are. In the best of the following pages I convey the messages of others, mostly the native or adopted island Irish. But my own experiences and ideas as a mixed-breed descendant of emigrant grandparents shaped the questions I asked and the places I went to ask them. My own story brought me to this project and shaped it. So I begin with a brief account of how Billy Flanagan from 52 Henry Street in Stamford, Connecticut, encountered Ireland as a place of shifting ideas and images.

The light was fading already on a late afternoon in early winter, 1976. For a reason I can no longer clearly recall I was standing in front of the Ryan family's institutional furniture factory on Glasheen Road in Cork, waiting for a lift home to the housing estate where I was living in the village of Blarney, a few miles outside the city. It is likely that the reason I was standing there in the chill damp was related to Ned Ryan, my friend and guide to organizing the details of my life in Ireland. From time to time Ned would cook up a special deal with one of his long-term cronies in his native city in order to make sure that I got this or that service properly provided. In the years before Ireland's economy took off, Ned's personal mission was to show the world that Ireland was an efficient place to do business, despite frequent bits of contrary evidence that popped up and got in the way.

Ned was the second-generation manager of the family furniture-making business. I came to know him as an honest sort whose life every day involved chatting people up, playing the angles, making connections, working the best deal, and "getting things organized," a favorite phrase of his. An example of his personal connectivity within the city emerged when it looked as though I might have to wait months to get a telephone. He rang up the local Posts and Telegraphs management and told them I needed a phone right away. In passing he referred to me as Doctor Flanagan. When the skeptical manager asked if I were a "real doctor," he responded truthfully, "Real? Why he's a P-haitch-D!" He said afterwards that he thought the term might have caused a momentary confusion, implying some sort of medical specialty in the mind of the woman at the office. But then he couldn't be sure that was the case, and he couldn't think on the spot of how to correct the "mistake" without creating a potential embarrassment for the woman on the phone. So he thought it best to let it go. If that didn't work, he was prepared to take the case higher until he found someone in the office he knew personally, and then he would simply ask a favor. In one of the exceedingly rare instances in which my degree in sociology actually impressed anyone, however mistakenly, the Posts and Telegraphs truck was outside my door the next morning.

Ned personally brought to life something I was told about the city soon after I arrived—that Cork at the time was really a village of nearly two hundred thousand people, a village where everyone appeared to know everyone else. One of the more colorful ways of saying this was passed on to me by a colleague, Theresa, who was originally from much more cosmopolitan Dublin and was often annoyed by how everyone in Cork seemed to know everyone else's business. She said it was common knowledge that if a young Cork woman were ever fortunate enough to lose her virginity, someone was sure to find out and return it to her mother.

But living in a village of two hundred thousand also had its more unqualified benefits. If your four-year-old son had a biting earache on a Sunday night, someone you knew knew someone who could call a *real* doctor at home, and you could find yourself standing in his kitchen under the good light at ten p.m. as he worked out what was wrong. His call would get the chemist out of bed in her rooms behind her shop, and she would meet you at the door in her dressing gown with the prescription at ten thirty. For me, Ned was often the initial contact person to get such favors "organized." If it needed doing, Ned knew someone who would do it right, at a fair or special price, who might owe him a favor, and he could tell you all that was fit to tell about their family, and might hint with a wink or a nod that there was more there that wasn't fit—but he was no gossip, and he'd keep that part to himself. In that way he was a little unusual.

I had been frequently reminded in the few months I had spent in Ireland at that point that Irish people love to talk, to tell stories of their lives, even details of family troubles—their own or another family's just the same. The proper telling of tales is an art, and all that is needed at minimum is an audience of one, and a story will emerge and begin to transform a conversation into a narrative. For the role of listener, a stranger or newcomer without local connections often seemed preferable, in contrast to someone local who could make good use of the information by adding it to their own stock of gossip. The art of storytelling has nothing to do with higher learning or a local reputation for special intelligence. Instead, it has to do with having an attentive eye and ear, a keenness for reflection about what has happened in a life, some native acting talent, the timing of a professional stand-up comedian, and an ability to slice through to the center and truth of the thing, but roundabout, holding the listener suspended, a partner in the dance. The storyteller's gift is often said to be found commonly enough among the native population, and my experience seemed to bear that out.

As a conversation was about to switch to the narrative mode, a storyteller might adjust his hat, smooth out a wrinkle in her apron or other piece of clothing, let out a slow breath to signal the significance of what was about to be said, or perhaps square his shoulders—as if he were about to step through a door into a room where the action was taking place. She might look straight ahead as if she were watching the tale unfold while describing it, shaping it with her hands in the air, with sidelong glances to see if you were following along. Or he might watch the listener the whole time, taking on the tone of a coconspirator, standing close, side-by-side, patting your arm, and maybe coming round to face you at a crucial moment, counting out the important points with a finger or two tapping your chest. Others simply let the language do the work.

I think it's true that there is a poetry in common everyday speech in Ireland, and students and friends there have at times mentioned that it is something they are aware and proud of. Maybe this is equally true for certain kinds of everyday talk anywhere, in the United States, for example. I'm afraid I never learned to hear the eloquence in everyday spoken American—probably through the fault of having been born there. But in Ireland I was often impressed by what had been communicated even in the briefest exchange, just a few words, even in the absence of spoken words.

As I stood outside Ryans' furniture factory, the smoke from coal and peat fires was sliding down the sloping roofs of the close-set houses that lined Glasheen Road, and the smoke hung just above the reflecting street, still wet from earlier showers. I was facing downhill toward the city center and the docks, and as the evening dimmed the scene and the damp gathered, the street lights came on, and the ground floor lights inside the two-story houses were showing brighter through the blue-gray haze.

Among the passing cars and trade vehicles a heavy-bodied draft horse passed, pulling an empty flat-bed wagon back down toward the docks, the horse's wide hooves the size of dinner plates clopping steadily on the pavement. The rubber tires of the wagon made no sound. The driver was sitting on the edge of the flat bed to one side with the reins lying loose in his lap, and he nodded and touched his cap to me, the stranger in front of Ryans'. I responded automatically with the peculiar head-wagging Irish salute, which I had picked up in my own American neighborhood, where Irish accents were mingled with those of Poland, Russia, Italy, and Greece. The returned wag and shrug from the driver was quick, and together we had exchanged something, unrestricted by the limitations of language: the hour, the weather, the workday, maybe all of that. What was significant was the ritual performance, the fleeting connection within the still common culture, startlingly fresh after the passage of generations. I watched the back of the wagon all the way down the road, as it slowed traffic and annoyed drivers with places to go and things to do, things and places that came from a different century, the twentieth, which was taking a long time coming to parts of this overgrown village, like a foreign presence at the gate, uncertain of its welcome.

This happened more than a quarter century ago. There is no particular reason to remember the scene, but, like many other glimpses from that time, neither is it likely to be forgotten. It has a photo-like quality, pinned to a board somewhere, where the things that suit my sense of Ireland reside.

THE PLACES WE ARE FROM

I taught in Cork for two years and then returned to the States. But for many of us who spend an extended period in a part of the world other than the one we start out and end up in, the in-between place left behind is carried around in our heads like a box of illuminated puzzle pieces, bits of images that shuffle themselves, unbidden, in and out of consciousness from time to time. The images in the box never change, but the places and the people left behind do. New generations come into being, saying and seeing things differently from the way previous ones did; the children of memory become adults; some of the living and speaking die, and their photographs, with frozen expressions on their faces and clothes increasingly gone out of fashion, hang on the walls of the houses of their now-grown children and grandchildren. Once living and breathing, the people on the wall are now sentimental antiques.

When a place is long left behind, the worlds of memory and of the present argue back and forth, contesting which one is the more real. For me, Ireland is the place I left behind a quarter century ago, as well as the one I return to each year, mixed in with the set of images I gathered from Irish people when I was growing up on Henry Street, thirty minutes from Fordham Road in the Irish Bronx, ten more minutes from the Saint Patrick's Day green-striped Manhattan, a generation away from Ireland.

The place-memories of the unsettled traveler, the person who has lived away and then returned home, offer just a glimpse into the contested reality lived by the true emigrant, the never-returned home-leaver, of which there were many in my neighborhood. Permanent un-settlement is the price paid for *absconding,* for the theft of oneself from the place that remains, to whatever extent, "home" in the memory of the heart, no matter how hard the life was there or how well considered the reasons for leaving. To the extent that each of us is a piece of commu-nity property, the theft of self — the act of permanent departure — can create an imbalance in the place left behind and a tension of memories between that place and the place of resettlement. Oscar Handlin, in his work *The Uprooted,* conveys the situation poetically.

Ceremonial salutations, *to my dearest* . . . to every him and her who filled the days of the old life and whom I will never see again. By this letter I kiss you. To the aged parents who bred and nurtured, who took trouble over, shed tears for me and now have none to comfort them; to the brother who shared my tasks and bed; to my comrades of the fields; to all the kin who joined in festivals; to the whole visible communion, the oneness, the village that I have forfeited by emigration; to each I send my greetings. And with my greetings go my wishes that you may have the sweet years of life, of health and happiness, alas elusive there and here. (1951, 259)

Often, something of the melancholy that attaches to the emigrant life lingers for generations. This seems to have been especially the case when that handed-down memory finds itself supported by a chorus of same-place attachments of many others, descended from those who left the same homeland, and found themselves clustering together in the factory neighborhoods of the new land. Immigrant colonies on adopted shores emerge by choice and not by chance, as co-ethnics are held together by seeking each other out and holding on together to frozen expressions of the distant homeland, like the ones that hang framed on the walls.

For the past few hundred years, especially, the world has been full of people who have within the span of family memory come from somewhere else. Today, this is as true about the world as ever before. Handlin chose the term "uprooted" to refer to the condition of the nineteenth-century waves of European immigrants, peoples caught between making their new land into "home" and the tricks of memory that reshaped their emotional attachments to the old homelands, now seen from a great distance. The same must be true for transplanted people the world over. The immigrant generation continues to live in a marginal cultural world, between the adopted home and the places that they have come from, the homeland, the old country, "back-over."

As time passes, neither home, the remembered or the adopted one, remains the same. The actual, physical place left behind changes in tune with its ever-emerging position in the world; it is increasingly different from the memories that are passed on to generations of offspring and grandchildren. And the new land becomes less new, more home, as the next generation grows up—particularly as they are seen by their immigrant parents—speaking the language and valuing that which is locally valued as flawlessly as the natives they have become. Nevertheless, within the New Worlds that the descending generations occupy, there often remains, to some degree, an element of where a people came from, and this element forms a part of their identity. For many of us, where we have come from, originated from, has a meaningfulness—a preserved, interpreted, adapted, shadowy, melancholy, stereotypical, collective yet personal imagery that people carry inside themselves.

During my childhood, in working-class neighborhoods of the cities in the Northeast, the idea of Ireland echoed along the generations as a harmony of images, accents, gestures, habits, religious practices, and prejudices, all reinforced by the lingering presence of aging first-generation immigrants and their stories of the remembered pieces of home. Some families tuned their radios to the two hours of Irish programming available on weekends in our corner of the greater New York City metropolitan area, a ritual as serious in its own way as the masses said in Polish in the Catholic church next to the parochial school across the street from the apartment building where we lived.

Ethnic group membership, although no one ever called it that on Henry Street, was a fact of life. Everyone was—at least through parent or grandparent—from somewhere else, and that fact helped to place you in the minds of your neighbors, your teachers, the grocer, the priest. My immigrant Hungarian grandmother with her labored broken English lived a few doors down the street, while my Irish grandparents were long gone, but my name was Flanagan, and that decided who and what I was in everyone's mind including my own. "Flanagan—now that wouldn't be Irish, would it? Ha ha." We second- and third-generation immigrants on Henry Street would have had a hard time explaining to you what it meant to be from a country we had never been near, but we would tell you it was important. People whose parents or grandparents came from different countries were different kinds of people; anybody there could tell you that.

In my generation's United States there was perhaps a decade when the accents seemed to fade as the generation of European immigrants aged and died out—the generation of our grandparents and parents. When restrictions on immigration were eased in the mid 60s and new waves began to arrive in the city, we were in our early twenties. The new urban accents were lost on us, as some time earlier the old neighborhood had filled with people of color, and one by one our families had moved away to other areas of the city, mostly whiter and farther from the core. They moved to the older inner suburbs and, in a few cases, even beyond to the real suburbs, from which commuters emerged to catch the train into New York every morning, at the railway station just a block from Henry Street. Tikey, who lived with his father in my friend Junior's building next door, attended the University of Bridgeport, earning an engineering degree and making so much money in his first job he was embarrassed by it. Junior's brother, Sonny, went to Julliard on a scholarship and bought a house in Old Greenwich. Joanie, downstairs, went to teacher's college and never came back. Only the surviving and aging members of the European immigrant generations were left behind in the increasingly black neighborhoods and Latino barrios that had come to contain our street corners and front steps in the South End, our old turf. Catholic masses across the street were said in Spanish. "Homeplace," in the autobiographical sense of a place of beginnings, of lived origins, became for us a more difficult concept.

The everyday habits associated with the American version of racial apartheid, inspired by varying levels of racism and fear that had caused the neighbors to scatter, made the old neighborhoods as unavailable as personal reference points as if they had been transported to a different planet. They were not places where we went anymore: *we* had emigrated. The loss of neighborhood place may have made it more possible for romanticized images of a distant homeplace, the place of our parents and grandparents, to become all the more real as an answer to the question of where we were "from" as we grew older. In the 1960s and 1970s, something of a nationwide ethnic renaissance developed; people of European origin in the United States sought out and revived their Old Country roots. For my generation this was a *classy* way to think about home ties, something that emphasized the substance, the "heritage," of your identity. Our ethnic rootedness was portable, the one thing that you could take with you from the old neighborhood, that you could always go back to—even if few ever did. It was not subject to neighborhood secessions and successions, because you carried it around inside of you.

An ethnic sense of belonging is handy, not at all something cumbersome to be studied or intellectually understood—unless you really want to make that kind of effort. Based as it is on selective memory, its elements of history and fantasy can be readily rearranged by each succeeding generation, according to what that generation finds useful. Being Italian might mean being proud of Italy as the cradle of the

Renaissance, a romantic affinity with gangster mythology, an anti-defamation stance toward those same stereotypes, a passion for pasta and one course of the Sunday meal set aside for sausage and peppers, or all of the above. "Irish" might mean an identification with the nationalist rebel politics of the homeland, a somewhat milder political affinity for U.S. Democratic Party politics, forcing your innocent children to attend parochial school and take Irish dancing on Tuesday nights, or a taste for green beer on March 17. Laying a claim to Irish (or whatever) ethnic rootedness meant that you got to choose what "heritage" meant to you.

Today, people who identify themselves ethnically as Irish in the United States represent the full range of demographics—in terms of age, gender, social class, even political party affiliation. An estimated forty to forty-five million people in the United States can trace an Irish ancestry. The Irish live all over the world. They all have stories about themselves. Some of them will identify with my tale of growing up on Henry Street, perhaps with going to live and work in Ireland as an adult; some will even have been academics who found themselves following a path similar to mine.

But my story of the context of my Irishness—a little of which I have told here—to whatever extent it may overlap with yours or that of someone you know, is unique to me in some degree, as is the case with all ethnic identification. If you, like me, are "Irish," what we share in common is the fact that we are *of* as well as *from* a small island in the North Atlantic, either ourselves or in the sense that at least some of our people came from there some time ago. Whether island-born or born into the diaspora, we share a history of a people where many more of us have been displaced by politics and economics than remain on that island. But the details that differ between your story and mine are also important in framing what your sense and my sense of belonging, our sense of "peoplehood," has come to mean. My Hungarian grandmother and plates of goulash on Sunday afternoons with uncles snoring around the living room after dinner are part of my Irishness, as is the fact that my Irish grandfather, whom I never knew, would never speak of Ireland and his life before he came to the United States (He died upon his return to the country as independence was won in 1922, long before I was born.) These facts are emblematic of my Irish identity in that I cannot conceive of writing about Hungary and the Hungarians—I have nothing to go on.

It was the family name that eventually drew me back to Ireland, that had set my re-emigration in motion, a name that had kept me tied to Ireland in the minds of the visiting graduate faculty, that suggested I was a logical candidate for the open teaching position at Cork. The name was the thread that had kept me tied to the common history of those who had left and those who had stayed. It is this history that I had come from, that eventually saw me coming back to the island (in a historical rather than biographical sense) just before the great changes of the present era. Chance and timing have framed my impression of Ireland, a place full of my peculiar meanings, built from my personal comings and goings.

The people who have shared their stories with me are for the most part island Irish, people who were born there and have lived through the recent changes. Our lives became reconnected as I listened to their stories with my passion to understand matching their passion to be understood. I think I could not have approached this project without having been away for a generation. For all of the people who have come from, through, or to the place, we are living a common history that has brought us all to where we are today. If there is geography in it, then it is a geography of evolving world events and personal identities. In that sense, there is no map of Ireland.

THE REAL IRELAND

The point is that with time the question of what and where Ireland is has become more complicated. Many of the millions of Irish who emigrated maintained a substantial phantom presence as members of the families and of the communities that they had come from. They sent home money for building, for education, for investing in business, for luxuries those who remained behind had not the personal means to afford—updated housing, medical care, musical instruments, meat on the table. They sent news of the possibilities and limitations of life in the world outside, geography lessons, expectations. The absconding migrants left behind a constant presence in the form of a question for friends, brothers, sisters: Become accomplices in the theft of self? Go or stay? Few enough were expected to return in the old days that the departing son or daughter might be "waked" on the eve of departure. Their photographs remained; candles burned; loved ones wept on birthdays and holidays. Their emigration was never complete—the tensions between the place of origin and destination never dissolved—until they and all who remembered them were dead. Even then, death would be a gradual process taking place over however many generations would continue to hear their fading story.

The saga of the journey from home and the loneliness so many emigrants endured were heart-wrenchingly rendered in letters, poetry, plays, novels, and, especially, slow Irish airs. The wailing of pipes or whistle that followed the poignancy of the singer's lines was enough to "tear the tears from a strong man's eyes," just in case the mercilessly melancholy lyrics had not released the flow. Here is part of "The Green Fields of America," a nineteenth-century tune:

My father is old and my mother right feeble
to leave their own country it would grieve their hearts sore.
Oh the tears down their cheeks in great floods they are rolling
to think I will die upon a far and foreign shore. . . .

As emigration continued during the twentieth century, the journey was different, becoming gradually less final, and after 1922 there was an independent Republic to return home to, if one cared to and could manage the journey (the year my grandfather Pat returned and disappeared from the family's sight). Thanks to what previous generations would have seen as miraculous developments, the transatlantic telephone and blindingly rapid and eventually affordable air travel, those who went abroad were not lost for good. With the telecommunications revolution of the last two decades and competition among the multiple airlines that now fly direct to Ireland, emigration had by the 1980s become as much a kind of long-range commute as an exit. It is common now for Irish emigrants working oceans away to return home at least annually for visits. And those who have been away for generations are increasingly able to find their way "home" for a holiday. Where earlier generations of Irish emigrants might have sat heavy-hearted in the "local" in Boston or Sydney, nursing an American or Australian brew, separated permanently from home by time and money, today's emigrant is a voluntary, temporarily displaced person who chooses daily to go or stay on a short-term or long-term basis, with the luxury of a Guinness draught at their elbow, wherever they choose to live and work in the world. Since the Irish economy boomed in the 1990s, many emigrants have gone back for good—or for as long as the good times might last.

Virtually every nation—certainly every nation in Europe—has become a more internationally linked place with fuzzier economic and cultural borders than even a quarter century ago. Many factors make this so: developments in global communication technology, the influence of an international mass media geared to both cultivate and appeal to the tastes of a global audience, the development of the powerful EU, the growth in importance of international trade itself, the worldwide operations of multinational corporations, the volume of legal and illegal cross-border migrations, expanded international tourism, and thereby increased intercultural shoulder rubbing at home and abroad. One cultural consequence of a single global market for mass entertainment and consumer goods is the tendency for all cultures around the world to become more alike, for tastes and preferences to converge, and for international borders to stand for less and less as boundaries that contain and preserve fundamental cultural differences.

While it remains the distinctiveness of the culture of Ireland, Italy, France, etc., that continues to draw short-term visitors every year, the international economy with its universal cultural baggage has arrived to take up permanent residence everywhere. The international economy is the new global melting pot of goods, tastes, ways of living—a force to level national distinctions. Of course, these are the early days of the internationalization trend, and it is far too soon to announce the death of distinctive national cultures, but it is not too early to watch the global mass market begin to dilute them. If you stand in a burger franchise in Milan, Beijing, or Cork, it is easy to see how each one remains different, yet how each is the same. You can walk out of these chain shops and into local eateries, but you may find international trends in customer service following you, in piped-in popular music, or in the people behind the counter who are trained to keep up with international standards of fast-food efficiency. We short-term visitors to these cities may decry the changes that erode the local distinctions in culture, or we may feel at home and comforted by them. In either case, we bring the changes with us, because that is what local businesses in Killarney or Limerick expect us to do; they see the world coming, and they want its return business.

Immigrants intent on settling in Ireland have been attracted by the Irish economy, and they arrive in their new home bringing their cultural influences with them. Within the past few years it has become routine to encounter substantial numbers of people of color, not only on the streets of major cities but in every small town and along country roads, and to hear accents from all over the world coming from behind the counters and over the phone. The native Irish themselves are manifesting a new dimension of social and cultural diversity, a serious divide. The division between rich and poor has widened with the nation's economic expansion: according to the United Nation's 2004 Human Development Report, Ireland was the world's second most unequal nation (the first is the United States), having the highest proportion of poor people in Western Europe. It is not that more people in Ireland are worse off than ever before, but the growing wealth of the well-off is driving prices through the roof, and so many are finding it difficult to get by. Affluence is more in evidence on the streets and in the shops of the cities; there is more available that is upscale, more that appeals to international style and taste. In crowded urban scenes, well-dressed young professionals dart through the sidewalk crowds on the way to important business, to meetings and dates with tight and unyielding American metropolitan-style time frames. Behind the wheel they help snarl street traffic in expensive flash cars that compete for space with increasing numbers of sensible Renaults, Fiats, and Fords. In cities and towns the street traffic at times barely keeps up with the slower class of pedestrians. In Dublin, Cork, and Galway it often does not keep up with foot traffic for long stretches on end.

Residential suburban rings grow around towns of every size, and housing costs spiral upward. Property crime and random violence occupy the public mind, church attendance and clerical vocations have fallen off sharply, and the sex scandals attached to the priesthood elsewhere are also present and well-publicized in Ireland. But by far the greatest driving force of change in Ireland has been the growing economy. In chapter 2 we spend some time exploring this factor, so that when we listen to people's stories later on, we have a framework within which to locate what they say. Many people, especially many of those who live there, will tell you that this changing and forever changed Ireland is the real one, finally on track, picking up speed in every respect. But many also know better than to think that reality is so simple a matter. Even some of those who have learned to ride the tiger find themselves looking back over their shoulder to a simpler time, remembering a different real Ireland.

CHAPTER 2

In the Teeth of the Tiger

On a visit to Galway, our daughter wanted to go to McDonalds,

which in fact was a Supermacs . . . indistinguishable from

McDonalds in every substantial respect. The confusion of

McDonalds and Supermacs, even to the keen eyes of a child,

epitomizes a broad historical process of homogenization of Irish

culture and identity wherein the local is transformed so that it

resembles the global.

(Kuhling and Keohane 2002)

In the 1990s the U. S. investment firm Morgan Stanley coined the now famous term "Celtic Tiger," dramatizing a remarkable fact: the expanding Irish economy had been outperforming the rapidly growing Asian Tigers for years. Ireland's astonishing economic growth has continued through the end of the decade and on into the present century. What makes this so noteworthy is the fact that Ireland had long been one of the poorest countries in Europe, with economic and job growth lagging behind those of the other nations in the region. Then, in the space of a decade, a total transformation occurred, as explosive growth translated, for lucky participants, into some of the highest living standards in the region and in the world.

Outside of Ireland the advance has been celebrated with single-mindedly jubilation. Finally the end had come to the long and dreary sweep of Irish history, which featured the suffering of the Irish at home, the crippling colonial legacy that had left the small independent nation economically off-balance. Generation after generation of young and ambitious people had left to make their lives in other countries, economic exiles driven from a homeland that could not compete with the rest of the world in offering the prospect of a decent living.

Not everyone is celebrating the New Ireland, however. Within the country the last decade and a half of prosperity has left some division and controversy. Sure enough, many have prospered, but large numbers of people did not benefit, and they faced ever-higher living costs as prices were driven upward by the growing incomes of the newly affluent.

The proportion of poor people in the country remained extraordinarily large in comparison to other European Union states. Many believe that government tax and spending policies, which were designed to promote economic growth, favored the wealthy and the international corporations to an excessive degree.

Paul Sweeney's 1998 book, *The Celtic Tiger: Ireland's Economic Miracle Explained*, is generally considered a balanced account of Ireland's economic growth and uneven prosperity. He attributes Ireland's success to a set of conditions in the international marketplace that fit nicely with emerging Irish government policy in the late 1980s. In Sweeney's terms, these external and internal conditions formed a "benign conjuncture" to produce the European economic miracle of the age. We recall the 1990s as the decade when the electronic information and communications revolution took off worldwide, enhancing the demand for personal computers, software development, and related services. At the same time the enormous marketplace formed by the European Union was about to begin reaching its potential as a free-trade zone with a common currency. Multinational computer and software manufacturers along with several other industries were poised to jump into the European market, and they all needed a regional headquarters. An Irish government coalition had just undertaken measures to offer foreign investors an inviting, tax-sheltered, incentive-rich, and stable economic environment. A revamped telecommunications infrastructure, a highly educated and native English-speaking population, and a reoriented educational system geared to providing graduates with in-demand technical skills rounded out the Irish attraction.

The multinationals came, including Dell, Microsoft, Hewlett-Packard, IBM, and Kodak. In the ten years preceding the mid 90s, computer-related exports tripled, while pharmaceutical and chemical exports increased six times, and even the long-standing trade in the export of food, beverage, and agricultural products doubled. Suddenly Ireland was importing labor, and young natives were staying home and going to work, a good number of them earning technical and management wages on the international scale.

By 1996 foreign companies were responsible for a sizable portion (45 percent) of the expansion of industrial jobs and for 71 percent of Irish-produced exports. According to Sweeney, the foreign corporate presence brought more than investment capital, tax revenues, and jobs.

Foreign companies brought a new standard of expectations about work performance as well, pushing aside the *"mañana"* or *"'twill do"* approaches to doing business that had allegedly been part of the traditional Irish business culture. Indifference was replaced by a confidence and willingness to help get things done, and this became the attitude expected of employees within a transformed business world. This attitude, of all pulling together for the common good, is consistent with a concerted effort on the part of government since 1987 to create a popular ideology, a spirit of cooperation, a common effort to produce mutual benefit for the wider society. This national consensus philosophy went a long way toward bolstering the image of a positive and stable investment environment that appealed to foreign capital and where good-citizen employees were willing and eager to dedicate their best efforts to achieve company goals. Meanwhile, the official government line promised that a buoyant economy would produce supply-side style benefits for all people.

It was important, indeed, to manage a positive national spirit during the boom years because, as Sweeney points out, the economic transformation meant the closing of some older industries and the displacement of their generally older workers. Troubling questions soon emerged— and they have persisted—about the fairness of policies that protect foreign corporate profits, tax structures that are not sufficiently progressive, the absence of measures that would help families cope with inflated housing costs, and the ineffectiveness of government to significantly reduce poverty.

Several critical reviews of Ireland's prosperity take up precisely this set of issues; among them is Kieran Allen's 2000 book, *The Celtic Tiger: The Myth of Social Partnership in Ireland*. The title tells all. Allen argues that the policies and consequences of a decade of economic growth produced a polarization rather than a harmonization of social classes in Ireland. He provides essentially the same analysis of the factors that led to growth as that presented by Sweeney, but Allen emphasizes the negative consequences of economic change, a change that has of course been driven by profit seeking, with government catering at every turn to international profit seekers. In Allen's view, the economic boom in Ireland occurred because, in the United States, smart money had learned that direct corporate investment in overseas operations—especially in stable advancing economies—returned high profits. With its poorly

paid and highly trained workforce, on the thresholds of both a consumer electronics revolution and the emerging EU market, Ireland was
simply in position to be taken advantage of. Multinational corporations,
struggling to keep their investors and to maintain stock values under
conditions of heightened global competition, followed the promise of
reduced costs and increased profits. In order to make Ireland a more attractive place to do business, government shifted the burden of sustaining the attractiveness of the economy to private taxpayers. For the many
who were not benefiting directly from the boom times, i.e., those who
were supporting themselves at bargain wages in the face of rising costs,
they also discovered that government-subsidized services and protec-
tions they had grown used to were being cut back or withdrawn.

Citing widely available data, Allen charges that during the period
of rapid economic expansion Ireland became a European tax haven to
multinationals by drastically reducing corporate tax levels — to the
resentment of its EU partner nations. At the same time it allowed to
stand one of the worst records in the EU regarding the degree of imbalance in income distribution and poverty rates. Allen estimates that
the number of workers who benefited most directly from economic expansion was relatively small (no more than 15 to 20 percent of all employed persons), while the majority of workers were left out. In addition
to the many who found themselves in positions where wage increases
lagged far behind inflated consumer prices, some were employed in temporary situations, a bulging segment of the workforce earned very low
wages, and a growing portion were not covered by pensions.

Allen's appraisal of the imbalance of the benefits of Ireland's prosperity was largely echoed in a 2001 report by the Combat Poverty
Agency, a body in part created and funded by the Irish government.
The report, *Rich and Poor: Perspectives on Tackling Inequality in Ireland*,
was the result of a study that set out to discover what connection there
might be between the two embarrassing features of the Irish success
story: the high degree of income inequality and the high levels of poverty in Ireland. The agency also wanted to discover whether government had been as effective as it might have been in promoting general
well-being during the growing prosperity years of the 1990s. The test
for whether the heavily promoted government program of social partnership was working, according to the agency, would be found in an

examination of the trade-off between lost revenues involved in providing tax breaks for businesses and the level of government spending on social programs that more directly benefited people in general. The social spending programs that the study considered included state support for medical care, education, housing, and direct payments from government to families to help them cope with increased living costs.

If this sounds like a critical investigation of the old argument that divides conservative supply-side and liberal social program politicians in the United States and elsewhere, it is. What makes the situation different in this case is that low-income Ireland has had a long-standing tradition of government support for average people's needs, and this provides a different starting point for judging balance and fairness in the most recent years. To withdraw existing supports once the majority of individuals and families are prospering might make sense, but to withdraw them during a period when many are finding it difficult to get by is something else. The Combat Poverty Agency concluded that the government's emphasis on managing the structure of taxes in order to maintain a competitive advantage in attracting and holding international capital had aggravated rather than reduced the inequality gap during the period of economic growth. The study's authors asked the following question: If the government was not willing to undertake to substantially reduce inequality and poverty—both of which remained at embarrassingly high levels compared to other EU states—during a period of sustained prosperity for business, then when would it be?

So there are cracks in the partnership idea. Reflecting the concerns of critics like Kieran Allen and the Combat Poverty Agency, the public has shown increasing awareness of the fairness issue. Questions are raised not only by activists and experts but by the news media, which regularly give voice to these concerns; they are also spoken about publicly by members of government and the clergy. In August 2006 the Conference of Religious of Ireland, a prominent official component of the social partnership, issued a report pointing to the unacceptable level of poverty in the country. Nearly 20 percent had slipped to near or below the poverty line, compared to 15.6 percent in 1994. Additionally, the report faulted government for failing to effectively provide fundamental institutional support, citing a functional illiteracy rate of 22.6 percent and inadequate spending for health care provision (*Irish Independent*, August 28, 2006).

In May 2006 the national Irish Nurses Association fought a plan to place beds in the hallways of hospitals' accident and emergency departments in order to accommodate emergency patient overflows. A part of the proposed plan asked staff to be vigilant and efficient in discharging patients at the earliest opportunity, and set forth a goal of having no emergency patient wait for more than twenty-four hours to be seen (*Irish Independent*, May 15, 2006). Earlier, the United Nation's *Human Development Report* (2004) had held up the high degree of inequality and poverty in prospering Ireland for the world to see.

In a mirror image of the UN report, the conservative U.S. Heritage Foundation and the *Wall Street Journal* published their *2006 Index of Economic Freedom*. The report enthused about Ireland that "the country has one of the world's most pro-business environments," noting that in January 2003 the government lowered the flat corporate tax rate from 16 percent to 12.5 percent, compared to the European Union's average corporate tax rate of 30 percent. The *Index* observes for 2006 that the country featured an individual tax rate that ranked "high" in international comparison, and a corporate tax rate that ranked "very low." The report did mention that there appeared to be a problem in health care provision in which costs were soaring and services were compromised.

While some in government would like to play down the potential divisiveness of class politics, there has always been a healthy left-leaning voice in Irish public debate. This is a voice that does not trust a coalition of successful politicians and businesses to keep the plight of the average worker uppermost in mind. A keen interest in class conflict emerges in conversations not only among academics and students in Irish universities but in discussions with all sorts of people. Segments of Irish society have paid the price of economic marginalization for the recent economic changes, which include those stemming from Ireland's membership in the EU. A series of large EU grants facilitated the economic boom that saw the growth in foreign investments and new jobs, but the transition has phased out some older industries and displaced workers. EU regulations have penalized smaller farmers. The reduction of those working directly in agriculture was already well underway in the last half of the twentieth century, before the new jobs made farming appear a poor career option for those ambitious young people with access to advanced skills and training. EU agreements also shifted subsidies and put farmers in direct competition with their continental counterparts. The share of the population employed in farming fell rapidly from 37 percent of the workforce in the mid 60s to barely 10 percent at the end of the century. Projections are for further drastic cuts in numbers as farmers give up or their offspring refuse to take over (see chapter 5). Can the "all for one and one for all" spirit be maintained in rural communities, in particular? Are the natives content with the changes? Some are.

BARRY AND MARY FIELDING, COUNTY WICKLOW

The Fieldings raised seven children, five sons and two daughters, on a modest dairy farm; all of them have earned university degrees. Their children's studies and work have taken them all over the world. None of them will stay on the land or carry on dairy farming. Barry himself gave it up some time ago and just runs dry stock—beef cattle—on the land, which he said was not really farming at all. How did it feel to have none of your children follow you into farming? Barry and Mary were delighted. A small farmer cannot make a living on the land, and both of them said so in separate conversations. No, they were not at all disappointed. They were happy that their kids were out in the world. The EU has made the prospect of farming bleak except for the largest operations, and this has helped open the door to a non-farming future for all the generations to come.

None of the Fielding children earned commerce (business) or technical degrees. Most or all (I lost track) studied language, as did their mother, and most or all added a concentration in the humanities or social sciences. "Wasn't that odd?" the parents asked. Barry took "credit," as he put it jokingly, for the lack of practical studies. He said he had no mind for science or math—beyond the considerable practical application required for farming and building, he should have added. He was happiest when at work building a new rental property on his land. He looked optimistically to the united European future as one that offered unprecedented opportunity for young people, his offspring included.

The Fieldings represent the spirit of compromise and patience that will be needed to support a united Europe and the Irish social partnership idea in future years. According to the master plan, in that future consumers will live better because large farming enterprises will be more efficient and economical producers, and people leaving the farms will earn the kind of living that will afford them a better quality of life. It will be a better life for the Fielding offspring in that they will not be trying to scrape by, as are the dwindling numbers of small farmers.

During the roughly thirty-year period that Barry and Mary worked on their dairy farm, farm families declined from more than a third of the population to barely a tenth. Barry, a keen student of his country's history, could fill you in with facts about what was happening in the wider world during the long tenure of his family's holding of this property and the ups and downs experienced by his predecessors. Explaining his acceptance, his enthusiasm, for the European future that his children have entered, he said that when the world is changing, you need to read those changes and get in step with them, and there is no point in looking back or digging in your heels to resist. He saw the present demise of small family agricultural holdings as part of the march of history reflected in similar patterns around the world. He believed that the trend was retarded in Ireland by the late demise of colonialism there, as some of the large holdings of landlords were broken up and redistributed in small parcels. Certainly, that was a good thing *then* because it gave people a living, but now the inevitable reversal of that redistribution is coming about through the irresistible logic of the world market. No, he had hoped that none of his children would want to stay in farming, and there was never much fear of that, given the hard work they saw growing up on the farm.

Today, Barry and Mary live in a comfortable modern bungalow. The older dwellings on the property are being restored and added to for rental. When foreign tourists come looking for a taste of traditional Ireland, the Fieldings will rent it to them, fitted out with all the modern conveniences. For the Fieldings themselves, their business is part of the New Ireland, which is a state within the new Europe, a place where a university degree in French and philosophy will get you further than the ownership of a working farm. A farm can be useful, especially in the provision of in-demand ambiance for a growing tourism enterprise. A farmer can come to appreciate a landscape he has lived all his life on if he can find the "scenic" in the familiar, if he can come to adopt the point of view of travelers looking for the real thing.

Looking for the real thing in Ireland means, for many visitors, looking to the rural Ireland of small farms and quiet countryside, the slowly changing place where generation after generation of the same family has worked the same acreage. On the surface, rural Ireland still presents such a picture, but it is a thinly populated one. Intellectually, we can all agree with the Fieldings and their far-flung and prospering children that this is a good thing, as the world opens up its opportunities for new and different kinds of lives for the home-grown Irish. In the old days, one son would have stayed on the land, and the other brothers and sisters would have "gone traveling" to find work in Dublin or Cork, or Birmingham or Boston, typically in construction or factories. Prospects are better for many today, but not all families will be able to provide university or technical college training; not all sons and daughters will be qualified for the limited number of spaces in postsecondary education.

Those advocates of controlled change, like the staff members of the Combat Poverty Agency, who want to protect the interests of *all* of those in the next generation to insure that they will have adequate incomes and a decent place to live, may be out of step with the realities of the global marketplace. From Beijing to Tokyo to New York the lesson has been that globalization brings a fickle and selective prosperity, and just as the fortunes of some are buoyed up, others are displaced by the widening inequalities that technical and economic change usher in. The future for many who have nothing special to offer the world economy is uncertain in Ireland, as elsewhere, and the real economic miracle will be how the government of a small nation, suddenly thrust forward into the center of the arena of unforgiving global competition, with its still emerging rules, will provide for the security of all its people.

SIGNS OF TIMES TO COME

And there is more that remains uncertain than whether or how comfort and privilege will be distributed equitably among the people of Ireland. Along with the economic surge has come a number of related changes for which there are no precedents, and that will test the coping abilities of individuals and the society itself. Among these are the effect of immigration on prejudice, discrimination, and racism; the correlation between greater levels of prosperity and upward trends in crime and violence; and the impact of growing wealth and materialist values as they collide with the influences of established religion. Nothing in this list of challenges is new to the world, but all are new to Ireland, at least in the dimensions that they are presently manifesting themselves.

Immigration and Race

In 2000 Kevin Myers wrote for *The Irish Times* that "we should know by now that the Ireland that was, is gone. Forever. We are going to be a multiracial society, and anyone who has visited truly multiracial cities anywhere will know that enormous cultural and culinary benefits lie ahead" (Myers 2000a). Food was actually not the focus of the article: Myers was writing about the need for the Irish government and citizens to squarely face the fact that their island had become a target for the globe's economic migrants, people—like the Irish in the nineteenth and most of the twentieth centuries—for whom there was little or nothing to do at home and who were bound by necessity to follow the economic action to far places across the world. Reflecting on the histories of immigration elsewhere, Myers predicted that the New Irish would over time retain many of their ways. Noting that in 2000 there were already more Muslims than Methodists in neighboring Wales, he observed that such elements of multiculturalism as neighborhood mosques might be hard for the Irish to get used to.

Maybe he goes *too* far when he asks whether working-class fans of Irish sports could someday soon be expected to tolerate immigrant groups openly rooting for Irish opponents in an international soccer match. It is not hard to imagine what the reaction of locals might have been if there had been knots of boisterous Cameroonian or German visitors in pubs watching Ireland play in the 2002 World Cup. By the same token, it does not strain the imagination to anticipate what the reaction in a neighborhood bar in Germany would have been to a throng of wildly cheering Irish tourists as the Germans watched victory snatched from them in injury time. But Myers's point is that the time has arrived when Ireland has to come to terms with such questions: "Tolerance is a complex thing. It is not a matter of dealing with stereotypes, but accepting people with different complexions, different ways and, most of all, different loyalties. We have absolutely no history of tolerating people with vociferously expressed loyalties different from our own; yet that [is what] we are going to have to do in the future. It will not be easy."

In the 1990s we were still not talking about huge numbers of people immigrating to Ireland, at least not by international standards. In the year 1996, early in the economic boom cycle, Ireland counted 44,000 newcomers, which overbalanced the 29,000 emigrants that left that year, for a net of 15,000 new residents. If we consider the worldwide dimensions of population movement, Ireland's share would barely deserve a footnote. Nevertheless, to indicate the significance of what appear to be very modest figures: the increase in Ireland's population added by immigration that year rivaled the net rate of population increase from native births. The country only had 3.7 million people at the time.

By 2006 the picture was somewhat different. With the expansion of the European Union from fifteen to twenty-five states in 2004, Ireland became a favored target of immigrants from the East. Only Ireland, England, and Sweden among all European nations opened their labor markets to the citizens of member states. Between 2004 and mid 2006, 150,000 newcomers arrived from Eastern Europe alone, with most coming from Poland. Polish-language advertisements are posted in shop windows, there are Polish signs on construction sites, and Polish foods quickly appeared in supermarkets. Ireland's population is growing at a rate of 2.5 percent annually, and two-thirds of that is coming from immigration. Yet Ireland's unemployment rate remained unchanged in mid 2006, at 4.4 percent, the lowest in the EU, despite the growth (Associated Press, September 12, 2006).

The numbers involved in what some have come to perceive as Ireland's "immigration problem" still remain relatively small on a global scale. According to the United Nations High Commission on Refugees, by 1999 over ninety million international travelers were looking for a place to live and work. The magnitude of such figures gives rise to concerns about where the flow of immigrants is taking the island. By the mid 90s, immigration — particularly illegal immigration — was a growing political issue for the EU countries taken as a whole. A decade later the issue has intensified, and the focus of concern has become migrants from countries where large proportions of the population are poor and desperate. Some international migrants are refugees fleeing their homelands as a result of warfare or persecution, and receiving nations commonly have provisions for granting asylum to limited numbers of this class of dislocated persons.

But many more international travelers are economic migrants, some who arrive at their European destination under various EU agreements, others with invitations and work permits, but some number come on their own, seeking work illegally. The latter find their way to prospering nations by whatever means and hang on to the edges of opulent economies, where there is at least the chance of relative personal security and a means of survival. In 2002–2003 there were some estimates that EU countries taken together might have been receiving three hundred thousand to five hundred thousand illegal immigrants annually. Reports of this scale of illegal immigration, of smuggling rings that transport human cargo by the truckload, the usual charges that the newcomers are freeloaders or worse, or that they will take jobs from citizens, engage in criminal activities, and so forth, have helped inspire support for reactionary, right-wing, national front–style political parties in Europe, putting pressure on governments to control immigration.

The issue was critical enough in 2002 for Britain's prime minister, Tony Blair, to urge that aid be cut to countries that refused to take back illegal immigrants, as well as nations that were particularly ineffective in preventing their people from gaining illegal entry to Europe without adequate departure documentation. Spain and Italy supported similar policies, but the idea of penalizing poor countries for failing to prevent illegal immigration to other countries was rejected by the EU representatives as unworkable and overly punitive (*Irish Times*, June 21, 2002).

Debates about Ireland's immigration policy swirl within this political sea. In this light, it is interesting to watch Irish politicians tread carefully on the immigration issue, unable to appear to be doing nothing, on the one hand, while avoiding the appearance of race-based xenophobic reaction on the other. Social critics are poised to pounce if anyone is perceived as drifting too close to racist pronouncements. For example, calls by a few politicians for health screening of asylum seekers in Ireland, primarily people from poor countries, led to charges by critics that such proposed measures were openly racist. The Minister for Justice, speaking in favor of developing an effective strategy to control illegal immigration, had to carefully make the case that such a strategy was needed in order to *prevent* reactionary racism. His argument was that if the perception grew of the EU's inability to control illegal entry, popular resentment against certain immigrants, including unfortunate refugees, might well increase.

In the 2002 general election in Ireland, the two local candidates who campaigned on an openly anti-immigration platform did poorly, gathering few votes as they went down to defeat. In an enlightened move, the major political parties had agreed not to introduce race or immigration into the campaign and largely stuck to the agreement. There were local efforts, such as those of the Irish People's Party, to exploit the issue, but these were outside the political mainstream (*Irish Times*, May 20, 2002).

But the policy of avoiding political issues that have the potential for becoming ugly is a fragile strategy at best. By 2006 political figures were still trying to figure out how to speak publicly about the issue of immigration, but opinion researchers were by then telling the leading parties that platforms that included stricter controls on immigration were potential election winners. In August 2006, when Labour Party leader Pat Rabbitte said publicly that cheap foreign labor threatened native Irish workers, his party quickly enjoyed a two-point jump in opinion polls (*Irish Independent*, August 26, 2006). A month earlier David Begg, the general secretary of the Irish Congress of Trade Unions, had put it more bluntly. He said it had been naive for the government to assume that employers would not take advantage of an abundant supply of vulnerable and compliant foreign workers, preferring to hire them at lower wages than to hire native Irish (*Irish Times*, July 18, 2006).

Although these are still relatively early days in the Irish homeland's brush with multiculturalism and multiracialism, there are signs that the public mind is increasingly occupied with the immigration issue. Writing in 1998, journalist Kevin Myers was not convinced that there was any reason to believe that the people of Ireland, when ultimately put to the test, would behave any differently from other xenophobes around the globe. He said that the claim that "we" are not racist is laughable, considering the way Irish emigrants and their descendants have conducted themselves around racial confrontations in the United States and Britain. He warned the people of Ireland that, with anti-foreigner street incidents and charges of official discrimination too numerous to be called isolated, they should mind any nationalistic tendencies to exclude outsiders and examine the ways in which their self-image of being open and accepting squared with the shadow already cast by the existing record (Myers 1998).

By 2006 the Minister for Justice, Michael McDowell, in an appeal to parties and candidates to be guarded and moderate in the way they debated immigration, could still say that the Irish experiment with immigration was going relatively smoothly. But then there was Ulster (*Irish Times*, July 18, 2006). In 2004 the increase in attacks on immigrants had earned the province the title "Hate Capital of Europe," a label often repeated in news stories about racial and anti-immigrant violence there. Nearly one thousand "racially motivated" attacks, some of them involving exceptionally brutal beatings, occurred in the twelve months prior to June 2006, a rise of 15 percent over the previous year. The attacks, which included assaults against Eastern Europeans, were widespread across Ulster and continued despite protestations and calls for unity and tolerance from government leaders. The police named racism their leading problem (Associated Press, June 26, 2006; *Belfast Telegraph*, June 27, 2006; *The Sun*, June 27, 2006).

Ulster is not the Republic, and the history of sectarian violence in the North may in some way provide hope that what has happened there will not be repeated in the South. While a significant minority of both Catholics and Protestants in Ulster admitted to being racist or anti-foreigner in a recent poll, self-reported bigotry was much higher (46 percent) among the members of Ian Paisley's Democratic Unionist Party (DUP) than supporters of Sinn Fein (19 percent). One of the poll's researchers, Chris Gilligan, said that it was possible that DUP members felt that they had lost out since the ceasefire and peace agreement and may feel that "the whole world is against them, the Catholics, the British Government, and now the immigrants" (*The Observer*, June 25, 2006).

Whatever the future may hold for race and ethnic relations in the North, in the Republic itself the peaceful integration of a growing immigrant population may well depend on the maintenance of conditions under which natives don't feel that they are "losing out." Whether it is fair to ask a people whose recent history has been so tied to economic emigration, whose citizens abroad were often ill-treated, to offer the world exemplary openness and tolerance when the tables are turned, can be debated. But surely the question will remain posed for as long as the prosperity of Ireland continues to draw a diversity of immigrants. The real test will come when the Irish economy cools down, unemployment increases, and Ireland finds itself a demographically changed multicultural and multiracial nation where natives and immigrants compete for the same job.

As it is, there is growing evidence that major employers exploit foreign workers, overworking and underpaying them in defiance of Ireland's employment legislation. In 2005 a Turkish construction firm was charged with underpaying Turkish workers in Ireland, and in 2006 charges were made that Serbian workers were being paid a fraction, in some cases less than 20 percent, of the industry standard at work sites that were contracted by the state's Energy Supply Board (*Irish Times*, May 18, 2006; *Irish Examiner*, May 15, 2006). Ireland's treatment of asylum seekers was publicly called into question when thirty-three Afghan men went on hunger strike, occupying Dublin's St. Patrick's Cathedral in May 2006. Scuffles broke out among the crowd that gathered when the Afghans were being removed by Gardaí after a week-long occupation, pitting supporters of the hunger strikers (including members of Residents Against Racism and left-of-center political parties) against local residents chanting "send them home." One young boy who was tearing down posters supportive of the strikers is quoted as saying, "I hate the Gardaí but I hate the immigrants more." Socialist Party leader Joe Higgins was also on hand. He addressed the crowd, saying, "Our government has a double standard. They are begging U.S. authorities to let the so-called 60,000 Irish illegals stay. . . . Why can't they do the same for a few dozen here?" (*Irish Times*, May 22, 2006).

Apart from the number, Higgins's statement is true. The estimated forty thousand illegal Irish immigrants in the United States receive support from various organizations working on their behalf, including the Irish Immigration Centre in Boston, similar centers in other cities, and the Irish government. Like other undocumented workers in the United States, the Irish are facing increasing pressures from legislation that restricts their freedom. Sister Lena Deevey of the Boston center said that the people she assists lead an underground existence, "You're always looking over your shoulder. You can't move around" (*Boston Herald*, July 23, 2006). Various rallies, which would include delegations from Ireland, were planned to try to influence the U.S. congressional debate on immigration in 2006, possibly to grant amnesty to the Irish illegals, to allow them to stay. The immigrants are made to feel at home by the American Irish.

Coping with Prosperity

There were sure signs of a cooling economy as the century turned and the dot-com and fraud-inflated Wall Street bubble burst, sending waves of distress across the Atlantic. In Ireland, corporate operations shrank, businesses closed, real estate prices faltered, related service and support businesses contracted, and some in the throng of newly affluent young professionals found themselves out of work. But for the nation there was no going back to the old, pre-economic boom days. The Irish marketplace had been transformed in the boom decade, and there remained enough economic vigor to sustain the mood of growing prosperity. And while the economy may not be expanding as rapidly as it was in the late 90s, in 2004 the GDP grew at a rate of 4.9 percent, which was enough to make the Republic the fourth most prosperous economy in the world, as measured by GDP per capita.

Indeed, measures of "consumer sentiment" remained high through late 2006, despite concerns about rising prices and interest rates (*RTE Business*, December 4, 2006). The seasonally adjusted trade surplus in March 2006 was running at 14 percent, aided by exports in the key software sector, which had reached a value of €15 billion in 2005 (*Irish Examiner*, May 19, 2006). Expectations had been set much higher than they were before the prosperous 90s regarding what sort of standard of living any reasonably successful person should anticipate—and there was a cosmopolitan acceptance among the young upwardly mobile of the high prices one could expect to pay.

And while the rate of inflation fell gradually from its highpoint in 1999, the cumulative effect of the decade meant spectacularly higher prices for most consumer goods. The cost of many items in Ireland is set to a great extent by external factors—such as the price of oil and expensive manufactured items like foreign-built automobiles. But part of the increase in consumer costs was home-grown, related to the modestly rising costs of labor in manufacturing and services. Prices were also tied in no small measure to the generous wages the international market afforded the managerial and professional classes. Taxes and duties added by government also raised prices. During the 1990s the Irish rate of inflation was a major concern to consumers and government, at times reaching double that of the average EU inflation rate. By 2000 there was a growing concern that the continued spiral of costs was undermining what was left of the delicate balance of the social partnership, as the typical worker's wage failed to keep up with the inflated prices pegged to the incomes of the professional and managerial elite. In July 2006 the rate of inflation was 4.2 percent, well ahead of the average rate for the EU. The price of housing, vehicle fuels, and utilities had increased 16.5 percent in a twelve-month period (Associated Press, August 10, 2006).

Ireland has become one of the most expensive countries to live in among all those that adopted the Euro, and the cost of living in Dublin is at or near the top of the major cities in the Euro zone (Cassidy 2002). Joe Humphreys wrote that "A new phrase has been added to the national lexicon in recent times—'Rip-off Ireland.' The label hangs so well, indeed, that it seems like the natural successor to Celtic Tiger Ireland as a badge of Irish identity" (2002). He cited a survey conducted by a consumer group, which found that a standardized basket of groceries in very costly St. Tropez on the French Riviera cost 23 percent less than the same items in a Dublin supermarket. Observing that a can of Guinness cost 60 percent more in Ireland than in France, Humphreys warned that despite "overseas perceptions of a happy-go-lucky people, the Irish are becoming ever more irritated by rising prices, a perceived decline in customer service standards, and a general feeling that shoppers are getting less value for money in a variety of sectors." A grocers' organization responded with its own study, which revealed that food was more of a bargain in Ireland than in many other EU countries. The grocers blamed everything from transportation to the cost of labor for any inflation in Irish prices. To this Humphreys responded with the words of a spokesperson for the Irish consumer group: "There is no valid reason why potatoes are half the price in Germany as they are in Ireland. . . . Labour costs are lower in Ireland than in Germany or France, and transport costs work both ways. I mean, how can you justify Irish beef being cheaper in France than in Ireland? The cows don't swim to France."

The difference between what consumers in Ireland and those elsewhere pay when it comes to what are commonly the two largest consumer expenses, cars and housing, is far from trivial. In 2002, despite the efforts of the EU's European Commission and the Irish government to level the cost of automobiles, Irish car buyers still paid among the highest prices in the EU. The same small Fiat cost €1,000 more to buy in Ireland than in Britain and €3,000 more than in Greece (O'Doherty

2002). Affordable housing is an even more fundamental need than personal transportation, and finding it has become an increasingly trying experience. People appear to be willing to go farther from their urban workplaces in search of affordable accommodation, with longer commuting times and distances the result, which means more cars on the road for longer periods of time on a daily basis, hence more snarled traffic in and around the largest cities and their growing suburbs.

Through the course of the twentieth century, housing had come to be seen by many in Europe as something of a social good, a right, although it was also understood that this right was often compromised: it has always been difficult for the combination of market-produced private and government-subsidized housing to keep up with demand in the major cities. Boom times have produced a period of extraordinary pressure on the Irish housing market—again, especially in cities. Young Irish workers going out on their own, people migrating from rural areas and small towns, returning Irish emigrants, and newly arriving immigrants all strain the available stocks of rental property, with the rental market responding to the law of supply and demand in the usual way. Rising rental costs were helped along by newly ambitious landlords who saw the huge profits and incomes being earned all around them, while the value of their own property advanced yearly by leaps and bounds. According to Ireland's Central Statistics Office, average housing costs for Ireland as a whole increased by 43 percent in five years from the mid 90s through the end of the century. Although the average industrial wage increased only about 26 percent in roughly the same period, the highest paid 20 percent of Ireland's income-earners enjoyed a 61 percent increase in their disposable income (Central Statistics Office Ireland 2000). The concentration of the income elite in cities amplified the effects of inflation there.

Dublin is the most extreme case of high housing costs, with rents increasing an average of 15 percent per year at the end of the 90s, putting even the most basic properties out of the reach of modest income groups. While the upsurge in rental rates leveled off in the past few years, even declining slightly, the average rent for a one-bedroom apartment in Dublin in January 2005 was in the range of €800 to 900, roughly the same as for the peak year of 2002. Families who needed more than one bedroom were, of course, paying much more. Competition among renters for affordable space in the major cities has been fierce at times. The tightness of the rental housing supply is aggravated by the fact that many of the young professionals whose salaries have been bidding up rental costs were themselves being priced out of the prospect of home ownership. The situation is difficult for any household, but for those with children getting by on lower incomes, it had become desperate by the century's turn (O'Dea 2001).

The rise in the purchase price of private residences also reflects the new position of Ireland in a global market where executive, professional, and high tech incomes are set at the international scale. Through a good portion of the 1990s, private housing prices increased at double-digit inflation rates, with those rates (certainly not prices) peaking in 2000, a year when the price of a house jumped 20.3 percent in Dublin and 18.9 percent in the rest of the country (Coyle 2002). Since 2000 the rise in real estate prices has been unsteady, escalating in fits and starts interspersed with brief stagnant spells. By the end of 2005 the average price of a house in Ireland was about €278,000 (compared to the average price in the UK of about €232,000 or the United States at €177,500), with values up by nearly a tenth over a year earlier. And for those who were not ready to jump at the bargain rate and waited until mid 2006 to buy, the average price had risen again, to €365,000. Understandably, real estate interests were encouraged by the resumption of the rapid upward trend in values, which, if sustained, would amount to an annual 14 percent growth rate, but this was not good news for buyers, especially first-time buyers. In 2001 Maev-Ann Wren reported: "A Dublin man recently wrote to me saying 'My daughter, who is a nurse, cannot buy a dog box, and my other daughter, who is a national school teacher, cannot buy a cat's cradle. In fact, the two of them together cannot buy a cardboard box in Dublin."

Such tales as this go to the heart of the partnership/fairness question of exactly who it is that is living well in Ireland. Wren believes that the government shares the same perspective as realtors, that rising prices are a positive sign. As it is, two good incomes are usually required to qualify for a mortgage. And for increasing numbers of people, there was simply no prospect of qualifying (Wren 2001).

Medb Ruane is a homeowner who is not single-mindedly jubilant about the increasing value of her property. She writes that in the space of a few years her Dublin house had "increased in value by such an exorbitant amount I could now refinance the mortgage to acquire a top-range

Porsche without much difficulty. . . . If I were to rent it out, the profit I could make over the actual mortgage cost would be at least double my outgoings. The potential for greed this encourages hasn't escaped me. Trouble is, how would I accommodate a family of five? We can't live in a Porsche" (Ruane 2000). Ruane speculated that without tough government actions to support common householders the country would soon face unprecedented levels of social unrest. In fact, inflated real estate prices may turn out to be good news for no one. Amid a flurry of speculation about the consequences of inflated pricing, with some experts warning of a major collapse in prices and realty interests expressing the hope that at worst the market might face a little correction, the International Monetary Fund weighed in on the calamity side of the debate, issuing a warning on the possibility of a collapse due to overvaluation (*Business News Digest,* September 15, 2006).

The rise in the cost of living that has helped to divide Irish society may be simply the inevitable result of gravitating to the prosperous center of the globalized marketplace. But the Irish can be forgiven for wondering why they must sweat the costs of such overheated prices for their own staples of shelter, meat, potatoes, and Guinness. Disproportionately high price tags also attach to "luxury items," that is, brand-name imported goods. In 2000 the British Consumer Association sent a team of investigators Christmas shopping in nine cities in Europe and three in the United States, finding substantially higher costs for brand name goods in Dublin than in U.S. cities. The Secret Message Barbie Doll cost more than two and a half times as much in Dublin as in the United States that year. A popular Britney Spears CD cost in Irish pounds £15.50 in Dublin compared to £9.88 in the United States, and the same Ralph Lauren short-sleeved polo shirt that cost the equivalent of £34.60 in the United States went for £53.98 in Dublin. The total cost of the brand-name luxury items was 63 percent more in Dublin than in U.S. major metropolitan areas (cold comfort was that the prices for these particular items in London were somewhat higher than in Dublin that year) (Byrne 2000).

Stress and Hustle

If living well means keeping up with international consumption patterns, then the high cost of keeping up means that we can expect to find a new level of hustle in everyday Irish life. Business people I have known in Ireland like to demonstrate, especially to American visitors, that they know all about getting things done efficiently. Apparently, according to Kate Holmquist, a kind of efficiency had by 2000 become a newly elevated value that dominated people's lives. She thinks that Ireland has become more Americanized in terms of hustle and pace than the United States itself. In her words,

> To think that when people used to ask me how I liked living in Ireland, I used to praise the quality of life. . . . Now I'm in the ironic position of going to the States to chill out and escape the American lifestyle that has taken over Ireland. We are all Americans now in our values and aspirations to earn and own as much as we possibly can. An American visitor told me recently how depressed he was to learn that all the Irish ever talked about was property prices. Everyone he met boasted about how much their house was worth. He had come here expecting a more spiritual, philosophical approach to life. (Holmquist 2000)

For Holmquist, the "so-called 'quality of life' has become a consumer item too expensive for most to afford on a regular basis. The possibility of spending 'quality time' with children in a stress-free atmosphere has become something you book with a travel agent." She was trying to figure out an alternative, a way to distance herself from the effects of prosperity. She might try St. Tropez—at least groceries there are cheaper.

And woe to those caught in the teeth of it, the prosperous participants who sell what those riding the crest of the economic wave have the money to buy. Where better to look for the benefits of prosperity than, say, a Mercedes dealer in Dublin? One Dublin dealer who was selling six thousand Mercedes in the year 2000, where he used to sell six hundred before the new prosperity, said that the demand for the flash cars kept him in his showroom from eight in the morning until eight at night. His American counterpart in Miami or Manhattan might respond, Sure, that's great. But the Mercedes man was not happy: "I can genuinely say it's not healthy for me or my family. I cannot be the husband and father I want to be at night after days like these, and I hear my colleagues around the floor say the same thing. We don't feel self-rewarded by the good times we're in" (Hoge 2000). This dealer's customers might commute forty miles out into the Dublin countryside, through areas being consolidated into metropolitan suburbs. Irish papers carried stories of the pressures of commuting along country lanes, the pressures of being caught for hours in traffic snarls, the aggravation of traffic congestion caused by ongoing road improvement construction, the isolation of people feeling trapped in new suburbs. Once again in a strange telescoping of time and space, twenty-first-century globalization brought about in Ireland the kinds of social concerns discussed in a suburbanizing United States a half century ago.

Change naturally brings questions about what is being left behind, as people struggle to figure out just what are the benefits supposedly brought in by the new arrangements. The official doctrine of partnership in progress has managed to encourage many to look on the bright side, to think about what is good for the country in terms of new jobs and better material standards. But even those who benefit most directly, who are proud of what the country is showing the world, those who are world-wise observers, can be caught worrying about what is being lost. Kevin Myers reached his limit some time ago. He exploded:

> No doubt we are all supposed to utter hoarse cheers of joy that the IDA has talked yet another American company into setting up here — this time in lovely, unspoilt Cavan. Soon lovely, unspoilt Cavan will be lovely, enbungalowed Cavan, every field a housing site, every junction a traffic jam, every village a dormitory, every pub a designer-chic drinks emporium, serving wheat beers, latte and bottled lager at £5 a go. Is this the future we are creating for ourselves: a commercial paradise, with not a corner of Ireland free of the fierce energies of industry, and road rage at every turn? (2000b)

It may well be. Unsurprisingly, one price paid for being drawn into the center of the global marketplace is that a place is bound to become structurally, behaviorally, and culturally more like the prominent economic poles of the global network — Tokyo, London, Milan, New York. Tastes, values, pace of life — these all twist into new shapes and speed up at the center. But despite the leveling power that the global culture has everywhere it touches down, it is itself an amalgam of all the cultures it affects. Ireland, with its dispersed cultural army of the millions of descendants of Irish emigrants, is influencing the world culturally, even as it is influenced in turn. The island's leap into prosperity has added a vibrancy to Irish culture that has in turn enhanced its power to communicate who and what it is globally, far beyond what might be expected of an island republic of four million.

THE GLOBAL PRESENCE OF IRISH CULTURE

By the mid 90s a new wave of interest in Irish culture was clearly developing around the world. By 1997 it had blossomed into a full-fledged distraction: on St. Patrick's Day that year the *New York Times* proclaimed, "From Poets to Pubs, Irish Imports Are in Demand" (Barry 1997). It was true, for better and worse.

Irish village theme bars, looking like bad Hollywood movie sets from the 1930s, began to pop up in major cities around the world, the worst complete with thatch, bicycle, and gas fire in the open hearth. Frank McCourt's *Angela's Ashes* along with novelist Roddy Doyle's works demonstrated a new Irish confidence in talking with fascinating irreverence about working-class and poor Irish experiences, as if to say, If you don't like us, you can leave us alone—we're alright. Maeve Binchy became a multinational cottage industry turning out non-threatening romantic novels that appealed to a worldwide audience. In Ireland the artistic version of industrial tax breaks was drawing filmmakers to shoot anything Irish. And Riverdance—emblematic of Ireland's newfound economic swagger—was breaking upon the stages of the world in a strangely sexy and breathtaking interpretation of a staid element of Irish culture, suitably amplified to catch the attention of an international audience. The world was turned on by step dancing, of all things. If Ireland's culture was going to be modified by global influence, then Irish culture was going to take hold of world culture on its own terms and carve out a generous space for itself.

Movies with international casts and distribution, like *The Crying Game, My Left Foot, The Commitments* based on a Doyle novel, Maeve Binchy's *Circle of Friends, Michael Collins, Some Mother's Son, In the Name of the Father, Waking Ned Divine,* and numerous others, signaled the Irish presence in the mass media in dimensions unheard of since the times of Barry Fitzgerald. In television, a weekly soap opera produced by BBC Northern Ireland generated such massive international interest that it astounded everyone associated with the show, but it fit with the burgeoning of worldwide fascination with things Irish. Set in a small village in Wicklow, *Ballykissangel* originally combined a taboo central theme, the romantic attraction between a Catholic priest and the town's cynical (female) publican, with each week's episode carrying several light subplots involving various ingeniously cast characters—who carried the show after the publican died and the priest went away with a broken heart. In no time, fans were flocking to the small mill town of Avoca, where the show was set, filling the main street and the shops wall-to-wall (see chapter 8 for more about the changes in Avoca). The show attempted to capture the life of a village where people were struggling to come to grips with problems besetting contemporary Ireland, and in the process it captured the imagination of people all over the world—as well as in Ireland itself.

As the world was discovering Irish arts, Irish artists were discovering a new creative buoyancy in an Ireland transformed in a historical minute by the new affluence, by government support of media enterprise, and by a secularizing culture that owed less of its identity to religion than to the dark backstreets of a rapidly urbanizing nation. The Irish playwright Sebastian Barry, comparing Ireland of the 1990s to that of the 1970s, said, "It's almost a new nationality now" (Riding 1997). The search for what it meant to be Irish in the New Ireland lent a new and appealing set of themes to the work of artists in a number of fields: there is nothing like drugs, sex, violence, and corruption to liven up a plot. The irony is that in order to become a self-sustaining financial success telling the tales of a small country like Ireland, you need an international audience with a sustained interest in your topic (product). Of course, the long years of emigration and Roman Catholic restrictions on birth control had provided an attentive audience of tens of millions of people of Irish descent around the globe. Some found it in the movies and books, others in the music. There was something for everyone in U2, Solas, Sinead O'Connor, Enya, the enduring Chieftains, Afro Celt Sound System, and dozens of others, including Irish performers who were not born or primarily headquartered in Ireland but who were springing up around the world reflecting the extent of the cultural reach of expatriate Ireland. In every area of the arts—novels and poetry, the theater, painting and sculpture—Ireland and the Irish had finally fully arrived.

The global dimension of Irish culture's appeal, not only in its spectacular performance or epic artistic proportions but in the everyday form of speech and amateur dance, is in some ways purely astonishing and difficult to overstate. A by no means exhaustive survey of people putting effort into sustaining and absorbing Irish heritage turns up the following sketch. An organization promoting Irish language study lists thirty-three states in the United States where you can take lessons, some strictly for personal satisfaction, some for university credit. For example, in New York State there are forty-one individuals, universities, community colleges, and other organizations offering Gaelic lessons, twenty-one in California, and twenty in Massachusetts. Among other states where you can get instruction are Mississippi, New Mexico, and Utah. The Riverdance production has inspired the growth of a full-blown industry in Irish step and other traditional Irish dance forms; there appear to be hundreds of schools and individuals around the world offering instruction. Kieran Jordan, former arts editor and writer for the *Boston Irish Reporter* newsletter, cites testimony from several teachers of Irish dance that the glamour and success of Riverdance has inspired a new level of commitment for young step dancers in the United States. While the instructors she spoke to in the greater Boston area were reluctant to attribute the growing interest solely to the popularity of Riverdance, they did indicate an increase in enrollments following the Hibernian phenomenon, and there had been a general trend in amateur step dancing competitions toward costumes and liberated dance styles that mimicked the flashy stage production (Jordan 2002).

And why not? If Riverdance and Michael Flatly's subsequent productions have come to stand as cultural symbols of Ireland and Irish culture, the world does appear to be watching—and wanting to participate. You can enjoy local step dance performances or take lessons in New South Wales, Sweden, South Africa, and Tokyo. Maria Cunningham teaches Irish dance in Nairobi, an American woman gives lessons in the Netherlands, and in Germany lessons are offered by an accredited instructor and a former step dancing champion of Trinidadian and Irish parents. She has full classes, and none of her students are of Irish descent (http://www.antoniopacelli.com).

Ireland and Irish culture are phenomena that have been and continue to be a product of a widening world, both historically and in our time. Today, a fabulously wealthy and powerful global market is providing a means of support for Irish culture and creative genius. In the new century we witness a strange flowing together of local and global elements that produce a many-layered and constantly shifting reality. The same can be said of any place—all are linked by the irresistible force of the global economy and its capacity to communicate, to have its way.

Commercial chunks of the global economy that get planted in among the intensely local sensibilities of the Irish countryside may create frictions and tensions, at least in the beginning: they are pieces of different centuries; they are not meant to fit together. And yet there is an inevitable logic to the remote economic forces: it brings those forces into contact with the local worlds and locks them in place. The wearing and chafing of time will reshape these local and remote worlds where they touch, forcing a mutual accommodation that over time will produce a future that is not quite possible to envision at the moment. The American performer Michael Jackson reportedly considered building a leprechaun theme park in Ireland (*The Mirror Eire Edition*, September 15, 2006). The project would synthesize the world-marketed cartoon imagery of Ireland with the authenticity of being able to experience that imagery right there in Ireland (Jackson spokespersons quickly denied the story, but the journalist, Paul Martin, assured me that his source was quite well placed). If the half billion dollars could be raised and the theme park built, the project would present a magnificent example of the power of the world to redefine little Ireland.

We may not be able to envision the future. What we can see with greater clarity is what a changing Ireland means to the people who are there. Now that we have considered something of the transformation of the island itself, we are prepared to look more closely at how people are experiencing change. People say and see many different things in Ireland—all of them true, because they represent the efforts of people to understand the meaning of things important to them. It is true what the business editor of *The Independent*, Brendan Keenan, says: "No one wants dear old Ireland back. Dear old Ireland was nice for the tourists, but not for us" (Hoge 2000). And it is also true what Colm Tóibín, the novelist, has to say: "I was much happier when this was a backwater because you could shuffle around without noticing it. Now you have to interpret everything that's going on to everyone you know. It's so much more exhausting" (Riding 1997).

It is much too simple to divide Ireland according to past and present, tourist and resident, reality and myth. Everyone's Ireland contains some appreciation of what is and what was, some element of nostalgia and a realization that things must change so that people may live better. Every individual is situated uniquely for knowing and telling the changes, and this makes all interpretations equally important, equally valid. That is why it is important to take the time to tell stories about ourselves and life going on, and to listen to others' stories as if the meaning of life itself depended on it.

CHAPTER 3

Strangers at Home

The day was never long enough for all we wanted to do . . .

anywhere and anytime we could find some pleasant occupation

or other. . . . Our chosen playground was outdoors and our

playthings the things we found there. Looking back I find

myself being sorry for the city children of today who are so

much cut off from that world of adventure.

(Danaher 1966)

In Ireland today, individual biographies intersect with a national history that has taken a sharp turn, as people everywhere in the world grope toward a dimly seen future driven by globalism. People make plans, place bets, engage in acts of faith that somehow, eventually, the future will all make sense, and everyone will live a better life. But there is much at stake in the changes that are here and those that are coming. Just as there is the hope that some of the hard edge of living day to day and the political rancor that was of the past can be left behind, there is worry. Among the many new things the Irish are not used to are happy endings. While there is a general sense that much is good in the prosperity of the present, people are uncertain about how, exactly, the continuing changes rooted in distant places in the world economy will affect their personal lives and are sometimes concerned about what is about to be swept away.

On Malin Head in Donegal, at Ireland's northern point, one family has for several generations operated Farren's Bar, the most northerly pub on the island, a stewardship spanning well over a century of colonial rule and independence. When I spoke to the youngest son of the family a few years ago, he was preparing for a career in software, reckoning that one or another of his brothers and sisters would take over from their parents when the time came. In Donegal, Republican nationalism remains a strong element of the local world view. The plastic and rubber bullets that adorned the shelves behind the bar at Farren's—with dates and places written on them in felt marker telling where they were fired at civilians in neighboring Ulster—were only recent artifacts of the long-standing conflict, part of a history that remains to be unmade by today's generations. There are feats of forgetting yet to be performed by many still living. Nevertheless, the prospering economies, North and South, are a major distraction from the legacy of sectarian violence, perhaps making it appear distant, even anachronistic, to ever more people, especially the young. Already the old enemies in Ulster seem to be turning together to face a new "other" conjured up by prosperity itself and common to both sides, as attacks increase on immigrants and people of color.

A short way down the narrow and winding road from Farren's, at Ireland's northernmost rocky outcropping of land, Banba's Crown, people have arranged large stones on the green grass to form messages they want God or some other airborne viewers to read. Some are the names of lovers enclosed in hearts, others the names of martyrs killed in the political strife next door; still others name themselves just to say that they had passed the place. The stone writers pilfer stones from each other's messages to write of loves and deaths and passing by. The constant, limited stock of stones is dragged into place to renew the same messages about different people, with the gaps in the works of earlier writers gradually making their messages illegible, more and more like the random scattering of stones. What do we say about change and constancy in this place?

Halfway between Farren's and the Crown, Teddy, having returned to his native Malin Head after a life away earning a retirement in a U.S. paper factory, tended his ancient family home. It was a thatched house standing by the narrow road, no indoor plumbing, only two rooms and a small kitchen. At his invitation I followed him inside as he stirred the banked fire in the old solid-fuel stove. Old pictures in frames hung on the ancient papered and painted walls, everything yellowing with time and yielding little by little to the dampness that creeps into the houses here—in spite of the eternal flame in the stove. The furnishings stood in their time-honored places, the mattresses were stacked together for the family members to pull out and sleep on each night, dishes stood on the cupboards, and the kitchen drawers were full of old pots and utensils. Nobody lived there. Teddy lived in the small modern house across the drive and up the hill, about a hundred yards away. His sheep grazed in between. He kept the family house thatched, painted, and heated against the damp because he could not bear not to and see it fall to ruin.

He did not keep it for show and remembered only one other time that he showed it upon request to a couple of young women from the United States who happened to be passing as he came out of the door.

There were five or six other houses in this tiny village, all built close together around a sharp bend in the road and all (except for Teddy's new retirement home) thatched. The one directly across the road had a view of the Crown and the distant sea. In the mid 90s it was renovated by a priest who owned it, then again by a Belfast lawyer who bought it from the priest. It sold for about U.S. $100,000 in 1999. The previous generations who had lived in Teddy's family cottage would be astounded at such prices, Teddy thought. In 2006 another of the renovated cottages was for sale for €230,000. What has been preserved here, and how has it been changed by preservation?

The little village at the turning of the road had a timeless quality as I passed through and stopped to look for someone to talk to. It appeared that nothing had changed there in a hundred years, a Brigadoon. But that perception was transformed as I talked to Teddy, as we stood in the empty family house with peat smoke curling from the chimney, a homey place where nobody lived, as we talked money and property and investment and the link between this seemingly remote place and the city wealth of Belfast and Dublin, in turn linked to the wealth of the world. In what way had my passing, our talking, the reciting of the value of a thatched house across the road, changed the relationship of the paper factory retiree, a man living on a fixed income, to his family cottage in a land of rapidly rising living costs? I thought about how the patterns of stones a mile away at Banba's Crown were continually being reshaped into new messages, the meaning of the old proclamations dissolving as their pieces were carried away. The piles of stones covered with thatch that were the cottages in Teddy's village held their place over the years. And still their meaning changed.

The journalist Fintan O'Toole writes often about how difficult it is to know and tell the story of Ireland, about how the place is changing. In the concluding pages of his 1997 collection of essays, *The Lie of the Land,* he talks about the Irish sense of home. He says that "home is much more than a name we give to a dwelling place. It is also a set of connections and affections, the web of mutual recognition that we spin around ourselves and that gives us a place in the world" (167). The words for "home" in the Irish language are never used to refer to a dwelling but define instead "that wider sense of a place in the world, a feeling of belonging that is buried deep within the word's meaning." Home is a state of mind, a sense of security, the familiar people around you. For generations, this sense of home was felt most keenly by those who had left their particular home in the world behind. Today it appears that some number of Irish natives are finding themselves left behind as their sense of security and place in the world departs, even as they themselves stay put and the world comes to them.

As Ireland, a society where deep memories of a modest rural past are only a generation old, becomes caught up in the web of the expanding global economy, as large segments of its population become materially richer, it might appear that people generally should feel more secure. But economic change is never even. Prosperity, when it arrives, may come to the few or the many, but never to all. And it always comes at a cost to some. Some can ill afford the prosperity of others. Income and wealth rise for some; costs rise for all. Those who were on the margins of the economy before—just getting by—no longer do, if their labor, talents, location are not part of the economic surge.

The Republic is a small place, where distances are relative to "infrastructure," and in the countryside, that has always meant the quality of the roads, although most recently it may also mean the broadband linkages the Irish government has worked to extend into every village as a matter of social equity. The secondary roads that run through the Irish countryside are still narrow and winding, and relatively short distances are magnified by the time it takes to get from place to place. People living thirty or forty miles outside Cork City in the 1970s might well have been living in a fairly "remote" location, where property values at the time reflected the kinds of livelihood provided by the local farm economy. Today, many of the secondary roads have not changed much, but we know that the meaning of distance as we see it in our minds has changed profoundly in the age of instant global communication. There are no remote islands in the global electronic sea: all points are bridged. It might take nearly an hour to commute thirty miles from home to work, especially with all the cars added by newfound prosperity to the crawling traffic in town and city, but anybody who has been anywhere knows that an hour one-way commute cannot be too far off the world standard for the suburban middle class.

In the last several years a kind of Manhattanization of urban real estate prices has occurred. In addition to the impact of their rising salaries on the value of city and suburban residential real estate, many members of the country's first generation to enjoy the new levels of affluence can afford vacation homes in the more attractive rural locations. Add to these the foreign visitors and returning pilgrims of the emigrant diaspora—seeking to wind themselves in ancient Celtic mists in the homeland of the heart, charmed by memories of landscapes and seascapes that follow them home when they leave. Many have the means to purchase a small rural building site or a house, to become part-time residents. And tens of thousands of visitors each year take a remote rural house at a weekly rate that inflates the value of any cottage with the potential for renovation to international standards of rustic holiday accommodation. Visitors collectively join other affluent agents of change in driving up costs in this changing place, where so much of what attracts them is what can be made to appear unchanged—with a proper cash investment in restoration.

Tradition, once it is sought after as a consumable, does not remain what it was, if for no other reason than that once it is purchased the price goes up. Even Teddy changed his ancient family home by maintaining it as a personal museum. The lawyer changed it by buying and then selling a similar property across the road for $100,000. I have changed it by telling you that you may be able to buy a small, unimproved cottage in Ireland for €230,000 if you hurry and shop around—and you may just have the means and the desire to do so. Many of the locals will not be able to bid against you.

PRICED OUT

In a small village in what is still Ireland's least-developed southerly peninsula, there were two modest shops, two bars, a church, and a national school. The shops have kept the same hours for years. One shop opened at two each day except Sunday and sold everything from farm equipment to groceries. The other was a grocery store that had somewhat more generous hours but was closed from twelve to three for lunch and doubled as the post office. The two pubs were open all day. In one of the two, Kate worked behind the bar. She had seen some of the world; she returned to Ireland after living for more than a decade in Boston.

Kate got tired of the hassle of having to work constantly expanding hours in the States to make ends meet, the hassle of two jobs, child care worries, and no time to herself. When her friend Jack bought the local bar, she came back to help him run it, and she made sure that the demands of work and home were balanced in a way that allowed her to retain a generous share of time for herself. For Kate "work" was a soft concept, better termed "hours of employment," which would include sitting outside the front door of the pub with the daytime regulars minding the passings-by and goings-on of the village and picking wildflowers along the road to decorate the bar. She had time to watch and to think, and that was important to her.

Her U.S. experience and a concern with maintaining a healthy balance between work and the other parts of life colored the way she thought about how things are changing for young people in Ireland. She believed that the rising cost of living was driving young couples to work more hours and more jobs just to get by, leaving little time for their kids, their marriage, and other relationships—"home" in the old sense. Something struck her one day as she watched the children at recess playing in the schoolyard a few doors down: every one of the children in the school was a first or second cousin to the others. Next she thought about how, because of rising costs, very few of those at play would be able to have their own homes in the local area—or anywhere else in Ireland, for that matter—unless they were lucky enough to go on to do technical or business degrees. She thought that was an unlikely prospect for most of these children.

Kate calculated—she and Jack did the figures together—what the minimum cost of putting up a very modest house would be if you were fortunate enough to have a parent donate the land to you and if you managed to put together a qualifying down payment (two contingencies that would be real obstacles for many locals). Even given these ideal circumstances, they concluded that most of the work available locally or in the nearest big town would not cover the kind of fixed overhead represented by monthly house payments. The only local men who could afford such payments would be those with established positions in the building trades and a wife employed outside the home. One plumber with his own well-established and bustling business, a mortgage, a family, and all the work he could handle scoffed at the suggestion that he might be able to afford to take time off for a holiday this year. He might risk a few days to visit a brother living near Cork.

As we three spoke, six new properties were being constructed in this village of perhaps fifty existing residences. All of the new houses were being built by "outsiders." I didn't ask for an elaboration; the term appeared to refer to any newcomer to the locality, whether from Cork City or Munich, and it would make little difference to the futures of the children in the schoolyard. The change would be hard on them, would change the meaning of home, but then didn't most people in the States rent apartments in cities? I was asked that question by three different people in the space of a few days in this village, and I had the sense that this was the talked-about solution to the problem of where and how the next generation was to live. If it were good enough for the Americans, maybe it was not so bad for the current local offspring.

Most of the new homes that would overlook the bay and be backed by the mountains here were being built on about the same scale as some of the larger existing residences. There were exceptions. A foreign family had bought an island in the bay and put a substantial house on one end of it, clearly visible, as if in a floating showcase, to almost everyone almost all of the time. I was told that some years the family might visit it for only a fortnight or so in summer. For the rest of the time the house stood fully furnished and empty, a little like Teddy's thatched family home in Malin Head, but in so many ways unlike that place. To the casual passerby, Teddy's house appeared to resist change, while the Tudor island estate declared at every casual glance from the surrounding mainland that change had arrived and that it had deep pockets. The house in the bay was testimony, the more so in its emptiness, to the reach of privately held fortunes massed just beyond the horizon.

Another house, a new and modern, low-masonry structure that was also empty most of the time, was located just at the edge of town, off a road leading out to the peninsula's point. It was built in what would be called "executive ranch style" in the United States: the windows had permanent bars, and the conservatory's glass walls were protected with the pull-down aluminum shutters that secure inner-city liquor storefronts after hours in the States. It echoed the message for those who would read it that the world outside had the resources to fundamentally change this village, that the world had noticed its existence and was coming here on its own terms. The outside world brings along assumptions of its alien and oppositional nature—an awareness that the opulence of its possessions will make it a tempting target in a land where it has no friends or deep ties to protect its interests and where it will be an absentee landowner most of the time.

SECURITY OF PLACE

The magnitude of the symbolic difference that empty barricaded property represents can easily be lost on an outsider like me who is used to concerns about "security"—how we protect ourselves and our property from each other. Security among neighbors in this village often means something far different. Mattie was eighty-two and lived on an especially narrow, grass-grown lane in a farmhouse overlooking the bay. She tended her beautiful garden daily and looked after the garden of a neighbor across the way. The farmer brother of that neighbor called on Mattie every day just to see how she was and "does she need anything." Mattie and the neighbor brothers were somehow related because long ago the various pieces of a single land holding were split among kin, with one receiving a house and property, and others receiving a bit more property and the agreement that a house would be built according to the now forgotten details of an established formula. The fact that these neighbors were related was quite unexceptional in a village where all of the children in the schoolyard were cousins.

The year before I met her, Mattie lost the brother she lived here with all her life; he was ninety-one. He was a keeper of ancient lore, and he and Mattie together were known locally as "true nature people." They closely minded the change of the seasons and could tell you what the weather would be like for the coming winter depending on variations from year to year in how the sun was tracking across the sky. The brother kept enormous bees in hives he fashioned from weaving hemp and the stripped outer layers of blackberry canes. The farmer brother described to me the making of the hives, explained in detail how the old man started with a coil of hemp in his hand and built the spiral outward, lashing the coils in place with the tough vines in a sequence of weaves that he alone knew. The completed hives were so strong that an adult could sit on them. At Christmas every year he was alive, including his last, the beekeeper would deliver gifts of honeycomb to friends and neighbors by bicycle, and the honeycomb would last the family twelve months.

The beekeeper also had a foolproof way of stacking hay to keep out the wet. He would build the haycock on a slab of stone or a cement pallet, using corn (wheat straw) layered in spirals that caused the water to run off, keeping the hay dry. It was a proven fact that if he built your haycock, the hay would be perfectly fit to feed for two years. When the traveling hay cutter with the massive combine came to the village, all the men followed him from farm to farm, saving the hay one farm at a time. They would all have to wait for the beekeeper to be done setting the haycocks on one farm before they progressed very far along in cutting the next.

Everywhere in the world that people have enjoyed the luxury of local peace for a couple of generations, country stories are full of nostalgia; they are stories about the decidedly good old days. But every village has its homegrown bullies and social climbers who want to punish out of meanness or to rise above the rest. When this outsider hears about the good old days in small-town Iowa or a village in Ireland, the skeptic's alarm goes off. But the farmer brother's story of the old man was invested with an unmistakable affection that spoke of more than the passing of a unique old timer, of past events and traditional ways of knowing and doing. It was a story about the meaning of time itself.

When Kate told the outsider about her worry that time was changing and people would not have time enough for each other, he nodded and said he understood, but he didn't. Here we glimpse something of what she meant. Time to watch over and over again the building of the hive, the stripping of the hollow briar, the way the first coil of hemp was held in the left hand, the way that the winding was done, if not the secret of the winding pattern that died—at least in this village—with the old man himself. Time to tell a stranger on a weekday morning in detail what was important about a long life filled with time, time as "time enough" in that long life to absorb secrets of nature worth knowing about hives strong enough to sit on and haycocks where the straw kept the fodder dry for two years, in which time the beekeeper on his bicycle would have made two rounds at Christmas delivering enough honey produced by special and happy bees one drop at a time to keep many families in honey until the next Christmas—until this past Christmas, which was the first without honeycomb and which came only as a small reminder, a sad anniversary, of their shared loss.

The story of time changing was full of spirals and cycles, of time encircling local lives and binding and stacking them together in recurrent patterns of things known and shared, suggesting the magnitude of what it may mean to break such a pattern. As a jaded sociologist and world-weary outsider, I am self-conscious about overdoing the images of spirals and harmonies here, images that my sophisticated social science colleagues in Ireland may well deride as the nostalgia of the displaced emigrant, a generation removed from real understanding. But there it is, in the way that it occurred to my outsider sensibilities, in the way I heard the story from people who were moved by the meanings of change. The farmer brother's two grown sons, who had been working and living away from the village for some time, were inconsolable when they heard of the old man's death, and they of all people, having been drawn away from the deep meanings of home by work and responsibility with the end of their boyhoods, felt especially keenly the finality of what this passing meant to the village and the world and to themselves. Many of the cousins in the playground in years to come will hear from a distance of the village that they knew dying one story at a time.

We could call the reflected pattern of close-by living and knowing and respect and caring "neighboring," but the word hardly seems good enough to someone like me who has lived his life next door to serial acquaintances. The point of my describing these intimacies of thought and feeling shared openly with me by strangers is to establish a frame of reference for those like me from the outside world who want to understand the meaning of change, to understand something of the depth of what is shared in a place where all the children in the schoolyard are cousins for this one final generation. Now people from the outside with understandable motives and a longing for a simple life are coming, people who can afford to buy islands or build fortresses with bars and shutters on the windows. They give a new meaning to "security" that Mattie and the people who care about her understood as a feature of the world of wealth that until now lived mostly outside small villages like this one. The need to protect property is arriving along with wealth's social distances, with the strangers who follow behind it, with the covetous stirrings it may kindle among the young people of the village whom wealth itself is shouldering away from this place.

The people of the village see very clearly that their place in the world is changing, and they waver between resistance and rationalization. Mattie's farmer neighbor and kinsman said that a lot of the changes dictated by European Union agreements had made it hard for small farmers, hurrying the demise of traditional knowledge and methods, making them irrelevant in a single regulatory stroke. He thought it might be better if foreigners stayed out of the local real estate market, but then the world was changing and you couldn't hold yourself apart from it for good. The new building in the village was providing employment at decent wages for some local men, and hadn't the locals made money off the foreigners by selling them rough pieces of land as building sites that weren't much good for grazing? He hoped the surrounding area might not change too much, that it would not be overbuilt, because that would change the beauty of the place and that would be too bad. But here he repeated the saying that you couldn't live off of scenery alone or take much nourishment from the fine salt air, and maybe a push was just what the young locals needed to get out into the world and have a chance to make something of themselves. There was still plenty left of traditional ways, he thought, and the men here still cut silage one farm at a time, working together, but for well over a generation now cutting and hauling with their own tractors — and no money changes hands in the process, no records kept, just a mutual sense of obligation and fairness. He had been out cutting and hauling until one a.m. that morning.

And when he thought about it, Mattie herself had been an agent of change. She introduced the practice of keeping a large decorative flower garden to the village decades ago, and people at the time thought she was a little touched because of it. But now they all kept gardens, and cuttings and seeds from Mattie's garden were blooming around houses from one end of the village to the other. On St. Patrick's Day every year people came to Mattie for the town's supply of shamrocks, and she was proud of that fact. They were lucky to have Mattie, for her own special qualities and to remind them of the importance of the old ways, he said. We stood in the lane and admired her neat traditional house and her beautiful garden, and I wondered how much we shared of what we saw, how the appreciation of the outsider differed from that of the one who had grown up tied by responsibility to this farmstead as familiar to him as his own. As if in response to my thoughts, he nudged me and pointed to a smudge of mildew high up near the eaves and said he had better get that cleaned up right after the hay was stored—Mattie had been after him about it since at least last winter.

Meanwhile a set of questions had been forming themselves in my own mind, inspired by the simple beauty of the setting, the unspoiled quality of this little house kept in the traditional way, the view of the bay and the mountains, maybe the age of its inhabitant: How many more years would she be able to reside here on her own? What might be the asking price for this "unimproved" property? How much time would my academic calendar free me to spend here each year—balanced against how little my academic paycheck might spare for a down payment? After all, someone would buy the place. But as attractive as the momentary fantasy might be, how could I take over the beekeeper's house and Mattie's garden with the farmer passing every day and not stopping? What was the "it" I would own by coming to this place as a part-time resident? What ownership ranks would I be joining? What would I feel compelled to do to protect this property I owned and thereby transform the meaning of "security" that attached to this place when Mattie had taken hers away with her?

HAZARDING PROSPERITY

Having drawn this sharp distinction between ways of thinking about security, I had better hasten to add that concerns over violations of property and person have never been altogether absent in modern rural Ireland. The outsider's concern with security is well understood on this sparsely populated southerly peninsula. There is a growing general concern with crime in the major cities and plenty of reminders that the city is no longer as far from the country as it once was. During my visit to that region I passed through the small town at the foot of the bay several times and noted an interesting antique shop. One day when I was passing, an "Open" sign appeared in the window, and I stopped. The shop was in an old building with rough floors and walls, but the merchandise was dusted and arranged with care. The totality of the impression as I entered was striking, the way the building and the pieces for sale and the proprietor all fit together. Old oak furniture and wicker pieces held the smaller things—utensils, decorative objects, and crockery. To one side sat the shop's owner, a woman with a pleasant and open face and her white hair in a bun. She was knitting. The picture, like a calculated stage set, remains in my mind as clear as a photograph. I bought two small pieces. She said she didn't ship from this store, but her daughter had a larger shop in the big town not too far away and could arrange shipping for the serving dish and candlestick. The big town was on my way.

The larger shop was easy to find, and I waited for the daughter to finish her conversation with a friend about recent declines in tourism. As the friend prepared to leave, she wished the daughter good luck with that day's court case and speedy recovery of the jewelry. Of course I asked about the court case. The previous year two women entered the other shop, wearing what appeared to the shop owner to be brightly colored saris, and they asked the pleasant woman with the white bun to unlock the jewelry case so that the younger of the two women, the daughter of the other as it turned out, could try on some rings. While she tried the rings, the mother offered to pay for a €2 item with a €100 note. The antique shop mother turned to check her cash box, doubting that she had enough change; the sari mother said she had changed her mind anyway about the purchase and called the antique shop mother to the back of the store with a question about another item. Then both sari women left. It took only a few minutes for the antique shop owner to finally convince herself that something that had never happened before had happened. Having left open the jewelry case and the cash box, she had been robbed as she went to the rear of the shop. The sari women were caught on a tip after they had finished a full day's work. Back in their apartment in Cork City the younger woman answered the police squad's knock wearing all of the rings from the jewelry case. She had hundreds of pounds in her purse, roughly equivalent to the amount taken in a series of complaints about two women running a variety of world-class cons between the little town and Cork City that day.

The antique shop daughter told me her mother didn't enjoy operating the other shop in the little town anymore. She didn't like having to be suspicious of everyone coming through the door. She was afraid that the robbers might be armed men next time and that they might hurt her. She had not had to think about such things before, about the danger of being alone in her shop. Just now the shop owners were anxious because if the woman who was in court today pleaded innocent, they would have to drop everything, lock up the shops, and testify. They had hoped never to have to see the alleged thieves again — it was nerve wracking, the daughter said, and with all sorts of people coming into the shop these days, especially in the summer, she had noticed more missing from her own store, where there were three stories and no way to watch everyone all of the time. It was awful to have to be suspicious about people. I asked whether she had done what some American shops do, leaving polite messages that ask people to be on their honor. Oh yes, and she had to take them down because her Irish customers nearly chewed her head off and threatened never to return because she was as much as calling them all thieves. She said that crime makes you think about people differently, and then they think about you differently.

The daughter needed to weigh my purchase from the mother's shop to determine the freight charges, and she did not have a scale in the shop. Would I, a complete stranger, watch the store while she ran the package across the street and down the block to the grocer's to use theirs? You think that you have found yourself in the very teeth of change, and then something happens, and you say to yourself that some things change very, very slowly.

When people talk about crime in Ireland today, they tend to worry about two groups: youth and foreigners. Only recently incorporated into the ranks of prospering nations, Ireland is concerned about whether young people will be able to handle bigger paychecks, which will buy more alcohol and lead to more trouble on the street. In addition, the nation is having to learn how to accommodate ethnic and racial diversity from scratch and in a hurry. One hears of racist incidents occurring in large cities, especially Dublin, but one doesn't need to go to the city to hear concerns about the growing foreign presence.

People in outlying areas of Western Ireland distinguished between more or less welcome hard-working foreigners, like those who may be found employed at eating and other service establishments in small towns, and those who, according to news reports, are arriving illegally by the ferried truckload or who slip in as bogus asylum seekers. Members of the latter categories risk being stereotyped as thieves or freeloaders. It seems inevitable in times of ethnic influx that one or another group will be singled out as the most troublesome in the public mind. Romanies, the Roma people, carry this stigma in Ireland today and elsewhere in Europe.

The mother and daughter who robbed the mother and daughter were Romanies. The pleasant elderly woman who was called away from her knitting and her sense of the world that day may today drop stitches each time a stranger fitting one of the profiles of the New Irish "others" comes through the door. The women, such a foreign presence in their brightly colored wraps, stole the confidence that allowed her to be alone in her shop in the little town. The knitting woman may this day be turning out sweaters and socks with dropped stitches because she is afraid of her life of foreigners, afraid that any day she might have to sit in a courtroom and look at the woman and say, "Yes, she took my rings and money because I fell for a silly trick," a trick that may have been rehearsed a hundred times from Milan to Manchester. It is one thing for the nation to be a great economic success and have the world beat a path to its door, but the world brings along rough tricks that change you inside. It changes the way you look at the world and the way it looks at you.

The world's rough edges have always been more evident in its cities, and this is true of Ireland today. One of the social concerns of authorities and citizens alike in Ireland is the increase in so-called random street violence, a kind of urban wilding where one or more youths attack and often do serious injury to passersby. The target may be anybody—other youth, foreigners, the elderly. In one instance an elderly man was pulled from his car in a car park and beaten to death by young people who took nothing and to whom he was a stranger. Like many stories picked up by the media, one wonders about the cause-and-effect relationships between actual and reported trends. There were some rough characters in Cork City twenty-five years ago, and if you found yourself in an isolated and vulnerable position, you might indeed find yourself a victim of "random street violence." But in the public and official minds, its apparent increase is clearly a problem associated with the new prosperity.

In the village pub where Kate works I watched a televised account of random street violence that included a video clip of a recent attack in Dublin. The video showed a well dressed young man in a blazer being punched a few times by a pair of thugs; the trio just an instant before appeared strangers about to pass each other on a fairly crowded city sidewalk. The police commander being interviewed explained what he believed was the cause of the general increase in violence: because of the booming economy more young people had more money for drink and behaved badly as a consequence of overindulgence. The economic well-being of the country appears to have become a catch-all explanation for every emergent social problem. It is probably a trivial point, but in the clip I watched the bashers were not particularly prosperous looking, while their victim was. On the basis of that footage, I would have entertained a different hypothesis about the divisive effects of economic changes that benefit some more than others and their connection to angry acts of violence. My speculation was interrupted by Kate's stand-in for the evening: "I'm afraid we're becoming a very uncivilized country," she said with a touch of embarrassment, as if we had just witnessed an unseemly public display of family bad manners.

I knew something about her. She had a son in his early thirties with a tumor. He had been fighting the disease for some time. People said it had taken a terrible toll on the parents. The son was a good-looking young man, tall and strong, a local athlete, and full of promise. The publican said that to see him in the pub playing cards with his chums you might not notice anything amiss, or, if you knew him well, you might notice a little something. The outcome of the cancer was still in doubt. The uncertainty was one thing, and then there was the expense. The son had just returned a couple of weeks earlier from another round of treatments at a specialized clinic in the United States.

As the reports of random street violence continued on the TV, tractors rolled past the open door of the pub pulling wagons piled high with green hay, all coming from whichever of the farms was taking its turn that day. The long summer day had finally begun to fade: the mountains that back down to the village on its western edge cast shadows that overtook the main street, and the gathering dark brought the light inside the houses out through the windows. In a small country place where events are woven together and everyone knows much of what is worth knowing about everyone else, in a short time you can gain an enormous wealth of insight into the way things are connected, if you happen to catch people in an open mood and if they see that you are genuinely interested in what they have to say.

As I sat in the bar in the quiet part of the evening—before the regulars showed up and the place got busy—wondering about the state of a nation with random violence in the streets because young people had too much money to drink, I knew a party was about to get underway that very night in the big town fifteen miles away, the town where the younger woman operated the antique shop that offered shipping. Plenty of money would flow into the till, and alcohol would flow out of barrels and bottles into young people (and people of all ages) who would stay late drinking and then go out into the streets. But it was a good bet that there would be no random violence from that crowd. The party was an informal fund-raiser for two local young men with cancer, one from the big town, and one from this village — the son of the woman behind the bar.

I didn't go to the party, with fifteen miles to drive in the dark after midnight on the narrow winding roads that ran above the water and linked the town and the village. But I heard that the event was a huge success. It complicated the whole question of the linkage between money and drink and the problems of a society where the economy gave some people too much money to spend on a good time, maybe some of them from little villages where they could not afford to buy a small house. The mysterious connection between drink and money was underlined by Jack, who would take none of my money that evening, being content with having passed the quiet time before things got busy in talk about the collisions between the great and small things of the world with an outsider who had shown a keen interest in the life of a small village.

The impact of globalization on a rapidly changing Ireland cannot be found in any one place: the story is too big to tell, and it is confusing to attempt to disentangle tradition and present and future and to talk about these things in a way that people will hear and understand. But we can find authenticity in the words of individuals trying to come to terms with their own lives, and we can make out something of the shadowy shape of change reflected in what they say. There is no one story of Ireland in change, but there are many stories of people, Irish and others, who are making journeys across a fluid global landscape, some of them making that journey while staying at home in small villages.

Some of what is taking place here has such a glaring irony that it hardly needs saying. In the past it was the poverty of the Irish economy that pried the generation coming of age away from villages and towns and sent them to find work where investment capital lived, elsewhere in the world. In foreign cities poor Irish immigrants along with immigrants from all of the sending points in the world had to come to terms individually and collectively with the insecurities rooted in change and inequality. Today, as wealth and the hypermobile global capital that generates it come to Ireland, new levels of inequality at home are having a similar effect, prying loose the next generation from local security and demanding quick adjustment to uncertain social and economic terrains. Some find that they are strangers at home, where new economic and social dislocations are settling in next door.

CHAPTER 4

No Traditions Without Change: Listeners Make the Music

"Where should we go to hear the best Irish music?"

"New York."

(Sonny, Ardara, Donegal)

There's nothing better than brown cake with a boiled egg and tea for supper. Boiled eel and potatoes are a sure cure for too much drink the night before. These are things spoken out of the past, from seasoned memory, things that are true for all time. Anyone who would challenge such revelations has not lived long enough to understand the manner in which true things worth remembering are known. Arguing that you had eaten a better supper or that there could not be anything particularly curative about the chemistry of salt eel boiled with potato would only prove the point.

It is hard to learn exactly what the experience of the world was like three-quarters of a century ago, not just because there are so few around who can talk about it, but because the pace and amplified scale of life today prepares the rest of us so poorly to hear what is said. Those of us who travel the globe searching for something in particular are disconnected from the people steeped generally in local matters, people whom we encounter in our search. There are the global passers-by with limited time and an agenda, hurrying along the road as if they know what they are looking for and where to find it. And there are the indigenous, the lifelong inhabitants, like the woman in her housedress, sitting on Fisher Street in the little town of Doolin to watch us go by.

I went to stand by her to see if she wanted to talk. I leaned on a van next to where she had parked her chair in the street by the curb. She was just down from the hill behind town, where she had gone to mind a few head of cattle, and she gave me the advice about brown bread and egg for supper, supper being on her mind at the moment. I got her own recipe for the brown bread to add to my collection of foolproof formulas for brown breads that I can never get to rise the way their authors can. She did want to talk, about the old days, and I was a contented listener. I'll call her "Annie."

Annie had lived in Doolin all her life. She didn't know the people she saw everyday anymore, and she didn't care to know them. It was not like the old days when you knew everyone and all about them. Annie talked about "blow-ins," which included anyone who had not been born in the village several decades (preferably generations) ago. Outsiders were changing the place. It had all been so different in her time.

I wanted to refocus the subject onto music because the busy street we were lounging in was, after all, in the center of the self-proclaimed "traditional music capital of Ireland." Annie made fun of my direct questions, the impertinence of a poor impatient listener trying to direct the storyteller, one of those passers-by with a predictable agenda. I immediately saw my mistake.

"Was there music? Of course there was music! There was always music!" She answered as though I had asked, "Were there cows?"

Were there well-known players in Doolin then? "What do you mean 'well-known'? Anyone who played was known very well by the listeners." I enjoyed the teasing and smiled at her. Then, patiently, and in her own time, she began, "In that time there was music made in the houses, in the kitchens and sitting rooms, and people came in to listen and brought a bottle of milk if they had a cow or a pot of jam if they hadn't."

With these few words Annie appeared to transport herself from the spot in the road where she sat, back to another place when that same road and all the people and things around us had a different look, when Doolin was profoundly different, worlds away from the present. She spoke to me and yet to herself, and I tried to reshape our surroundings in my imagination so that they matched the pictures she was seeing. "The houses in town would different times all be full of people and music and dance. Fresh tea and bread or scones would be served twice a night to everyone, and that way they would all be happy. Once at ten, and again late."

This was the story of traditional music, music that wasn't a thing apart from everyday life, music that had a life of its own and yet wove in and out of the wider fabric of life so that life in general and the music could not be separated from one another—back in the times that today's music had come from. Now that original music was as mute as an old fiddle under glass in a museum showcase, a thing to be told about rather than heard coming out from a crowded cottage. The connectedness of it all died with the old players and listeners who lived when the town was the way it was when Annie was a girl. Listening to the music in Annie's memory may be the closest we can come today to hearing the music of the past that was exchanged among the common people of Ireland in the little towns. You cannot make that music anymore; you can just imitate the sounds the player made.

All the people were fishermen in those days and all the houses were thatch, even the pub. We girls would go out to a dance, maybe near the cliffs, but we wouldn't think anything of walking to a dance fifteen or twenty miles there and back, linking and laughing and shoving each other, ten or fifteen of us coming down the middle of the road in the middle of the night, getting back at three or four in the morning. Do you know how it was then? We'd be getting back and want one more fag, before we went into our own house. You couldn't let your mother see you smoking, because she'd kill you. The doors of all the houses coming through the village would be latched, but never locked. There was never a lock on any door. Because they was all fishermen having to rise early, the coals would be raked together in the hearth the night before. So we'd go quiet into a house, they'd all be asleep on settle-beds pulled out, and you'd go to the fire and light the end of the fag in the coals and go quietly out the door. Nobody would think anything of it. Could you think of such a thing today? No, you couldn't! I don't know any of these people around here. All the ones I knew are gone and the place is changed. The children in the school above? All blow-ins!

Maybe an excusable exaggeration. There were still plenty of the old families in the area, and they did have kids. But the point was sound, expressed as it was for emphasis. There were still the O'Connors, Murphys, Flanagans, and O'Briens, who had supplied new throngs of children to the general population and the school for generations, but now there were many others, and that meant that the threads of community that had woven the families of the old Doolin into a unity of kin, friends, and feuds were loosened, no longer the same. We were straying from music, but I had learned my lesson. The music and the people were the same, and this was Annie's tale.

In her youth all the families had ten or twelve children. All born at home, all without the services of a doctor. The women served as nurses to each other, midwives; all had attended birthings dozens of times. They came to her mother when she was giving birth, and she went to them when they were in labor. "To live all your life in the same place and depend on one another in this way makes a different kind of connection between families than you have nowadays. Do you know what I mean?" I could only reach for what she meant. What it meant to be all your life in the one place delivered into the world by neighbor women who watched your every move as you grew—the essence of that experience seems beyond the reach of imagination for most of us today.

"All the doors was open, and you'd just walk in." As I sat in a house just above the village, writing the passage that included Annie's words, a voice called "halloo" from the dining room. Martin, my landlord, had come to say there had been a phone call for me. The door was open, so he let himself in. I explained the circumstances of the call—a daughter was traveling and not feeling well; I had left Martin's number in case she needed to contact me. He said that there was a little anxiousness in her voice; he thought it wasn't an emergency, but maybe I should call her straight away. I did and later let him know that all was well. He was relieved to hear it.

I knew from our first meeting that Martin was disappointed that circumstances did not allow any of his children to carry on farming, that his lands were now rented to different farmers and the productive output was all divided. That didn't feel right to him, but what could you do? I had quickly learned that among his neighbors there had been a legendary musician killed in a car crash a decade ago at a traffic circle on the way to Galway. The musician, Micho, had been a great world traveler, and his young namesake, Michael, a great-nephew and sometime whistle player, had eight pints that Sunday afternoon but still thought he would be back that night to play at O'Connor's. (He wasn't.) His friend Pat Flanagan, who spent his days traveling around visiting and singing for people, whom I had met under what for me were emotionally charged circumstances, did sing that evening, and another unrelated Pat Flanagan, also a musician who had played with and taught Micho, had the next—next farm over to Martin's beyond Micho's. Old Pat had been dead for forty years, and the place had just the four walls left standing, its two rooms converted into a cattle confinement pen. I knew Micho's brother Gussie, who had never left the island and also played the whistle, was not as famous as his brother but still kept the farmland in between Martin's and Pat's. I had learned the eel and potato cure from Gussie. And I knew that I was only a transient who did not even merit the disdainful label "blow-in," indigenous to nowhere and nothing, a blow-by. But I also knew that an occasional nod or eyebrow raised would keep a story going for a good while, and you could learn quite a bit.

I had come to Doolin because it was a place much changed by its musical reputation, which drew droves of visitors each year. They packed the hotels, hostels, and B and Bs that were going up as fast as they could be built by local and distant capital. I had come with no plan but to listen to what people said so that I could get some sense of this musical place. Annie talked about the village's musicians as she had known them, and their lives were of course seamless with those of the general citizenry. In her words: "There were some players that were good men and they'd been missed by this village when they were dead and gone. Micho Russell was no young man when he was killed in the car accident just about ten years ago, but he's badly missed. He was a very good man. And his brother Gussie is still alive," as I already knew. In fact a kind of shrine to Micho Russell, with photographs and writings, covers the walls of O'Connor's pub on Fisher Street. The whole family was connected with music—not unusual in this village. Micho, the stand-out, helped establish Doolin's "traditional music capital" claim. Annie thought that brother Gussie was getting a bit feeble. But the man was in his eighties; he might be forgiven.

By chance I came to know Gussie. "You spoke to Gussie Russell? Well, you've had the great honor then! I've been his neighbor for thirty-five years and never had a word out of him!" Cathleen, Martin's wife, was telling me how Gussie kept to himself. He had always been that way but had become more so in the past ten years. His niece who lived in the house above his old cottage might receive no more than a flap of his arm in greeting. Cathleen repeated the gesture for us: a sidelong abrupt extension of the arm that ended with a slap on the thigh that said "go away and leave me alone" as much as anything else. Other neighbors had had equal luck, but I had the greater luck, since Resmiye was traveling with me on her first trip to Ireland.

It was she who first encountered Gussie at his gate. She is a pediatrician, well used to getting information out of people (littler ones) reluctant to communicate with her. Gussie had been his usual dismissive self when she approached to ask who he was and what he was doing. He was obviously repairing his farm gate that had fallen to pieces. She first attributed the awkwardness in their meeting to the possibility, given his advanced years, that he might be more comfortable speaking Irish. He did not respond to her the first two times she asked his name, pretending not to hear or not to understand, or simply ignoring the friendly request. In her best persuasive bedside manner she gave it one last try. In a coy manner she said, "I'll tell you my name if you tell me yours: my name is Resmiye." He gave in. "They call me Augustin—Augustin Russell."

By the time I came down the road ten minutes later, they had established an acquaintance of sorts. He was thin, angular, a little bent. His eyebrows worked up and down as he learned my name. Flanagan. There were a lot of them, and gesturing in general directions he located half a dozen in the space between where we stood and Lisdoonvarna. As he spoke to us of his life of farming, fishing, and cutting turf, he would walk back and forth from one side of the gate to the other, prop up one foot, consider his words carefully, and then let them out with a sense that this might be a useful piece of information he was sharing, a historical insight about fishing from the rocks or turf cutting or farming. Absent any sense of self-importance, it was a kind of oration.

Gussie said that as a young man he sold turf cut from his own bog, carted to town and neighbors by a long lineage of donkeys he had kept over the years, good but not always willing beasts. Not a big living, but steady. A donkey brayed as we talked, and Gussie pointed back to where the sound came from and said he still kept one. No, he didn't work this one, "for he's young and still not trained." After a time Gussie had given up the turf business to work in the Doolin stone quarries. He said that in the old days he and his father fished off the rocks at the back of their land, on the Doolin side of the cliffs, for something to have with their potatoes. You would need to be a good fisherman to make it work, and he and his father were. Pollock and mackerel, with the odd this or that thrown in, whatever you pulled out. It was at that point that I received the formula for the cure for the common ailment—eel and potatoes. He didn't eat the eels he caught himself but gave them to a neighbor, who salted them. "They used be all white hanging down stiff from the roof inside that house, always there if you needed one."

The old family home was more than a bit run down now, and he lived over the hill in a different one. He rode a motor bike between the two and wherever else he needed to go. He did say a few words about music, that they had played out here and there. Micho was the great musician and world traveler, said Gussie. (Micho had toured with the popular group Clannad as well as others.) Gussie said he himself was never interested in touring far from Clare. Micho and Gussie were up in Donegal in 1979 for a music festival when Lord Mountbatten was blown up on his yacht in Donegal Bay. The IRA claimed responsibility. The Russell party came back down to Clare through Derry Town, and the border guards stopped them and gave them a hard time. He made a simple reference to Micho's death in 1994 as he turned back to his work.

Micho and Gussie were as different as night and day, Cathleen said later on. Micho would keep you talking if he saw you along the road or if you gave him a lift. If you were in a hurry, you would want to watch yourself, or he would make you late. Gussie had always been the opposite, and since he had to give up the music, he had become reclusive. That was about the time that Micho had died. Gussie developed a malady that had something to do with the chest or throat. Before that, the odd time you would see him down in the pub with his whistle. Afterwards he stopped coming because they would keep after him to play when they saw him, and he couldn't anymore.

The brothers' relationship itself had not always run smooth. They didn't speak for long periods. I was told it had got to the point where they had separate entrances to the same house; Gussie put in his own. Like the village itself, the Russells were held together by feud as well as blood. In a place where people live all their lives on top of one another and there is so much time and opportunity to become an annoyance to one another, music might have a job to do to bridge the little distances. Whatever difference there may have been between Micho and Gussie, and between Gussie and the rest of the world, the sounds the musicians made are still there to hear in recordings, the way it was learned and played in and around the houses in Doolin, in the times Annie remembered. There's "Campbell's Reel," "The Walls of Liscarroll" and "Battering Ram" jigs, "The Connemara Stockings" and "The Westmeath Hunt" reels, with Micho holding forth on flute or whistle and Gussie in support (O Róchain

1989). Brother Pakie Russell, who died in 1977, and neighbor Pat Flanagan are also there. All but Gussie were dead in 2003 when I met him, and Gussie played no more. His playing style, in his time, had been described as "smooth and racy."

On this visit to Doolin, as I always have done, I put in some time listening to the music as it is played today. Local players as well as players from all over the world had come to sit in during the informal evening sessions at the packed public houses. What a lot of good players there are in the world now, playing many of the same tunes that Micho, Gussie, Pakie, and Pat played. Some of the players are well-known. I thought about Annie's question: "What do you mean, 'well-known'?" These would be accomplished players whose playing — quick, subtle, solid, lively — has responded to outside forces, as the art form has been pushed forward by an international competition with broad appeal and the force of a world market behind it. These are the great players and singers in a time when the appeal of Irish music has spread around the world.

In fact, when I listen to the simple renderings of Micho and Gussie I wonder if they would be much noticed today, maybe even in Doolin. The singing and playing has such a homespun quality, as if you were listening to somebody singing or playing at a gathering of ordinary people in some cottage in a small village. It is easy to see scones being passed around. The homeyness of the setting, the familiar faces and voices, and the sharing would give you an ear for the music that might not translate into the electronic age of celebrity performance. What would you be expected to hear if you didn't know the players as neighbors delivered into the world with the help of your own mother, without knowing how each one fit into the local map, where a man might reasonably choose to stay home and cut turf and stone rather than to join the international music competition and travel the world? What would you hear off a CD of music recorded decades ago, if you were a world traveler for whom a fresh egg and a slice of brown bread washed down by a mug of tea might pass your lips as an unexceptional snack on your way to the pub to listen to the music of well-known strangers?

To raise such questions is not an exercise in playing with words. When we ask how Ireland is changing, has changed, we enter an important discussion about how many of the still and quiet societies in the world have been changed by being drawn into the broad flood of global attention. Just as music was not separate from the life of the island in the past, neither is it separate from the question of what is happening and what has happened to Ireland today. Given the importance of music to the people of Ireland, wherever they may be, we follow this thread, this piece of the weave of culture, here for a little while to see what it can tell us about how this one place and the wide world reach into and alter each other. The process has been underway for some time.

THE LISTENERS

Cultural pilgrims journey to Ireland each year in search of an authentic Irish music experience. The pilgrims include not only Yanks but people from all over the world, drawn by the strings and pipes that strain to be heard above the din of pub chat. We bring with us enthusiasm, expectations, and plenty of foreign currency. Thereby we take as much of a hand in the creation of the traditions that we have come to hear as if we sat in with the players. In fact, if we stayed home and listened to the music on our own electronic audio systems, we would have pretty much the same effect. The listening changes the music.

Today, all music is played upon a single global stage with such a powerful ear that it can reach back into the past and change the fingerings, drummings, and marrow-deep aesthetic of musicians and composers dead for a hundred years or more. For traditional music purists the idea that the traditions they love will inevitably be changed by their own devoted attention, and that this is neither good nor bad, may be difficult to accept. We can take some comfort from the knowledge that foreign influence on Irish music is not something new. Foreign invaders, many of them pointedly hostile to the local culture, have influenced Irish traditions during centuries of comings and goings. Today, the invaders come in homage to the music and players in an electronic age in which all cultures are simultaneously invader and invaded. Everywhere, we listeners take away, and we leave behind, as itinerant culture carriers always have.

When I first came to Ireland in 1976, it was not as a fan of Irish culture but for the teaching job in Cork. The requirements happened to match my specialties in sociology—none of them having anything in particular to do with Ireland. One of the members of my new department and her husband gave a welcoming party so that I could meet other faculty in various fields and be made to feel at home; for those who knew a little about me, it was possible that I was simply a returned emigrant, one generation removed. At the party I received a crash course in nineteenth-century Irish history from John, my host. He cleared his throat and asked if I knew this song from the famine.

Oh the praties they are small over here, over here,
oh the praties they are small over here.
Oh the praties they are small,
and we dig them in the fall.
And we eat them coats and all, over here, over here.

The room had gone quiet. As John continued his singing, in a pleasant, high, slightly nasal manner, I sensed what I thought was the awkwardness of the moment, with this sophisticated professor of philosophy sitting with eyes closed and head and voice raised. I wondered how the others in the room would bring graceful closure to the moment when the song was done. At the end of it the room remained quiet for an instant, followed by some subdued encouraging murmurings, and then John began a second, picking wild mountain thyme all around the purple heather.

He had had a little bit to drink, not much, but he was a slight man—maybe he just couldn't hold it. At the end of the second song, the room was quiet for a few seconds, the others waiting to see if he were done. He was. Then people shouted congratulations and "Good man!" and John elbowed the person next to him with a grin and said, "Go ahead." A song was produced. And then the next person, and so on. As I sat listening to the singing and to the stories and recited poems from those who couldn't trust themselves to carry a tune, I was overcome by a chilling realization. There were twenty or more people in the room, all sitting backs to the wall, in a kind of circle, and the cue for performance was passed to the left like a plate of vegetables around the dinner table. I was in that circle and would be the last singer.

When my turn came, I begged off. I had no traditional party piece, no Irish song that I would sing in public, certainly no poem, nothing that would fit in this warm Irish parlor with the fire and the low light, a room full of performers, if not uniformly talented, certainly more talented than I. I had found myself unexpectedly in the midst of an oral tradition of cultural elements deftly rendered by natives who as adults were able to take satisfaction from joining in and turning out an artful performance, full participants in a convivial and familiar ritual. My cultural background was irrelevant. I was inauthentic, not very Irish after all.

I had initially been embarrassed for John. Now they all seemed embarrassed for me. "What happened at American parties?" they asked. "Was there no music?" Well, yes, but it came out of stereos, not people. Those must be boring occasions, they said, as my breaking of the circle was dismissed, rather than forgiven, I thought, as a foreigner's failure to know how to behave properly. At subsequent parties I learned to avoid embarrassment by strategically timing a run to the bathroom, and I usually found myself in the company of one or two skulking stage-frightened nonparticipant natives hanging around outside the parlor or lounge.

But it was my loss on these occasions because I loved the songs and recitations, especially the music, and I missed the chance to enter the circle—but not sufficiently to overcome my performance cowardice. Within the group each offering was a gift from each person to the whole gathering. I liked the way the songs sounded a capella, coming from these people—academics, well-off people of towns and cities, business people and professionals—many of them as distant as I was from any folksy rural Irish roots. And despite the little self-deprecating protests that might precede or follow a piece, during the singing the singer at times appeared transformed, dedicated to getting it just right in the way that he or she knew it.

I soon encountered pretty much the same spontaneous songs and renderings in the small villages of County Cork, up in the pubs around the Boggeragh Mountains. This was not the Irish music I had grown up with in the greater New York region, where St. Patrick's Day parade festivities and the weekend Irish music radio programs featuring touring show bands defined an ethnic musical tradition that I had not found particularly attractive. I had discovered in my first days in Ireland something deeper and more authentic. I wanted more of the authentic thing, and so I innocently became complicit in changing it: I bought it, on tape.

Soon I became aware that there was a bickering among the performers whose works were represented on the recordings, about which were the more traditional, which had committed more unorthodoxies in order to cater to contemporary audiences who wouldn't know the difference but might be drawn to purchase the changes. Even a mild purist would hesitate to refer to the work of the Chieftains, for example, in any serious conversation of Irish music, given their middle- to late-career progression away from traditional playing and flirtations with international and pop influences and artists. But on the world stage, where the Chieftains were able to tap into a market in which the growing popularity of musicians from Ireland playing various kinds of Irish music would reach previously unimaginable levels, the debate over orthodoxy quickly became irrelevant, replaced by material measures of success. Many young musicians were pulled along by the global market and abandoned the affected long skirts and peasant shirts for the authentic denim and black leather of the international pop music aesthetic. During the next two decades the power of the world market would redefine the music of Ireland, and those like Gussie Russell, who hung on as the traditional players of jigs and reels on concertina or whistle, would occupy the smaller venues, the corner tables in small pubs. Their tapes and CDs sat on the dusty shelves of only "serious" Irish music collectors, as the music of Ireland became too big to be contained—or even to rest both feet—on the one small island. It would be lured onto the international stage, even as Micho had gone off to play on the same bills as the innovative Clannad and other popularizers.

In the 80s and 90s the most influential voices of Irish music would increasingly merge what was identifiably Irish with world music influences. Enya would reinvent the mute Celtic past in Gregorian harmonies ethereally remixed for a new "New Age." The Afro Celt Sound System would wire electronic audio technologies to traditional instruments and enter the mainstream of the World Music industry by fusing traces of African, Irish, and world beat elements. But cultural mix is something that has occurred in waves over and over again for a long time in Ireland. Contamination is a long-standing and authentic part of traditional Irish music, as it is of Irish culture in general.

WHERE THE MUSIC CAME FROM

The Republic has been a free state for only just over eight decades, Gussie Russell's lifetime minus a few years. At best, colonial rule had previously neglected preexisting Irish traditions as inferior while it superimposed upon the culture of colonial cities and great houses the formal arts that reflected the highest achievements and good taste of the imperial homeland. At worst, colonial rule meant the suppression of native culture and expression, as in the seventeenth century, when Irish musicians were hunted and persecuted and their instruments destroyed. As Marie McCarthy reminds us in her 1999 book, *Passing It On: The Transmission of Music in Irish Culture,* from the mid-sixteenth to mid-seventeenth centuries the British Empire brought to colonial plantations in Ireland thousands of English and Scots immigrants with their own musical traditions. In the world of art music, Dublin was said to have been second only to London as a center of imperial high music culture, and the music of European composers was performed and admired there. When the trained Irish musicians of the Gaelic tradition were driven from the cities and the patronage of the great houses, some went underground and blended in with country players and thereby influenced rustic expression.

With the new popular music of cities and towns adapted to the language and sensibilities of English patrons, and with the spread of Scottish and English influences through the countryside, we begin to see some of the difficulty of identifying what we might want to recognize as an unmolested body of purely Irish tradition. There are still further complications.

Rionach Ui Ógain emphasizes the fact that many of the instruments we associate today with Irish traditional music are neither precolonial nor Irish in origin. Certainly, the harp may be traced back to ancient times and appears to be a home-grown artifact; however, it is the rare stage-produced traditional anthology or pickup pub session today that features a harp. Some form of pipes can be dated to eleventh-century Ireland, but the characteristic uilleann (uill'an) pipes—the Irish bellows pipes—took on their current form only in the eighteenth century. The fiddle was imported in the mid-seventeenth century, and the melodeon, concertina, and accordion arrived in the first part of the 1800s. As we take account of these "foreign" influences in the formulation of Irish tradition, we should consider the effect of emigrants to the Americas and elsewhere, whose little fortunes allowed them to send instruments or the means to purchase them back home. Without the diaspora Irish, there would have been fewer (and maybe different) instruments to make music with in the countryside of former times. Ui Ógain reminds us that the poverty of the colonial countryside, a poverty that sent so many out of Ireland, prevented the typical household from owning a musical instrument. In poor Connemara in the eighteenth century, musical instruments reportedly were virtually nonexistent; on the Blasket Islands, fiddles were fashioned from driftwood.

The tangle of native and foreign historical influences in the music of Ireland is in large part due to the fact that we are considering a colonial history. It may well be impossible to know how the cultural heritage of Ireland might have looked and sounded if the nation had been politically independent and culturally isolated for the last several centuries, but that would also make for a highly unusual piece of European history. How much of the melancholy of the slow airs, how much of the defiant buoyancy of the jigs and reels, which draw us into the music today, is rooted in native conditions under a particular colonial experience? Both McCarthy and Uí Ógain offer the view that the very suffering of people, both musicians and audiences, may well be responsible for the haunting beauty and the heights of achievement. These colonial times are the very times that produced a distinctly Irish music that emerged and was retained in sorrow, opposition, and defiance.

Our knowledge of the details of the history and evolution of this oral and thereby largely not-written-down native music must remain indistinct and incomplete. This was a body of lore shared from person to person and generation to generation, in villages and in the open country, where storytelling, poetic-recitation, myth, and music were the core elements of a collective oral memory, the body of work that is the foundation of the tradition celebrated today by the fiddlers, pipers, and singers on festival stages or around the corner tables. What has been handed to us by past generations comes through the filters not only of centuries of changing tastes but also of foreign political and cultural influences that are a part of today's music no less than the foreign English language in which it is sung and discussed. The nature of tradition is that it is always modified by generations of change.

ACCEPTING TRADITION AS CHANGE

Every regional music today is a pure and honest production of its particular history, and that history is bound to be a blend of local and foreign elements. What if it is hard to tell whether a piece—in the form that we receive it—is originally from Scotland or Wales or Ireland? As music historian Frank Harrison has written in a little essay, *Irish Tradi-*

tional Music: Fossil or Resource?, a music tradition is a living and therefore changing body of practices and sensibilities. He draws a contrast between "folk music" and "traditional music."

> A "folk music" is a careful archive-like preservation of the way something was done in the past. Folk pieces are protected museum relics, produced some time ago, within a distinct cultural setting that can have a line drawn around it in time and space so the thing in question can be kept as it was, the same for all time. A folk piece can't be sustained out in the real world, especially the contemporary world, because people will always be changing the thing, bringing it up to date, enhancing its appeal for a changing audience. Folk has to be kept in a museum, it can't be let out. (Harrison 1988)

A "tradition" is a different matter: Harrison talks here about the "natural maintenance of tradition" as a continuous process of evolution, "where over periods of time and in changing circumstances, some elements will be lost and others acquired. . . . *The essential point is that the mixture continues to be characteristic of the people who mix it at the time it is mixed*" (1988, 19; emphasis added).

If we extend this idea a little by drawing again on the observations of Marie McCarthy, we can begin to develop an appreciation of the Irish music tradition and what our role is as the living mixers—wherever we may be listening. McCarthy offers the idea that a music tradition is something shared within a "community." It is easy to envision the idea of a music community as any small rural village (Doolin in the past, for example) where a local body of tunes is shared by familiar voices and players and where children may grow up possessing this music as a part of who they are, aware of it only as music and not some kind of cultural legacy to be preserved. We can picture the Russells growing up hearing the playing of Pat Flanagan next door and others, for example. In such places the distinction between performer and audience is blurred, as all find themselves on occasion pressed into service as performer and strain to get it just right according to local standards of the moment. But McCarthy also invites us to see that "music as community can also be experienced in the more imagined, abstract sense of belonging to a regional, national, or global community by virtue of common musical interest or expanding consciousness. This is increasingly made possible by electronic mediascapes, which facilitate the creation of communities worldwide" (1999, 24). This latter sense of community applies to that far-flung and otherwise loose collection of us who find kinship in the difficult-to-name thing that Irish music does for us.

There are interesting conclusions to be drawn here about the Irish music tradition. When we put together Harrison's idea of tradition as a living and evolving body and McCarthy's inclusive standards of community membership, we see that a tradition is a people united by common cultural interest who remake that tradition in each generation, and they make it just as they see fit. No one can stand outside a music tradition as an expert deciding what is or is not admissible. For better or worse, anyone who is moved to feel themselves a member of that community is helping to decide its present and future content. Scholarly concerns are set aside about where the music actually comes from; instead, the tradition is determined by whatever it is within our community that roots our cultural sense of ourselves. We have license to include, free-form, whatever musical noise we find characteristic of that tradition at the time we add to the mix. Here is serious anarchy with a touch of democracy: the relatively small body of living native musicians of Ireland have no more influence in determining the mix today than their enormous audience flung worldwide that constitutes a community of musical interest, an expanding consciousness, which in an age of instantaneous and continuous attention brings to the never-ending session its passions, its tastes — and the huge store of money with which it pays for what it likes. Our dedicated appreciation of what is "just right" has eclectic foundations, and we may participate only as listeners, but on the global stage our numbers give us an enormous power to draw forth from tradition what pleases us.

All of this raises interesting questions about what we hear as tradition today and about what that tradition will sound like in the future. Among other things, it places in context the serious consideration of Riverdance as a significant episode in Irish tradition. It brings into our discussion the Eurovision song contest, which, if we had begun with it, would have appeared an odd starting point in a discussion of authentic traditional music. But if we ignore the 1994 Riverdance Eurovision event, it becomes the elephant in the living room, the thing that needs talking about, however uncomfortable that may be for some members of the family (that is, the music community).

THE FUTURE OF TRADITION

The annual televised Eurovision song contest had been going on for years and was already an institutionalized piece of European popular culture when I was living in Cork in the late 1970s. I happened to be back in the country in 1994 when it was Ireland's turn to host the TV spectacular. The event is built around a contest featuring one pop performing act from each participating nation, all of them vying for selection as Europe's top act or top song for that year. Exposure via Eurovision can substantially boost performers' fortunes, as ABBA demonstrated in the 70s. And having its offering selected as the year's best gives the winning nation first-among-equals pop culture bragging rights for that year.

As a part of the televised extravaganza, the host country selected for the broadcast (the home country of last year's winner), in addition to offering its own contestant, puts on a show that provides a backdrop for the European-wide broadcast. The show is in the popular performance vein but often communicates something about the national cultural heritage—repackaged for a world market. Ireland's offering that year was the Riverdance chorus line, the inspired step-dance-meets-Broadway conflation. It is an important detail that the original male and female dancing leads were from Boston and Chicago, and the male lead, Michael Flatley, was also one of the show's creators and chief choreographer.

That year Ireland's musical backdrop to the Eurovision extravaganza stole the show, and the world literally went wild. There is genius in the original production, a production that lives on as a virtual performance industry in touring companies and dozens of licensed reproductions across the stages and Irish-culture-themed entertainment venues of the world. The genius is that Riverdance embodies something of the fractured, disjointed, and blended cultural adaptations of Ireland-as-homeland to a great body, a community, of the scattered fans of Irish musical traditions. The production's eclectic music and dance elements represent faithfully no particular cultural place on earth, yet remain identifiably "Irish" in derivation, in their primary cultural code. In this way it is authentically "traditional," an element of evolving tradition.

What Riverdance most faithfully represents is what happens to a musical tradition when it steps on the global stage. Riverdance tells us about the accelerated pace with which the powerful world culture is dissolving national borders. In a recently bygone era, those borders were marginally more effective in insulating and preserving regional cultural differences. Today's world culture continues to celebrate its various national roots while distilling out local elements that are too peculiar or idiosyncratic to fit the emerging mass appeal in a seamless world market. Just listen to the recorded music produced by Gussie and Micho playing together, if you can find it. Try to fit those sounds, well suited to the parlor or the pub, with the thundering tap and electronic fiddles of the music and movement of the monumental scale of Riverdance Incorporated. Riverdance is the newly authentic representative of the spaces that are to be taken up by things Irish in the new tradition built by what the paying audience wants to hear. The world stage is the contemporary ethnic melting pot, dominated by Euro-American tastes and style, and the compelling economics of the market dimension of cultural globalization.

As a result, what most of us popular culture consumers encounter as music traditions will be a version of national and regional cultures as they are offered for sale in the new marketplace, offerings that are already filtered through the fine mesh of global production and marketing considerations. They are as much an authentic representation of a global aesthetic as they are a representation of a particular place-tradition or people-tradition. In this sense we may say that identifiably distinct regional or national styles are becoming more "ethnic" than "national" within the single emergent culture to which all national cultures are electronic immigrants.

In a world market in which even the enormous corporations of the last century became too small to compete successfully and have had to merge, art is pressured to adapt to global formulas if it is to sing successfully for its supper. When potential financial rewards take on global dimensions, the criteria for "success" are altered. Cultural traditions must remain identifiable but at the same time appeal to the tastes of a new, global audience. Two very successful Irish writers, Roddy Doyle and Maeve Binchy, have achieved their particular level of success because "the Irish authenticity" of their stories is perceived as such by readers and moviegoers *outside* Ireland. The images of despair conjured up in Frank McCourt's *Angela's Ashes* were questioned in some quarters in Ireland, because people there thought it presented the world with an overly Dickensian picture of the conditions under which some Irish lived. But McCourt's story resonated with many outside the Republic, providing some of us who fancied that we had lived martyred childhoods with an opportunity to claim insider's knowledge about what it *really* meant to be Irish. What made the movie version worth making was that people outside of Ireland thought that McCourt had got it right. The movie was crafted in Hollywood, where a movie that earns $100 million on the world market may still be considered a relative failure when compared to other ways the capital involved in its production could have been invested.

The Eurovision contest perfectly embodies the internationalization of cultural expression: the stage is the visual electronic ether that we all live and breathe, and the language is the common pop culture that we all speak. The world market consumes Riverdance as a very attractive packaging of traditional music and dance and wants more — more of what Riverdance offers. Riverdance, a synthesis of technology, art, and the grand scale of the contemporary stage, becomes the standard for what a particular musical tradition is expected to offer if it is to succeed on terms set by the financial requirements of the mass media industry that sponsors it. Traditions have to change, continue to change, if they are to be heard amid all the pleasant noises competing for attention.

In the early summer of 1994 some fellow travelers and I had not heard of Riverdance, a point that shocked our Dublin hosts, and they quickly treated us to their videotaped version. It was like nothing I had seen before, fascinating in its totally bang-on sense of itself, its presence, its lack of ability to be located in the United States or Ireland or the rest of Europe as a cultural document. Now, years later, as Riverdance productions that once, like powerful culture magnets, drew innumerable tour buses to innumerable performances around the world begin to fade into an Irish tradition, the cultural event threatens to merge in terms of its "everybody" symbolism with green beer on Saint Patrick's Day. I still hold onto the significance of that moment when I first experienced it, sitting on a living room floor in a Dublin suburb. Our hosts were clearly moved by the fact that the male and female leads were Americans — and such brilliant dancers. And the experience shared by Americans in search of authentic Irish culture and the Dublin couple with a son in the United States, where kids learned brilliant step dancing, was all the evidence we needed that we Irish were all just one people, after all. We mixed Riverdance into the tradition that included the common experience of all of us in the room, this element of *our* shared culture, with sedate step dancing transformed into a thundering chorus of hoofing in time to the billowing strains of electronically enhanced instruments—and that was perfectly OK, "brilliant," in fact, and we all said so.

It has been quite a few years since we all were first confronted with the Riverdance phenomenon, time enough to recognize its authenticity as a central piece in Irish music tradition. I still struggle with the idea, but only when I forget that tradition neither lies in the past nor belongs to me alone. I am no judge; the community of Irish music lovers has not asked me to arbitrate. But I secretly resisted. I assumed that the American dancers in Riverdance had learned their skills at step dancing classes in American cities, thereby learning a distant imitation of a native art form that is somehow different "contextually" from what children in Ireland must learn. But McCarthy tells us that as long ago as the eighteenth century the native Irish were receiving formal instructions in their native dance from itinerant teachers from outside the local community, and I don't suppose it makes any difference whether a child today is cajoled to follow in Flatley's clattering footsteps by a step-dancing stage-door mother in Clonakilty or Philadelphia.

One other notable, nontraditional feature of Riverdance is its alternatively acrobatic and sensuous dance form, a violation of the reserved tradition of step dancing; the innovations make it more like modern American tap than the "real thing." Yet we can find tradition circling back upon itself here again, as the indigenous American tap dancing art form emerged in mid-nineteenth-century urban slums from the confluence of Irish step and African-American southern shuffle traditions. This makes the episode of toe-to-toe confrontation between black and white Riverdancers a kind of homecoming. And where Riverdance went on to include boldly eclectic southern European influences, "southern European" compositions were included in the repertoire of the legendary blind harpist Turloch O'Carolan, who performed works by Corelli and Vivaldi that he had learned in his travels in Ireland.

CHANGING WITH TRADITION

I am about ready to set aside concerns about whether something really fits with tradition or violates it; I am nearly prepared to let it be what it will become with or without my consent. But there may be some use in critically monitoring what is included, what direction change within tradition is taking. Michael Flatley's association with the Riverdance production became something of a brief Irish soap opera when he left the company shortly after its huge initial successes. His next production, *Lord of the Dance*, pushed the envelope of a changing music and dance tradition yet further onto the center of the global stage. However, according to Fintan O'Toole (1996, 155), the dancer stumbled, demonstrating that one can make mistakes in modifying tradition, even when tradition is seen as changeable. In *Lord of the Dance*, Flatley employs a particular air that commemorates a mass tragedy, which is injected into the performance without reference or context, constituting what O'Toole considers an act of cultural vandalism, amounting to dancing on a mass grave.

But how many in the audiences will realize the faux pas? On the world stage, culture is performance, not history. *Lord of the Dance* is part of the "more" that a widening community of Irish music fans seek. Its relevance is in how it makes people feel, how it connects with where they are, not the untidy details of where it has come from or other details of translation. We are not interested in the trivia of what is being represented, beyond a quick read of the liner notes. Perhaps there is some law of conservation of cultural physics operating here. As a tradition expands to fill the void created by wider, ultimately globalized demand, it becomes lighter. Links to the past become harder to see, at times even vanishingly transparent.

When I lived full-time in Ireland twenty-five years ago, you might be hard pressed to find people playing "traditional" music publicly on a given weeknight, even in a fairly large town like Cork. No more: pubs of every size in towns of every size have become music venues, either featuring a pickup collection of musicians who do it for drinks and tips, or a named group that plays for a fee, a cut of the door, or a share of profits from the volume of drink. In large towns live music spills out of the doors of every other pub on some streets, mingling in the open in a kind of mad thrumming. In small towns, at least one pub on at least a couple of nights a week, especially in the high summer tourist season, will have traditional music. How does culture change when it is spread out this way?

One thing that happens is that once you can find the sought-after thing anywhere, some fraction of the global audience will begin to demand to see the real thing, the best example, where it is properly linked to the past and done right. Again, that search is likely to take them to Doolin.

CHANGING IN PLACE

Today many informed travelers have taken to staying away from Doolin during the peak touring season of summer because of the crush of visitors. Easily accessible from Shannon Airport and Galway City, the self-proclaimed and widely self-promoted traditional music capital draws large numbers of enthusiasts. There are still just the three bars, and if you can manage to get close enough to hear it over the drone of the crowds, there is very good music played in them.

Here in the little worldly town on the Clare coast is found an appreciation for a mix of music. Widely differing styles follow one another unannounced, except for the loud shushings that mark the start of unaccompanied voice music. One of the local musicians pointed out the who's who of the players to me one Saturday night in late June. He was not sitting in tonight because there was such a crowd of musicians in the house (I counted twelve playing at once). He had played last night. Was I there? No. Sure, you missed a great evening of music with a group of players in from the East.

The fellow had an unusually long name hard to hear over the music and shouts. He preferred it shortened to "Sky." He said he was a "trad" (traditional) player, but he liked the fusion of trad and world music, especially Afro-Celt. He had picked up traditional music playing in England, where he had lived for three years, a product of family and local influences. He was originally from the United States, a fourth generation Irish-American African-American. What kind of a reception did he get in Ireland as a person of color *and* a trad musician? He was comfortable in Ireland because he felt less categorized, stereotyped; people let you be who you are and treat you accordingly. Sure, you find the odd hopeless idiot anywhere. And as far as the music goes, some people, especially Americans, are a little taken aback at first, but after a few minutes of listening they're appreciative, alright with the idea of a double hyphenated Irish-African-American player here in the traditional music center. He was more at home in this small community in the West of Ireland than anywhere else he had lived, where he could pursue his music and other art reasonably free of labels.

I shifted over to talk to one of the musicians who had been playing all night. She was a fiddler who excelled on the slow airs, played with her eyes closed, locked into the music—I noticed she listened to the other musicians in the same way when she wasn't playing. In the one piece she had led she got a very respectful hearing from the other musicians as well as from the crowd, and it was easy to detect something like formal training. She had been playing Irish music for seven years. She and two of the other musicians sitting in that night were on holiday together, seeing where they might join with other players as they traveled around Ireland. They were from Germany. At various times they had played Irish music with different bands there. I had to ask who the other two Germans were. They were indistinguishable in appearance, dress, or the music they played from the local Irish players.

A more unusual presence was a group of three young men in black ties and tails who had listened respectfully to the others. Eventually they produced instruments, set up in a separate corner very near the pickup group, and during a pause launched into an accomplished but intentionally comic string of frantically rapid pieces on their own, getting in turn a good-natured hearing from the circle of musicians who did not venture to join in. Not surprising: they were playing a nonstop medley of Eastern European music embellished with a sort of bobbing and spinning choreography. People in the crowded room stood on chairs and benches to get a better look and listen, thundering their appreciation. The men were from Dublin, previously from Eastern European countries. By day they were guys with office jobs, by night musicians who played with a larger group that toured Europe occasionally raising money for orphanages back home. Once a year on holiday they came out to Doolin to sit in and mix in their influences. Their performance appeared to add to the atmosphere without changing it, the circle of musicians applauded with the rest, and the Irish music resumed.

The one other musician from outside the main pickup group was a young native Irishman in his twenties with a shaved head who wore a European football jersey. I had talked to him earlier at the bar, where people around him bristled at his vulgar pushiness and familiarity, especially with women who already had male company for the night. He wasn't challenged outright: he was squarely built and tough looking. With the same overly familiar style he borrowed a fiddle from the players and fired off a piece or two, before doing a respectable-enough job of unaccompanied singing—which might have gone better if he knew all the words. He was on the verge of overstaying a polite tolerance when he moved on, presumably to another of the town's pubs to sit in again.

He was an odd presence: his bold manner in this place of blended aesthetics, mutual cultural reachings, the stark shaved and shining scalp and red, white, and black sports allegiance. The other musicians hung back from his playing—parting, withdrawing for a few minutes, cautious, patient with the demand for attention. He got it but seemed never a part of what was going on, except by offering a contrast, foreign. Sky had said something earlier about this kind of music being the real hope of bringing people together, of the people here accepting people from anywhere who wanted to play. I wondered about how the football guy fit into the picture, stirring things up, then moving on. Here was a reminder that bringing people together necessarily meant all people, with some being easier to accommodate than others. There was a global/locality/foreign/familiar insight here that might take another pint to get to the bottom of, but might better just be left to stand on its own.

Two of Doolin's pubs sit across from each other in one section of the village, while O'Connor's is in the other, on Fisher Street, closer to the pier. On a Sunday evening at O'Connor's, John, a Clare accordionist of note, had left his instrument in the hands of a Japanese student while he went about his business of socializing with friends and strangers at the bar. He was now retrieving the box from the student, teasing her into giggles, retaining his accustomed role as the center of attention in the room, at the same time carrying on a conversation with a singer seated at the opposite end of the room from where I was sitting. Suddenly the world changed. John gestured dangerously in my direction and, looking right at me, bellowed, "Now Flanagan here, that man is a *great* singer altogether!"

Was this some kind of curse connected to my public performance cowardice? Here, sitting in O'Connor's pub, directly under the Micho Russell commemorative wall shrine, in "the traditional music capital of Ireland," was I about to be forced to pay for all those sessions when I had ducked out of parlors and sitting rooms to avoid performance? Was I to atone for my cowardice at last in a public house where I was wedged in, my back to the Micho Russell memorial wall, behind a heavy table and with no hope of escape? I had met John the night before at McGann's, in the two-pub section of the village, late into the session, a time when John gets very sociable, but he was meeting and introducing himself to everyone in the room at that point of the evening like a man running for office. He couldn't know my name—I hadn't told him.

I turned to the young fellow who had only just come in a few minutes before and sat beside me, and I asked his name. Pat Flanagan. Another Pat Flanagan. *He* was the great singer. Life was good. I introduced myself, and we matched spellings. He probably attributed my enthusiasm to my having met a potential kinsman by chance rather than to my relief. There were loads of Flanagans in Doolin, he said, and maybe we were cousins. We were both content with the myth for the time being and began catching up on family branch histories.

Yes, Pat Flanagan was a singer, and he sang all around Doolin. What did he do for a living or during the day? He paused for a moment, "I travel around locally and visit people. Sometimes I sing them a song, or just talk to pass the time." Pat travels around and visits and sings, and that is what he does.

We seemed to have interests in common. He was agitated as he talked about the direction that change was going in, how people were changing, in the world and in Ireland. They had no time for each other. The cost of living was out of hand, driving people to work harder and rush around, and they wanted to buy and consume, with no thought for the state of resources or the environment. The amount of money at stake led to corruption in government and to the division in society where a few people did well and the working people had to struggle with all kinds of jobs "going down." Nor could you make a living off of farming anymore. He had the whole picture there in a nutshell. I thought, "Flanagan, maybe there's a gene for politics," and the idea that we might be cousins seemed a surer thing.

He said again that all of this hustle for the almighty dollar or Euro was not for him. So he went around visiting confined people, whether in the hospital or in jail, singing them the old songs, or new, if they liked. Music was the thing that connected everyone, joining us at some deeper level. It filled a need, and the need was particularly strong for him. When he heard a good song, he would have to learn it; it became a permanent part of him, as if it were programmed into his memory, and he could sing it right off any time. He had quite a store of songs, like an old-time fiddler. He hummed and sang verses of things softly as they swam into his thoughts or came up in conversation. Pat said that all people are really good at the core and that music travels to that goodness, brings it out, whether a person is sitting in a pub, sick in the hospital, or locked up in prison. That was why he did his visiting rounds. I told him that he sounded like a priest, making music sound like a faith, a religion. He said that he thought so—that was true; that was the kind of work he did alright. I thought that he was the closest person, of all I met, young or old, to the way of the music of the past in his town.

Pat was called on to perform later that night and did two unaccompanied songs, popular current pieces. The music came from somewhere deep, as if indeed it were stored there and just needed letting out, and singing was just the act of letting out the sound and the message. As he began, there was the loud shushing of the large and noisy crowd from the people closest the musicians; I turned and loudly hissed my shush in the direction of the bar. The crowd was quiet. He was well received.

John was the major draw for the evening and rattled off traditional pieces with winks and grins to the crowd. A young man had come up from another town with his concertina; I don't need to say which town or what his name was. He eventually joined in and played with a pounding heel and driving intensity, his body bent angularly, muscles taut. He pressed every quick tune forward furiously, picking up the next phrase an instant before its time. He didn't smile or talk across the group of musicians; he didn't look at John, the man he was playing with and junior to. Instead he looked down at the floor or straight ahead.

Was this a competition? From time to time John broke off playing and smiled around the room. After two or three pieces in which he fell behind the concertina player, he shifted out of the circle altogether. He took his accordion with him. A little while later he took the extraordinary step of starting up on his own, on a stool by the bar. He never came back to the other players. This is one way tradition may be passed on and changed. The sounds coming from alongside the bar were softer, more lilting, decidedly "old fashioned" in contrast to the sparks flying from the concertina of the challenger.

On a different night Christy Barry, another prominent traditional player with a well-deserved reputation as a genius at the whistle, was at O'Connor's. The playing within the circle was inspired. Young players joined in tentatively at the margins of the group, quietly at the more familiar and repeated passages. They would raise their flute or whistle to their lips, starting and stopping several times in a piece as they looked across at Barry, whose fingers danced along the whistle to produce a liquid blend of more sounds than could seemingly be produced from the limited instrument. There were no challengers in the group, only young people who were learning what was possible from a master of the art. Both evenings tell us something valuable if we want to understand the meaning of tradition, how the music is passed down, preserved, how it is changed.

There is one last evening of music to describe that may help illuminate the nature of tradition. It dates from a few years ago. If Doolin is the traditional music capital of Ireland, Killarney is the tourism capital. In a certain bar a group of hired young players performed night in, night out. The place, popular with young locals as well as tourists, is divided down the middle, with the bar to one side and tables on the other. Young locals congregate along the bar, people who come to listen to the music at the tables.

On the night I was there, and perhaps most nights, the local customers were audibly contemptuous of the traditional music played by their musician peers, probably past or present classmates and acquaintances. The musicians appeared self-conscious about the shtick they were obligated to render for the tourists while being alternatively loudly derided or pointedly ignored by their friends at the bar. The single woman among the players was the only one who appeared engaged by the music. When she sang—being assigned by gender to the particularly plaintive slow airs—even her fellow musicians needed to communicate through exaggerated takes that they were alienated labor in this process of turning out the tourism product.

The critical tone of the bar crowd softened a little to a mixture of good-natured ribbing and a slight lowering of voices when one young local was dragged from his place to hold forth on the borrowed concertina. He was less practiced, what he played seemed older and simpler, and there were pauses and glances from the bar side while he played. By the end of the second and last piece, a few of the patrons had turned completely away from the bar toward the player, good nature and encouragement on their faces. Some noisy appreciation followed the playing.

But it was when a second reluctant volunteer was cajoled to take the stage that a serious transformation came over the place. The tumult of cheering and words of encouragement abruptly ceased as the young man took a seat near the stage, a little to one side. I watched the audience again and saw all fifty or more of the young patrons turn away from the bar and face the stage in total expectant silence. You could have heard a hiccup from the far end of the long bar in this place, where seconds before you had to be a lip reader to carry on a conversation across a few feet of space. What were we about to experience?

The fellow by the stage was boyish and handsome, very fair-skinned in contrast to his dark hair combed back. He had deeply shadowed eyes, sculpted sideburns. He took a few seconds to brush back his hair with his palms and compose himself. All was silent. As he began his a capella performance, I continued to watch the crowd as it watched and listened with near reverential respect. He was an Elvis impersonator, and he was good. After his second song, "Are You Lonesome Tonight?" the house came down. He declined all attempts to get him to continue and sheepishly accepted handshakes, back slaps, and shouts of "good man" from friends in the band and in the crowd. I left as the hired group took the stage again.

The search for authenticity is fraught with trick questions posed by experience. Ireland has a musical heritage that many of us feel passionate about preserving, but a thing preserved is not really the thing itself but the thing preserved, like the thatched cottage where no one lives on Malin head. Young people may at times make poor preservationists and at other times good ones. The paid musicians in the Killarney pub are traditional music impersonators whose hearts may not be in their work. But the Elvis impersonator's heart is truly in his work, and he is better at sustaining a tradition that is not in its origin an Irish tradition and not precisely a Presley tradition. It is in the worldwide tradition of Presley impersonation, which, because it resonates with (young) Irish people, certainly those in the pub that night, made it the most authentic thing going on there. We were witness to a local tradition, in part a Killarney tradition, in the making. The Elvis impersonator, known to the local people, part of the community, would never be allowed to leave a public house without a song or two.

This takes me back to, of all places, the welcoming party for the young American faculty member many years ago, where I failed to demonstrate I was as Irish as I was American. I did not join in the singing because I thought I didn't know any appropriate songs and because I didn't sing in public. But none of them were singers that night, any more than I. They didn't sing in public but shared in a tradition of reciprocated performance that had parts of it set to music and needed to be sung to be expressed. Of course I had a stock of songs in my head: Lennon and McCartney, Woody Guthrie, Aretha Franklin, and, yes, Elvis Presley. After the age of fourteen or so I didn't care much for Elvis, and you couldn't really know how it might have gone over with that particular audience that evening, but if I had worked up "Heartbreak Hotel" as my party piece for all those gatherings, it would have made me more Irish, less an outsider, more authentic, more a part of the community. Who can say that it might not have become a kind of comic tradition in Cork, with somebody picking up where I had left off when I went back to the States in 1978? I might have returned to Cork years later to find people doing Flanagan doing Presley as a comedy piece, especially those who were unable to carry a tune, something I can picture as a very satisfying entertainment in the traditional sense.

Tradition, that thing rooted in the past in the manner that it is expressed at present, represents a stage of change in the same way that all culture will continue to pass through stages on the way to the future. We can say that what is perceived as tradition is changed because we know all traditions are dynamic, alive, evolving: once they are sought *as* preservations they become something else ("folk"), a different nature of experience than they were before they became self-conscious of themselves as preserved. To preserve a thing, such as Irish music, takes a different kind of effort and produces different sets of motives in musicians and those who provide them with their performance venues than existed before, when the idiom was just music. Once we begin to examine ourselves as an object, we no longer live the moment in the same way. So whether it yields to the global ear or attempts to defy it, traditional music represents change, and there is no point in going into the past to look for it.

I know this, and yet I went to Doolin. I wanted to see tradition, to talk to it, because it is so hard simply to find it in the music. I found Annie and Gussie Russell. And I went into the pubs to listen to the sounds associated with the music in the ways they are expressed nowadays. I have become a better listener, I think, but I know that the more I listen, the more I will change the music. When people come into my house, people who like Irish traditional music, and I have Micho and Gussie on my modest three-CD changer, they say "What's *that?*" The question is the same as if I had invited them over, promising them the best supper they would ever eat, and gave them a boiled egg and slice of brown bread with tea.

CHAPTER 5

Passing on the Farms:
From Family to Euro-Business

*We were standing where the paths cross near the houses—Donal,
the Yank, old Eoghan, Tadhg the Joker and many more of us—
chatting about the ways of the world. Who should come along but
Séamisín, a bag across his back with a handful of Blacks to sow.
Anyone who did not know him would swear that he had been a
beggerman ever since he left the cradle. The figure he cut brought
a smile they could not repress to everyone's lips. Dear as clothes
are at present, no one there would have given sixpence for what
he had covering his bones.*

*No one could muster enough courage to speak to him but since
he is Séamas' uncle he greeted him.*

"God save you uncle!" said he.

"The same God save you," the uncle replied.

"Is it potato sets you have there?"

"It is."

*"Isn't it great courage you have and to be planting them in this
class of weather?" . . .*

*". . . I cannot tell what God will do with these, and all we
could ever do was put our trust in Him," was Séamisín's reply.
(Great Blasket Island, Spring 1920)*

(O'Crohan 1986)

PART I: FARMING AS IT MAY HAVE BEEN

The business of planting potatoes was a simple matter a century ago on Great Blasket Island or on any small farm in Ireland. When the time came, you did it and hoped for the best, with only survival hanging in the balance. No matter how complicated the story of the present-day Irish, the present has grown out of the soil; it begins with people living from the land. The standard image of Ireland is rolling green farmland dotted with little white houses and shaggy sheep. To many, this is the real Ireland, the place of origin.

Politically, access to the land itself is a symbol of the colonial struggle. Historically, the capacity of small farms to produce little more than subsistence was the impetus that drove millions away to other countries. Biographically, many of the people of Ireland begin their personal stories with reference to the small farms on which they grew up. This was certainly the case in the past and is still so today.

It is no error of memory or perception that ties the image of Ireland to the land. When I was living in Ireland, I asked a friend who was traveling in Europe if he would stop for a visit. "No thanks. I've driven it once, and it's just one big cow pasture." Many of the young people growing up in rural Ireland have shared a similar sentiment regarding rural life. The dullness of prospects in the countryside has driven farm boys and girls away to the cities to live and work, and this is true now more than ever. In that respect it is the same in Ireland as in other wealthy and rapidly changing countries of Europe and the Americas: the title to a piece of farmland that for countless generations meant work and life itself no longer offers an attractive option to young people. Eking out a modest living from the hard work of farming, as noble an existence as it may be, is only an attractive choice when balanced against other choices of limited promise. And twenty-first-century Ireland offers young people lots of choices.

In the first part of this chapter we dip into the past a little so that we can understand the kind of change that farming and rural life have undergone up to the present day. Each of the features of life that we focus on here—the common identity of family and farm, cooperation, conventions for passing on the land, close ties among farmers—are selected based on how much these aspects of life have changed, and that is the focus of the second part of the chapter. To understand the significance of the land in the past, we need only look at a few of the images in the black-and-white photographs from the time of the land evictions in the 1800s. They show families standing by cottages reduced to rubble by the authorities, the faces of the displaced conveying a message of absolute desolation. With the end of access to the land, life itself was in doubt. Today, the wider world is again driving down the number of Irish farmers, just as relentlessly as ever.

In the old days, along the coast of Clare, there was a saying, "fighting for Tim Flanagan's title." The phrase applied to anyone's struggle to keep what was theirs, especially land. It described the resistance of a legendary figure, Tim Flanagan, a farmer with ten grown sons who would not go quietly when the eviction order came. With regard to the plight of the current Irish farmer the legend offers a telling contrast. When people were evicted from the land in the past, a person like Tim might at least look his enemy in the eye. Today, farmers—not subsistence cultivators, but small and large farmers alike, efficient producers—are again driven from farming. They go quietly, if often with great bitterness. There is no immediate enemy to face, no matter how many strong sons you have. The sons would be away, anyway, perhaps with university or technical college degrees, working in town, where the global economy makes its regional headquarters. The aging generation of parents, who see what they have worked so hard to keep now devalued by their own offspring, ask, What was it all for? The two generations came of age in Irelands that are now worlds apart.

The Tim Flanagan reference is reported as an incidental piece of local history in a little book, *The Irish Countryman*, published in 1937. It was written by Conrad Arensberg, who together with Harvard colleague Solon T. Kimball, spent two years observing and writing about country life in and around Luogh (pronounced "Luke"), a strip of coastal farmland between Doolin and the sea cliffs in County Clare, the very place where Micho and Gussie Russell lived. Arensberg and Kimball interpreted country life in terms of the balance and harmony they perceived in those early days of Irish independence. I knew of the books that came out of the study when I first went to Ireland to teach sociology in the 1970s. By then, the social sciences I represented had moved on from the perspective that framed Arensberg and Kimball's works. We were much more interested in getting to the roots of the economic and political conflicts that we believed stood at the heart of all social relationships, as we had come to understand the world forty years after Arensberg and Kimball.

At one point during the time I was teaching in Ireland, the Irish Labour Party member of Seanad Erin and lecturer in sociology at University College, Galway, Michael D. "Mick" Higgins, came to Cork to present a thorough critique of the old Harvard-based study. Higgins handily roasted the authors and their work. The outsiders from Harvard had erred fundamentally in assuming that they were examining longstanding traditions, and they made too little reference to colonial history. They ignored the influence of the powerful Catholic Church. They emphasized harmony and balance among neighbors while they should have been attending more closely the conflict among large and small farmers. Worst of all was the legacy of the study: for years afterward, virtually all examinations of rural agricultural life in Ireland found it necessary to start out by arguing in a major or minor way with Arensberg and Kimball's interpretation. The problem was not whether the Harvard scholars found the right answers to the questions they asked, but that they had asked the wrong questions. We applauded the critique.

After Higgins's talk, my colleague Paddy O'Carroll led me over to introduce me to the speaker. Given the thrust of Higgins's just completed lecture, I had misgivings. Would I be perceived as a foreigner who thought it his mission to enlighten Irish social science students at

University College, Cork? Higgins looked the fledgling scholar from the United States up and down, said, "Oh, yes . . . ," and turned away. He might actually have sniffed; I can't say after this number of years, but that was the effect. There I was, another outsider to get it all wrong for Irish sociology students. In my heart I was thoroughly diminished by the experience, and still feel slightly scalded by the memory. Higgins went on to be a government minister and in his career championed many of the causes of working people that I identified with.

Well, here we are seventy years after publication of the damaging Harvard studies. But I am at a loss to see how we can begin to explore how farming has changed in Ireland without a brief reprise of Arensberg and Kimball's work. Readers are forewarned of the dangers. In this case we will stick to the descriptions (rather than the analyses), which, after spending two years in the community, the authors may have got nearly right. What can it hurt? It is just another set of stories told by local people to outsiders about the way the local people themselves understood life going on. In that, it is very much like my own work.

Farming, Family, and Community in Clare in the 1930s

This story of a farming community in Clare in times past is appealing because it presents a detailed and homey account of a life balanced through friendship, kinship, and simple repetitions of things done a certain way. It is the story of life lived according to principles of integrity based on loyalty, reciprocity, and obligation. It has that timeless quality characteristic of anthropological description, and presents a social order where things change very slowly, if at all, from generation to generation. In this tale, change came slowly in part because the world in those days had mystical properties that have abandoned us today, unseen forces and mischievous beings, that would get you if you didn't get it right, and "right" was doing the thing as it had always been done.

This is a story that fits neatly into a nostalgic view of old Ireland. But it comes directly from observations of how people lived and what they said about it. And Arensberg displayed a certain sensitivity in letting the tale unfold. According to him, an observer just had to sit back and let it happen. "We are left then with what we can hear and observe about the present. To question upon anything else is to get nowhere;

it merely starts a chain of obscuring generalities more inspired by the question than by what Luogh thinks and feels and does." Thus Arensberg and Kimball were quite careful in their observations. Below I summarize Arensberg's descriptions of what they saw in the rhythms of work, the harmonies of continuity between generations, and communal cooperation.

For the smallholders with farms under fifty acres, the family was the farm. As a general rule, Arensberg's impression was that the very smallest farms tended to have the very largest numbers of family members. This was a time when just over half the population of the Irish Republic gained their living from the land. And earning a living from the land was literally the case, for eight out of ten people living from agriculture drew no wages but shared instead in their family's subsistence. The larger farms of two hundred acres or more were businesses that produced beef and employed labor; the smaller ones were mixed garden and dairy operations that employed family labor and produced for sale, in addition to milk, calves that went to the larger operators for fattening and finishing and for eventual sale to England.

The small farms were found all over Ireland but were concentrated then as today mostly in the South and the West of the country. The most numerous were in the fifteen to thirty acre range. While it is true that through remote connections the calf sold from such a farm might eventually end up on dining tables in England, Arensberg says that the livelihood gained from small farms was "little connected to the outside world." Instead each of the farms made up little economic worlds in themselves. The farm family "spends its entire life" on the holding, "sleeping, eating, giving birth and dying there. . . . The countryside knows the farm as a unit. The farm shares the name of the family working it. It is inalienably associated with them." Beyond the family name, each farm was also known and referred to according to the number of cows it kept—as a place of this number or that number of cows.

The work of the household was divided and ordered according to the hours of the day, the days of the week, and the months or seasons of the year—with special attention paid to Holy Days that marked a particular date for specific tasks to be begun or completed. Work was divided by age and gender. The men had the work of the fields and large livestock, and the cutting and preparation of turf from the bog for fuel.

The senior farm women had the work associated with domestic life, including milking the cow or cows and the care of the chickens. The life of the woman of the house was regulated by the days of the week, those of the men more by the months of the year. One woman represented the order of life in recounting her typical round as: "On Monday I do the washing, on Tuesday the ironing, on Thursday I make butter, on Friday to market, on Saturday I get ready for Sunday, and on Sunday I go to Mass and do as little as I can."

The wider business of the farm fell to the man of the holding. "He is less free to choose the date of sowing than his wife the hour for dinner. Long-established tradition and ancestral experience imprint upon his mind the best dates for planting, for reaping, for harrowing, for breeding cattle and so forth." Arensberg more than suggests that a belief in supernatural forces reinforced the strict observation of dates and the following of ritual practices that prevented or cured bad luck. People might deny a belief in mischief-making beings or omens, but they also followed custom and applied remedies as wise precautions.

The work of the fields and stock regulated the rise and fall in the intensity and pace of labor for the whole household, with the entire family, even young children, pitching in at planting and harvesting times. Nevertheless, there was otherwise in that time a more or less strict segregation of the sexes in what specific contributions each made to the work and business of the farm. While husbands would tell the authors that the key to any farmer's success was a clever wife, the operation of the wider farm enterprise was the men's domain. As a rule, women never touched the heavy implements of farming, nor men the objects of housekeeping or domestic chores, as each sex was unlucky to the other's enterprise.

Supplemental labor during busy seasons was supplied by neighbors. Sons were an asset to any farm in part because their labor could be lent at times of harvest. Arensberg speaks of the institution of "cooring" (*comhair*, in Irish), where families lent support in the form of the mutual sharing of labor or equipment at busy times of the year. No record was kept of who had helped whom or on what occasion or for how long, but each had a general sense of the balance of efforts that had been borrowed and lent among friends and kin. Such support integrated the families within the community in a vital manner.

Among senior men, mostly those with complete families who thereby had "responsibility on them," another type of social integration took the form of regular visiting patterns, typically to the house of the most senior and respected among them. In that house they would sit, with each assuming his regular place, closer in or further back in the half circle around the hearth, depending on some combination of each man's age and reputation. The meetings were the forum in which men shared their thoughts on the events facing the world and their community. These gatherings were important sources of camaraderie, deliberate get-togethers, a source of identity and consensus building. As one man said, "a man would feel lonely" if he didn't regularly go out on such visits. When the young men who previously had no place in the circle came of age and had land and a family, they would come around to the meetings of the older men or form their own circle in time. "It wouldn't suit the young men to come in, but when we get old and they get married, then they will gather just as we do. That is the way it always has been and that is the way it will always be."

The prophecy that this is the way masculine society would always operate in rural Ireland did not foresee a time when the business of the world would reach into the rural community and accelerate the pace of life and magnify the size of holdings. One day in the future, Irish farmers would speak of the loneliness of their life, would have forgotten the old means of conviviality, would have no way of finding their way back to the conventions of a socially richer age.

The young men, whose heads were full of card playing and dancing in the 1930s, might well have been expected to settle down when the time came. Succeeding their fathers by becoming the proprietor of the family farm was the only means of attaining a place of full honor as an adult male in rural life at the time. And the transfer of ownership among succeeding generations was a very serious business. For a farm to be reckoned successful meant much more than that it be able to provide a modest living year after year: the farm unit needed to produce heirs, preferably in the form of male offspring. Anything other than a complete family unit on the land was considered tragic, although of course fate and differences in marriageability among bachelors meant that there would be a few incomplete family units in a given locality in any generation. But these units were considered exceptions — unfortunate, afflicted, malformed.

So every farmer wanted a sensible and strong son to follow him when his days of farming were done, but not too soon. Sons interested in farming, those who hadn't migrated to the city or emigrated to the cities of other nations, could be expected to be anxious to be getting on with their own lives as farmers. As long as the father was in charge, the son remained a boy or a lad, which had its drawbacks. For one, he was at his father's command and mercy. He had less than full adult stature in the community. And he was not able to marry until he became the man of the house, which, if his father was in good form, might mean that he would be a little old boy himself when the time came. The father had incentive to continue on as the active head of the family. This was the way to retain full status within the community and the control of finances. Retirement meant, under ideal circumstances, that the old mother and father would be permitted to retain for themselves the west room of the house, a garden for potatoes, and enough grazing to keep a milk cow. They would otherwise be supported by the work of the new generation. But there was one added incentive put toward retiring: the retiring farmer would retain a substantial share of the dowry brought in by the new daughter-in-law. The system was reported to work as follows.

When the father was ready to consider retirement, he would begin to look around for a suitable match for the son who had been chosen to inherit the farm, and, given what was at stake, the son was likely to take a lively interest in surveying the pool of prospective candidates himself. When a good prospect was found, the son might send a friend, a "speaker," to the woman's family to explore possible interest in the match and to ask what "fortune" (dowry) she might bring with her. At the same time the speaker could be expected to build up verbally the suitor's character and his prospects. Following the initial discussion, assuming that it was successful, a meeting of the interested male parties from both sides would be arranged at a public house. The following is an account presented by a farmer from Inagh:

> The speaker goes with the young man and his father that night, and they meet the father of the girl and his friends or maybe his son or son-in-law. The first drink is called by the young man; the second by the young lady's father.
>
> The young lady's father asks the speaker what fortune do he want. He asks him the place of how many cows, sheep and horses

on it? He asks what makings of a garden are in it; is there plenty of water or spring wells? What kind of house is in it, slate or thatch? Are the cabins good, are they slate or thatch? If it is too far from the road he won't take it. Backward places don't grow big fortunes. And he asks too is it near a chapel and the school, or near town?

If the match could be agreed to in principle, and if the young woman and man were found to suit each other, her people were invited to dinner on the farm where they could be expected to "walk the land" or carry out a general inspection. The man from Inagh continued: "The day before the girl's people come to see the land, geese are killed, the house is whitewashed, whisky and porter bought. The cows get a feed early so they look good; and maybe they get an extra cow in, if they want one." The last point was meant to convey the idea that the groom's family might borrow stock to match the claims made about the place in the expansive early stages of negotiations, which may have been animated by drink.

With the match made, the farmer signed the land over to the son in a formal process overseen by an attorney. The bride's family was investing in the son's, not the father's, enterprise. The dowry would come to the father. He would retain some of it for his retirement, distributing some to the groom's brothers and sisters, who had put in time and labor on the place and who now had to travel to seek their living in the world. And indeed, he had to set aside shares to augment whatever he might have managed to lay by for the dowry of any of his own daughters who were in hopes of marrying into farms themselves. With a wedding followed in good time by the birth of a first child, pointing the way to the building up of a complete family unit, the bargain was complete.

The marriage bargain may make it appear that family was largely an extension of the land itself in the 1930s. This is precisely the point that Arensberg and Kimball want to make. The continuity of the holding that carried the family name from one generation to the next lent an order to the countryside, balanced the books intergenerationally and among in-laws. The institutions of cooperation and social integration grew from the land, as did the crops and the livestock. While such an order provides stability, this is not the same as saying that it made life easy for all who participated in it. It simply meant that tradition provided the answer to the questions of "How is it done?" and "How do I belong?"

The memoir of Jeremiah Murphy, who as a young man fought in both the Irish war for independence and the civil war that followed, opens with a conversation between his mother and his paternal grandmother. The conversation took place on the Kerry farm on which he was born, in the same year that he was born. For all of its brevity it supports and suggests some interesting variations on the standard pattern described by Arensberg's farmer from Inagh. We must imagine that the conversation that took place in the first month of his life was recounted to Jeremiah by his mother years later, although he doesn't say.

In the spring of 1902, two women were talking about the outlook for the current year. One was about 25 years old, the other about 60 years. They were discussing farm business because that was their way of living. The younger, a returned Yank, had gone to the U.S. seven years before and having saved enough money to pay the dowry or "fortune" (as it was referred to in that part of the country) had married a "small farmer" (owner of a small holding) the previous year. Owing to the peculiar marriage arrangements which were the custom and the law, the older people could retain the ownership of the farm by agreement, for a year or two after the young couple got married. The purpose was to try to save some money to tide them over their declining years. Old age pensions and social security as we know them now did not exist in those days and people, especially the elderly, were forced to make their own arrangements. In this particular case, the older woman was deploring the fact that the previous year had not been very profitable and in a few weeks she and her husband would be turning over the farm to the young couple with very little on which to retire. The younger woman countered by remarking that she had very little too, but during the past month she had a son born who would be very little help with the spring work. She added, "He and ten shillings and the clothes on my back are all I possess but he will be a man someday." This was absolute optimism but it was typical of the people of that part of Ireland. They trusted Divine Providence that every year would be better than the one gone by. (Murphy 1998, 19–20)

Murphy's account of the conversation between his mother and grandmother allows us to slip behind the closed door of custom and feel the tensions that live there. We are reminded also of the narrowness of the economic margins that surrounded the lives of the people who lived in the rustic settings that today attract visitors to the Irish countryside.

Luogh, the site of Arensberg and Kimball's study, is a particularly attractive section of the Clare coast as it rises to the Cliffs of Moher above Doolin. It struck me that I knew someone there, Gussie Russell, who might remember the Harvard researchers and be able to tell me how they were received and whether they had gotten their story right. Gussie would have been one of the young men in the area at the time of the study, the last person alive from that era in that place.

I drove up from Tralee to look him up again in May 2004, to see how he was doing and whether I could get him to talk to me again, this time about what he may have remembered of the strangers camped in Luogh for months in the 1930s, asking the locals about everything, prying into everyone's business. But Gussie would not be able to help me. He died on the morning I arrived, as I quickly learned in the grocer's.

Apparently reading my disappointment, the women asked if I were related. No, I just needed to ask him something about the old days, the 1930s. Well then, there is no one left to ask about those days now, they said. He was the last of that generation. I was directed to a couple of others who might have some secondhand information, but no one had ever heard anything of the study. I went to look for Annie, who I knew liked to talk about the old days. She was not old enough to remember the 1930s, her girlhood of dances and carrying on with the boys having come a decade or so later. I found her at home.

"Yes, it was awful about Gussie," Annie said. "Bad timing for you. But he had been in hospital, then home for a bit, riding his scooter around town until the end—not safe for anyone, that. He'd have been the only one to tell you of Luogh in the 1930s. But I can tell you, if strangers came to do a study of the local customs, they'd be well treated by the people around here—if they were decent and well mannered."

I guessed aloud that they probably were, given their mission.

"Then they'd be taken to every dance and music evening and card game and meeting. Just for showing interest. As scholars they would be treated with the greatest respect." It struck me at that moment that very little mention was made of music in the Harvard study, reinforcing the impression that in those days music was simply a seamless part of the life of Doolin.

Annie's own knowledge of local lore straddled the decade of the 1930s. She knew many stories told her by older people of when the British irregular occupation force, the Black and Tans, were active in the area, way before her own time. Then there were her own memories of girlhood, when she and her girlfriends with linked arms would span the width of the road and walk miles to the nearest dances, coming back in the morning to howling mothers. But it was worth it: she said the girls were so mad for the boys, pairing off with them. "We'd risk anything." I wondered, Were the girls so wild in Arensberg and Kimball's time? If they were, we don't hear about it.

Telling Annie I might see her again in the evening if I stayed on in the area, I drove up the narrow road through Luogh, past Gussie's old place, where I had met him mending the gate the year before. There the old house sat alongside the ruins of Pat Flanagan's, both houses occupying what locals call "the hole," a hollow on the sea side of the road. The signs of neglect were already showing on the Russell house; they would, without intervention, reduce the simple cottage to the same sort of roofless shell as Pat's place within a decade or so.

I stopped in to talk to the O'Connors, who had land on both sides of the road. In the time of the study, Martin O'Connor's kin had owned a good deal of the area, divided among several relatives, all the way down to the Russells' holding. I explained what I was doing back in the neighborhood. Terrible about Gussie, but he had not been at all well and was depressed, and Cathleen O'Connor had been worried about him driving that motor scooter—dangerous for him and anyone else who met him on the road for that matter. So I had wanted to talk to Gussie about farming? Martin's own recollections ran back as far as the 1950s. Yes, there had been great cooperation among the farmers in the past, in Martin's own time as well as in more distant days. He had learned of the web of cooperation in the old times through the stories handed down. He also recounted the system of courtship and marriage in the old days, mirroring what was laid down in Arensberg's account.

The O'Connors no longer farmed. Martin had a map of the lands in Luogh dating from the 1800s, which showed how the long strips of fields were all held by different branches of his family; the pattern had persisted until nearly modern times. The lands that were the treasured link to livelihood in the 1930s were today rented to other farmers. What is true for Lough is true for all of the Irish Republic. Small holdings have been consolidated into larger ones, or they are leased to larger farmers. Long gone is the kind of farming described by Arensberg and Kimball. The annual sale of a few calves and mutton, a couple of tins of milk sold to the local creamery, a plot for vegetables — these had not provided for much of a life in terms of disposable income.

"In the old days there was no money in this country," was the way Martin put it. When, as a young man, he was deciding to continue farming in Lough, he swam against the tide: in that time, he said, "there was a flood of emigration from this area." Martin was part of a liminal generation, one that stood on the threshold of a new age. He was not old enough to have been part of the people and the time that Arensberg and Kimball had documented, but he had been born into the lifeways of that era. When he was growing up, "the turf for heating the household and cooking was very important in those days. . . . Nobody cuts turf any more." When he wrote to me a while ago, he was reflective about how life was changing in Luogh, even as the O'Connors prospered under the present circumstances. The personal narratives that could light up the past are being lost with the elders dying out; one spark at a time, the past is becoming sealed up. Martin wrote simply, "I miss Gussie and Micho very much." People recalling their country childhoods of decades ago have said to me, "We didn't have much, but we never thought of ourselves as poor. We were well fed, and happy, and satisfied with the life." But they never add, "I wish we could go back to those times."

PART II: FARMING AS IT IS

Farmers Wanted: Substantial Risk, Uncertain Future, Modest Prospects

Few of the young people who grew up on small farms were sufficiently satisfied to choose that life for themselves. The story of young people leaving the farm behind is a well-worn theme throughout the Western world and beyond. From the middle of the nineteenth century through today, Ireland may be able to lay some sort of claim to a kind of thematic preeminence here. Large families on small farms that would eventually be inherited by just one of the offspring guaranteed that the farm-to-city migration story would represent the typical early life career experienced by Irish natives. In the many decades of the twentieth century that were characterized by high unemployment and underemployment in the cities of Ireland, emigration to the cities of other countries was simply a logical geographic extension of the journey. In the last decade of the twentieth century, with more to do in the building and technical trades in Irish cities and towns, the economic calculus of the farm-to-city movement shifted in favor of migration for all of a farm family's sons and daughters.

At the same time, the maturing European Union, a vast economic empire, began to provide subsidies to European farmers, Ireland included. For some well-placed farmers, farming suddenly became a reasonably attractive business opportunity. At the same time, EU regulations meant that the successful farmer would have to be nimble, clever, and lucky to balance the new expenses of doing business with the timely acquisition of subsidies and profits. With new regulations coming from remote Brussels, many failed or became fed up and quit as the playing field tilted this way and that.

In a generation or less, farming in Ireland, as elsewhere in the world, took on a new character. The farm was no longer a place synonymous with the family name and a local reputation for keeping this or that number of cows. In fact, the farm was no longer a place located in this or that village or parish. The farm had become a business located in a global marketplace, a balance of assets and liabilities depending on its size and what it produced. Success means being able to cope with changing demand and remote competitors scattered worldwide, and it also depends on European agricultural policy decisions that shift from one to another priority as conditions change and EU membership expands.

The story of Irish agriculture today doesn't begin on the farm. Instead it requires a focus on international trade agreements in a united Europe and an appreciation of the dynamics of a global economy in which huge foreign-based agribusiness conglomerates are matched with corporate marketing and sales groups based in Ireland. In the world of agribusiness there is room for only the most incidental consideration of the impact of world trade on the Irish (Chinese, American, French, etc.) farm and rural community. The nature of the work of the Irish farmer, and farmers throughout the world, is now more than ever the consequence of global economics, international power structures, and shifting technology.

Even in the time of Arensberg's study, calves were produced in the West and grew up and were finished for market going east, the whole chain of production dependent on the British demand for beef. And Arensberg noted some big changes in the technology of the era that seem primitive and barely noteworthy today but would surely have produced their own ripples of change in community. In particular, horse-drawn mowing machines imported from England were replacing the hand-held scythe on a few farms. Still, he was able to conclude at the time, "modern tools do not shape the life of Luogh," although "they work a slow effect." Gone are the horses, and the little tractors that replaced them have now become antique curiosities in today's farm culture. Change came more rapidly after the mid-1930s, much more rapidly, and the consequences are easy to see.

The way of life described by Arensberg is long gone from Ireland, with only traces of practices and old memories left to indicate it ever existed. In the passage that opened this chapter, Tómas O'Crohan describes Séamisín's planting of potatoes on the Blaskets in 1920 as an act of faith. What is Irish farming if not rows of potato mounds? Séamisín was planting in bad weather because in his estimation there was little choice in the matter but to plant the cut spuds and put your trust in God that they would be looked after and would make a crop. They still grow potatoes in Ireland, and the island's per capita potato consumption leads the world. But we can no longer picture the potatoes in the pot coming in from the back garden. They come in plastic bags in the produce section down at the VG Market. In 2002 there were only 832 commercial potato growers left in Ireland, and 70 percent of the potato acreage was controlled by just 160 of them. Teagasc, the agricultural research and advisory body, estimated that most of the remainder would quit the business in the following five years.

Like all serious farming enterprises, potato production in Ireland has become a market-oriented science. Teagasc's potato breeding experts favor biotechnology to improve the development of new potato strains that are tailored to shifting market tastes. Old-fashioned traditional crossbreeding methods take too long (ten years from experimental plot to market), and market trends shift quickly. Targeted improvements favor the production for export of seed potato varieties for the United Kingdom, Mediterranean, and north African markets. According to Teagasc's advisory bulletin, current shifts in demand that need to be followed are from bagged potatoes to baby roaster, spiller, vacuum-packed, and boil-in-bag compatible varieties. Progress in the field of potato research was reported: these included the genetic fingerprinting of variants of potato blight and elevating the levels of CO_2 within potatoes to resist the damaging effects of ozone depletion in accordance with expected climate change scenarios. Nothing was reported on aligning production strategies with a trust in a higher power that had been a part of Séamisín's strategy for success.

Other sectors of agriculture, now far more important to the Irish economy than potato production, show an equally dramatic shift away from locally determined and familiar practices toward business strategies that flow from advances in science and policies geared to global economics. In contrast to Ireland's 832 potato farmers, 39,000 sheep farmers contributed just under 10 percent of the value of the agricultural sector in the early 2000s. The number of breeding ewes in the nation had increased from 1.5 million in 1975 to 4.2 million in the early years of the twenty-first century, which meant that there were more breeding ewes than citizens in the nation. The reason for the dramatic population growth was the opening of the French market to Irish lamb, with France importing 80 percent of the 2.7 million lambs exported each year. According to the Irish agricultural advisory board, the big challenge in maintaining or increasing the production of mutton was the change in consumer tastes and lifestyle. Mutton is red meat, falling out of favor with consumers in general, and lamb (global marketers never say "mutton") has the further liability that by contemporary standards it takes too long to cook and is thus simply not an in-demand convenience food. The challenge to Irish sheep farming, which really has nothing to do with the Irish farmer, is to improve the image of sheep meat in the world while engineering a microwave-compatible product. Just as there is little role for the farmer in enhancing the future of marketable meat product, there is little that farmers can do about the fact that wool is continuing to lose out to synthetic fibers in the world clothing industry.

Beef and dairy farming make up the vast share of Ireland's agricultural economy, and these production modes have also been affected by consumer demand and the expanding and maturing European economy. A complex and ever-changing set of EU direct payment policies has kept these sectors alive, but the number of farmers engaged in the production of beef and dairy products is plunging at a dramatic rate. The number of dairy farmers has fallen especially sharply in the last three decades, and the further reduction of numbers in this nearly necessarily full-time occupation is inevitable. Evolving hygiene standards for milk production have meant that progressively more efficient cooling systems must be located at the point of milking, and increasingly strict standards regarding permissible milk bacteria counts (which, with an eye on consumer squeamishness about bugs in food, must never even be mentioned) mean lockstep increases in the cost of dairy farm operation. Each decrease in the maximum permissible bacteria count means the farmer must purchase more expensive rapid cooling equipment. Whether or not a farmer can afford the next level of required improvement is determined by the number of cows being milked on that farm or, more precisely, the volume of milk the farm produces. This, of course, eliminates smaller farmers every time standards change.

Beef farmers, dependent on EU subsidies, have faced a need to increase efficiency in order for their enterprise to remain viable. For years, the EU direct-payment scheme was based on the number of cattle produced that year. Presently this is being converted to a fixed payment decoupled from production: instead the farmer is subsidized at a level based on the average value of cattle the farm produced for sale in the years 2000–2002. In other words, farmers will be given a direct payment for what was produced in years past, rather than what they are producing presently. The rationale has to do with the laws of supply and demand: providing an incentive to produce fewer cattle will control retail beef prices while allowing farmers to speculate about whether it makes sense to produce additional unsubsidized beef at the moment, given anticipated market conditions.

Meanwhile, the admission of ten new nations with large and poor agricultural sectors to the EU in 2004, coupled with the fact that the EU has a fixed total budget for direct payments to farmers through the year 2013, has Ireland's farmers duly worried about the future. They assume that the bulk of subsidies will go to farmers in the new member nations. As world market conditions shift, EU policy changes accordingly. The future holds who-knows-what market trends for beef prices and demand. BSE ("mad cow disease") and foot-and-mouth outbreaks have required total traceability for each head of cattle, and, despite the huge increase in record keeping that this has meant for farmers, there is no guarantee that future outbreaks will not either squeeze supply or poison demand.

Every year there are fewer farmers, and there appears growing resignation among them that government can do little to help. Yet critics continue to demand some sort of action. A Sinn Fein TD (member of the Dail, one of the two houses of parliament) from Kerry, Martin Ferris, speaking before the Dail in early 2003, charged that the year's cutbacks for farm sector supports apparently meant that farmers were being excluded from the "social partnership," the government's promise that it was committed to looking after the well-being of all citizens as the Irish economy grew. Ferris argued that "income levels have continued to fall and this has placed thousands more farmers on the poverty line or facing having to leave farming." In particular, Ferris was troubled by cutbacks in support for agricultural education and the government's failure to support young farmers. The specific incident that drew these comments was the prospect that Mellows College, one of the remaining schools that specialized in agricultural training, would be closed (*The Kingdom*, February 12, 2003). While eleven such colleges were operating in 1998, only six were still open in the academic year that ended in spring 2003. The number of technical programs and training institutions serving other sectors of the economy were expanding in the same period.

But the pace of closure of agricultural colleges only matched the rapid declines in the number of students taking agricultural courses. Those who were still attending were not optimistic. A survey report by Macra na Feirme Society (a government program supporting young farmers) found that more than three-quarters of the students in agricultural colleges in 2003 did not expect to be able to farm full-time, even though a similar number wished that they could. The cohort of active Irish farmers was aging as young people became reluctant to venture into the field. In that year only 10 percent of all farmers were under the age of thirty-five (*The Kingdom*, January 14, 2003). The following year saw a significant drop in agricultural college enrollments. Only 738 young people enrolled for the 2004–2005 academic year, down from 837 the year before.

By then, interested young people would certainly have been acquainted with the substance of a report submitted to government in 2000, ominously predicting a reduction of full-time farmers in Ireland from forty-four thousand to twenty thousand in the next ten years. An optimistic interpretation of this projection matched the perception of agricultural students that the chances of becoming a full-time farmer were slim: the government report speculated that some of the reduction in numbers could be explained by full-time farmers deciding to become part-time farmers. It was thought that many would take advantage of the expansion of new and attractive non-farm work opportunities that would augment farm incomes to meet the higher standards of living that people now expected. The bleak interpretation was that the number of farmers was sure to continue to fall below twenty thousand, and that eventually a small number of large ranchers, many of them not native Irish, would come to control large areas of land for export beef production (*Irish Independent,* April 5, 2000).

Among farmers, themselves, the most troubling aspect of all this was the sense that there was something inevitable about the loss of farms, that there was so little to be done. The story from the small town of Mountcollins is typical. Three decades ago there were 180 commercial milk farmers in town. By the time of the study projecting a reduction from forty-four thousand to twenty thousand farmers, only twenty-two milk suppliers were left. The number of Mountcollins's full-time farmers at that point might have been two or three. By then, the community had already become a much different place from what it was just a few years before. Fifty-two students attended grade school, where there had formerly been 107. Two grocery stores remained where there had been seven. A local man observed, "Five years ago . . . four of us trained an under-sixteen football team and won the county final. Today we can't even provide a team."

No less than the reduction in educational resources or retail and other services available to the town was the loss of the intergenerational continuity in sports, which signaled a serious quality of life transition in a rural culture in which leisure and tradition are built in no small part on sporting pride. Maybe, for a town with only six farmers under the age of forty, and none under age thirty, the question of fielding teams of school-aged young people to play soccer appears at best a secondary concern. But the inability to field such teams is a good indicator of the declining vitality of the community, of social integration, of the quality of life. And people have reported feelings of anger as well as futility surrounding the perceived inevitability of it all (Feehily 2003).

Shrinking profits, rising costs, and the uncertain future were taking a serious personal toll on farmers' emotional health. The cattle and sheep sector was producing an average annual income of only €7,500; there were the accounting pressures of having to produce increasingly detailed records; and then there was the trapped feeling of knowing no other occupation or way of life. The declining number of farmers meant that many of those continuing on the land felt isolated; they might not have anyone to talk to from one day to the next (*The Kingdom*, March 26, 2003). The farmers in Luogh in the 1930s, locked into patterns of cooperation and regular visiting, might be astounded that neighbors struggling along on adjacent farms could be living lonely lives. Yet this feature of farming in modern Ireland is mentioned over and over again as one of the hardest costs of the work.

An executive with Ireland's farmers' association, Simon White, issued a plea for farmers to watch for signs that farmers in their neighborhood might be facing hard times. The winter of 2005–2006 had been particularly hard, and farmers pushing the productive capacity of their holdings were running out of feed for their stock. Silage was running €40 per bale. Often the first public indication that a farm is in trouble comes in the form of animal cruelty, when dead and wasting livestock come to the attention of authorities and the farmer is prosecuted. White said, "The problems in farming today are enormous compared to what they have been. Farmers are becoming more and more isolated, and it is important that every one of us keep in touch with our neighbors to make sure that when people are having problems . . . that we keep in contact" (*Irish Examiner*, May 18, 2006).

It's a cold world that the Irish farmer lives in, and the factors affecting life and livelihood are remote and unyielding. But, once again, we might be advised by those who see the future clearly in terms of the realities of the international marketplace to take the broader view, rather than wringing our hands over the past and what has been lost, the declining family farm and the former richness of rural life. In this view, a superior understanding of agriculture begins with an appreciation of the fact that the rationalization (that is, worldwide integration) of raw material supplies and marketing strategies extends to every region of the globe, turning the world into a single efficient supermarket for inputs and profit taking. And organizing global resources takes organization on a very large scale.

For example, a quick look at the Kerry Group Annual Report and Accounts yields some idea of the magnitude of the forces at work, and additional insight into the nature of the world in which the Irish farm is situated. The Kerry Group is an Ireland-based corporate marketing, promotion, and finance consortium listing ninety-nine "principal subsidiaries all wholly owned" and located throughout the world, including, in addition to Ireland, the United States, United Kingdom, Netherlands, France, Germany, Italy, Poland, Hungary, Australia, New Zealand, Canada, Mexico, Brazil, Singapore, Malaysia, China, and Thailand. The subsidiaries range from consumer products and raw material supply and processing centers to investment, finance, and management services. The group's overall mission statement includes the clause that the company "will be a major international specialist food ingredients corporation, a leading international flavour technology company and a leading supplier of added-value brands and customer branded foods to the Irish and UK markets." In addition, "Kerry creates, produces and markets lifestyle and nutritional foods, flavours, and ingredients, meeting today's consumer demands for healthy, convenient, tasteful food and beverages" (Kerry Group 2003).

Of course, the bottom line is that the company is in business to make a profit from products that begin as raw agricultural materials. The purpose of the year-end report was to show how well the conglomerate was doing just that. That year the group did €3.7 billion worth of business, €308.5 million of that in profits, €113 million of the profits from sales in the Americas. According to the perspective of the global marketers, this is the proper size and scope for understanding agriculture in a global economy. The consumer dollar is what moves the system. Punch up the flavor, make it convenient, extend the shelf life (never mention bacteria), and let the farmers know how high to jump to clear the bar, if they want to stay in the game.

A copy of the glossy report is circulated to all farm households that contribute raw product to the company's operations. I borrowed one from friends in County Kerry who supplied milk to the Kerry Group and who believed, despite the fact that they milk a large number of cows under up-to-date conditions, that they would probably be priced out of dairying in the next round of regulatory changes. But that is the nature of change in the global marketplace. The family farm will do all right if under global product marketing, regional regulatory, and local labor market conditions it remains competitive enough to get what it needs and produce at world-competitive prices. If not? It's a cold world.

On the Edge of the Family Farm

Today, there is no "family farm" in Ireland, lots of different kinds of farms have some sort of family attachment. Nevertheless, as elsewhere in the world, "family farm" remains a strong value, an image of how things ought to be, here often followed by the thought "as long as I don't have to be stuck on one of them." The values implicit in the family farm image have to do with continuity, integrity, productivity, commitment, community, tradition, and mutual obligation—a way of connecting the present to the past, the notion that at least some things never change, or only change slowly. There is a sense of security in this idea, not only for the family farmer but for the whole of society: you can point to the existence of family farms as a kind of bedrock, as anchoring a common heritage, even if you have never set foot on such a place. When I went to talk to Ireland's farmers, I found a mixed story regarding the struggle to keep going.

When I first met and interviewed them in winter 2002, Adam and Lorna Gleasure were dairy farmers in North Kerry. The Gleasure name had been on the same land for generations, and Adam, who had carefully built his herd of big Holstein-Friesians, was milking fifty cows. Farming had changed substantially over the twenty-seven years that the Gleasures had been married and raised three children. Regulations designed to protect consumers and farm animals had been translated into a staggering schedule of record keeping for farmers. Lorna said, by way of comparison, that while Adam's mother might have been required to record the price received for the sale of a cow in her own time, "today you have to register every cow and every calf—I mean the sheer amount of records! Five times a year we have to fill out a complete account of what we have. And you have to identify every animal, every calf within the first week, and the mother's number." This is the set of requirements that ensures the complete traceability of every animal, introduced in response to concerns over BSE.

Lorna continued, "Once I slipped up and notified them that the wrong cow had just given birth to a calf—and some time later that cow did give birth. I saw my mistake, but thought that the record did show two cows and two calves—it was no big deal. But the next year they called up. The cow that calved first was actually recorded as the cow that calved second. Well, the next year she calved first, and there wasn't a long enough time between the births (to satisfy animal protection regulations). And they'd got us!" I asked what the outcome was. Lorna laughed and said, "Well, I thought at that stage that honesty was the best policy—I wasn't going to try to lie my way out of that one. And they said, 'well, as long as you've recorded the records that way, then we'll just put down that this year's first was born prematurely.' Well, that was a lesson to us, and that has been the big change. Everything has gone into regulations."

The one regulation that has put the greatest economic pressure on dairy farms stems from the milk quality standards, the key variable being the time it takes to cool the milk as it comes from the cow. "No matter how clean you were in maintaining the milk parlor, and even with the system that we had, the immersion cooler, it was taking four or five hours to cool the milk. You just couldn't achieve the levels set." The incrementally higher cost of each improvement in the milk-cooling technology has been responsible for the elimination of smaller dairy farms at each stage. The first to go years ago were those who milked a few cows, soon followed by those who milked fifteen or so. Lorna recalled her early years in the local area with a glance at Adam. "There was a wee woman down in the village, and she had the one cow and would leave the one can by the side of the road for the lorry. Do you remember, Adam?" He did. There was no place for such a charity in the present age.

Lorna and Adam had complementary qualities to one another. She spoke reflectively with compassion and humor. Adam communicated in a different manner. He had the philosophical quality of some country people who have lots of time to think while their hands are engaged in tasks made familiar by a lifetime of doing them. He kept his verbal observations simple and direct, but you wanted to watch him closely as he spoke because the gesture or nod with which he completed a sentence was an elaboration of what he intended to say. He was a man whose work had enforced a reflective patience, as that work was appended to the rhythms of nature and the experience of life beginning and life ending around him. I had the sense that he had gathered and stored a lifetime of ideas that come when you are working alone and communication offers no interruptions. The evening of the interview, with a tape recorder running, he sat and thought, looking into the fire, as Lorna did most of the talking. He would glance at me frequently with a small nod or other expression of emphasis, in this way questioning whether I had understood the significance of what had just been said.

Adam had seen the world change from his farm in Kilflynn, and Lorna explained how. His grandmother might go as far as Tralee, the big town, fifteen miles down the road, maybe once in three months. Now Lorna often found herself going in three or four times a day. A great change came in Adam's father's time, when he bought a motorcycle with a side car to travel the rutted roads. Lorna said that there would be no farm couple today that could do without two cars; she and Adam each had their own. Also typical of farm couples everywhere in Ireland, Lorna worked off the farm. She was the director of the Tralee branch of the Samaritans, a benevolent organization that assists people in need, and she was on call virtually all of the time. That was why she carried more than one cell phone. As she mentioned this, she jumped up and hurried from the room, realizing she had left her phones in the kitchen. "Here, I'm back," she announced, "clutching my phones to me," and the farmer's wife cradled them like an armful of eggs. Adam's eyebrows went up. "Four?" Apparently they had been proliferating out of view. She said it was becoming a challenge to find clothes with pockets large enough to accommodate her high-powered existence.

When I asked about change in the local community, the couple agreed that they were in fact more oriented to the big town of Tralee rather than to the village they lived in. This might be especially so in their case, they speculated, because their children were grown. A family's usual school-aged agents of local involvement were absent in this household. Also, they didn't drink, so they were not involved in the social circles that grew around the village's two side-by-side pubs. And finally, they were not Catholic, and the local Church of Ireland had closed for want of parishioners in 1979 and was now a community center. But if they could talk about the entire region in response to my question, there was a sense of change taking place, even if, as Lorna said, you might not see it day by day for being a part of it yourself. There was frustration with traffic in town, where a while back you never thought in terms of "traffic" at all. There was noticeably greater affluence, and maybe a bit more concern with crime, which the Gleasures were not at all preoccupied with. Lorna said that when her on-call work took her into Tralee at a late hour, she had no fear of walking the streets by herself. When their daughter, Rosemary, was still at home and working down at the Grand Hotel late at night, they did worry, sometimes. But her mom told her to walk to the roadside edge of the sidewalks on her way to her car, and they believed she would be perfectly alright that way. It was a modest precaution. No, crime was not a problem, and Lorna thought that a lot of the concern about it was coming from people's overworked imaginations.

But the expanding economy was bringing one big change to the farm gates all over Kerry. From the gentle rise that their farm stands on, you can look across the plain to Banna Strand and a thin sliver of the sea at the horizon. They said that ten years ago all you could see in that direction was the green of the land dotted with a few farm buildings. Now the plain was cluttered with new housing, not farmers' houses but houses built on land sold by farmers, built mostly for people working in Tralee. There was building going on all the time, and at night the lights from the houses broke the darkness as these suburban outposts marched across the fields, a luminous metaphor for the world crowding in on the farm.

Lorna remarked that a young fellow choosing to follow his family into farming would be nearly a rarity nowadays. When we first met, their three grown children were at home, but it was just for a Christmas visit. Their oldest boy had earned a PhD in chemistry and was making his way in industry in Cork, only reasonably comfortable, struggling with the rising costs of housing and everything else. Their daughter was doing a second degree, adding business management to her degree in biology and ecology. The youngest son was working in special effects in television, at the moment specializing in death-like cadavers molded from latex—we passed around a couple of sample body parts, very lifelike, which had been featured in television productions. The future might be uncertain in his profession, but for now it suited him. We sat around the dining room table one morning when they were all present, and the fact that none of them had chosen to follow Adam in farming came up. There were efforts to treat the topic humorously, but Dad was silent, and Mom wasn't smiling. That's when the partial cadavers came out, as conversation pieces.

The future prospects of the farm were clouded, to say the least. The fifty milk cows were pressing the limit of the land owned by the Gleasures, and the EU milk quotas limited any enlargement of the operation. The next change in milk quality standards, which Lorna and Adam were expecting to come in any time now, would almost certainly involve new costs that would be beyond the farm's capacity to sustain. Even a farm as large as theirs was potentially obsolete in the new world economic order. When Lorna married Adam in the 1970s, there were 7,500 dairy farms in their North Kerry dairy association. By December 2002 there were fewer than three thousand. At that time, Adam estimated that he could hold out for another year or two. We stood one day looking down the road toward his farm gate. Adam said he could not imagine what it was going to be like, that last day, when he gave up the stock and milking and was no longer a farmer, when he finally let it all go. He wasn't looking at me, and I had the sense that he was trying out the sound of the words, saying them to himself.

I returned to see how the Gleasures were doing in 2004. Adam was still milking his fifty big black-and-white cows. He greeted me with his new dog, a terror of friendliness, who chewed my hands and shoes the whole week I was with them. Lorna greeted me as she would an old friend, and we resumed the conversations of a year and a half ago as if it were just a week and a half. Things hadn't changed much. But now Adam was the very last man left milking in the entire township. He still thought he had another year or so left in it. The son in TV special effects had returned home, but he was doing some sort of applied engineering degree having nothing to do with farming. Of course the lack of interest in farming among the three offspring remained a sore spot, a sentimental rather than rational one, given that the end was in sight for whoever was running the farm. Lorna said she felt it not so much for herself, but for Adam. His family had been so many generations on this land. It was a sad thing to be leaving off. She felt that they had held out as long as practical. But the latest idea was that maybe Adam would try beef cattle for a while when the milking was done.

She was concerned that their story, while sadly typical, would not be the only one I should hear. She had a brother farming in Derry who was earning £28,000 in EU subsidies alone, which came to quite a bit considering the conversion rate of pounds sterling to Euros. Too bad I could not interview him, but she had in mind someone local I should talk to. Robert Groves was a dairyman doing very well. He was chairing the Kingdom County Fair (the County Kerry agricultural fair) and was run off his feet at the moment, but maybe when the fair was over next week, he might have an evening free. She would talk to him. Meanwhile, I would take in the fair.

Of course an event like the fair received a big buildup in the local papers, promising that it would be bigger and better than ever. "Huge Crowds Expected" read the headlines. At the fair there were farm implement exhibitors, contests in stock handling for the young people, livestock judging, sheep dog trials, vintage tractor and farm machinery exhibitions, crafts and cookery competition, and best-dressed-ladies prizes. It would be an old-time country fair with a new message for the new age: the two main messages to be delivered, according to Chairperson Groves, was the new emphasis on quality breeding of stock, and that there was a good future in farming. Robert was quoted by *Kerry's Eye*, "There has been a lot of negativity about farmers leaving the land . . . so this is to give a positive outlook to farming" (*Kerry's Eye*, May 13, 2004).

I arrived at the grounds early, before most of the stock were there, and I watched them come in and be unloaded. Two or three good-sized heifers gave their handlers the slip, but just one at a time; they careened through the exhibits in one-cow stampedes with farmers jumping to contain the animal and shouting directions at each other: "Head her into the wall, send her toward the gate, send her back into her comrades, let her stand quiet—would you look at the eedjit with the stick!" But otherwise, the excitement of the day was restricted to the recipients of blue ribbons, and, all in all, the event was a well-ordered success. The sun and the crowds came out together; the vintage machinery sputtered and came to life—including an ancient, giant thresher/bailer; and a number of events took place simultaneously throughout the day.

A rural version of class conflict—which of course excited this sociologist—did threaten to emerge when gentlepersons on their show jumpers rode onto the sheepdog trial meadow, confusing the dogs about just what it was they were supposed to herd through the trial gates. The sheep men were of a much different cut from the booted, coated, and capped mounted gentry. In response to the public address request to exit the dogs' field, two of the three intruders slowly rode back to their proper practice area, while the third paid no attention. The PA repeated sharply: "Would the lady or gentleman on the horse in the dog trial field please exit?" No immediate response, but slowly and gradually the rider retreated, with some teasing reentries, sauntering and sidestepping back and forth on the edge of the field. The sheep men bristled. "The arrogance!" one next to me said. "Walk down there and tell them to get the hell out of it," another urged the man with the PA system. And there were other remarks about what the person might do with himself.

The day was warm now and the air close in the hazy sunshine. I walked back to watch the old thresher working bales. A half-finished pint of black liquid sat on one windowsill of the thresher (the machine was the size of a small house), and that gave me an idea on this late Sunday afternoon. As I left the grounds, I noticed a tall woman dressed in a leather suit with enormous heels that made her even taller. She was climbing over a confinement fence to tend her goats. I wondered why she had dressed that way to bring livestock to a county fair. Then I remembered the best-dressed ladies' competition. I looked forward to meeting the man who had organized it all.

Successful Dairy Farming: Staying Just Ahead of the Posse

Robert lived with his wife, Betty, and a grown son in a fine house at the end of a long private lane. The house is on a rise, and the Slieve Mish Mountains on the Dingle Peninsula filing away west toward the horizon fill a magnificent panorama. Robert welcomed me warmly and brought me into the sitting room. He was a squarely built man of middle age with a soft voice and a mild, even gentle, manner. He made me feel very comfortable immediately. I said a few words about what I was doing there, and he said that he had a good idea of what I had come for. His narration linked past and present and provided a hopeful view of the future. He leaned forward, elbows on his knees, and started this way:

"My story is to be told, Bill, going back to nineteen and fifty-seven. I come from a family of nine: four boys and five girls. Just a small dairy holding about five miles from here. And as I was about to leave school, I saw that there was no great future. I came sixth in the family. I wasn't the oldest; there were two boys older than me, and of course, in those days it was the common practice that the eldest of the boys on a family farm here would stay on the farm. That doesn't work that way any more; times have moved on and times have changed. And now it's the individual who's interested, regardless of where he comes in the family, if he's interested in farming, then that's the boy—or the girl—who'll take over the mantle and keep the reins of the holding at home.

"I should say, forthwith, that farming to me—I looked at it as a way of life then. I wanted nothing else, whatsoever; I was going to be a farmer. I was sent off to college at Gurteen, the agricultural college, which was founded by the Methodist Church in Ireland away back in 1948. I remember quite well: it was the first Tuesday in October. I was put on the train from Tralee, [and traveled] away up the midlands, and the principal met me at the door, and he says, 'Your name?' he says. And I said 'Groves.' And he said, 'From where?' And I said, 'From Kerry.' And he says, 'Now, young Groves, will you behave yourself while you're here?' He was a very, very precise man. I could have turned on my heel and gone back to Kerry. But I stuck it out, and I was glad to have.

"I took to it like a duck to water. Everywhere I looked around, you know, there was interesting things going on. And I hadn't ever seen the likes of it before, and I was meeting people. And to make a long story short, I put in my two years—it was a two-year course in agriculture, both theory and practical. And you were assessed—not an ongoing assessment, but you had exams, and we had an assessment at the end of the year. And for me, lucky I suppose, after my two years were up, I was invited by the principal, believe it or not. Would I like to remain? To stay on the staff. And of course, well, I jumped at the idea—and I won't tell you the wages—but that was never really of interest to me, I was out for experience. Now, people of course get large money. But that, Bill, was it. My first leg up. And at the end of two years, judged from the staff, I was awarded the trophy for Character and Leadership. I never thought much about my commitment to things, but I suppose people saw something there, and that's why, I suppose, I got invited on the staff.

"From there I carried out a year in dairy, a year in the pigs, and a year doing machinery. And at the end of my third year, low and behold, the farm manager departed. And I had a real grasp of the running of the college. We had 308 statute acres, and students coming in every year— and you know it 'twas like home to me, 'twas just a community in itself. You know it was all a community spirit. And I was offered the job. And I had full responsibility of the farm. Of course I had great back-up service from the principal and vice principal, and they were always in touch with me and I with them. We got on great."

I asked, "So it was the perfect thing for you then?"

"It was the perfect thing for me, to gain the knowledge because at that time farming was, you know, it was a way of life. And ten years after that farming began to change, and farming became a business, and the way of life went out of it. And then the pressures came, and I could sense where it was coming from, with people getting out of farming. But what I saw in mind was the more you committed yourself to acquiring knowledge, and everything else, the more you were rewarded for it. I never worried about holidays, or the revenues or an increase in the wage or anything—I liked what I was doing, and that was my first priority. And I liked meeting people and so on.

"I left the college after five years, with a certain amount of reluctance in one sense. I was sad in leaving, but I had to move on. I had this ambition of owning a farm of my own. I had this ambition, and I went to work for an uncle of mine, up in the midlands in County Kildare, and the plan was in maybe a couple of years—he was in the building trade, and he had a farm, and he had a son, and I could see they had a lot on. And he did say to me, 'Robert, you never know, we'll see after how things get on and maybe I could assist you in acquiring a farm.' But in eighteen months I could see that wasn't to be and the area wasn't for me.

"But you know, going back to the college, the appointment of that farm manager, he was from Scotland, and he found it wasn't the place for him, and he decided to move on. And low and behold, wasn't I invited to become farm manager. And so I did, I put my name in, and I acquired the position of farm manager back at Gurteen. After leaving a place that I loved, and after eighteen months here, I was back in this lovely building in the center of the whole thing with the full responsibility of dairying and everything around me, and college work, as well as anything that went wrong at the college, and you know I had my fingers in a lot of things. I went into the classrooms once a week—and this is coming from a very practical base now—I wouldn't have the qualifications to lecture or anything at all like that, now, but I was invited in by the principal to demonstrate to students what was happening in a practical way. I loved that, and they questioned everything, and you know I got on great with them. And that went on for eleven years.

"And then the whole thing of the EEC started coming on stream, and Robert Groves began to get a little bit unhappy. Unhappy from the point that I was inclined to get a little bit settled in where I was at. And I would love to get my hands on a farm or land—I wanted to get a farm that I could build up, that I could see progress! The next thing was that I had come back to Kerry for a week's holidays, and a friend of mine says, 'Robert, there's a little farm outside of Tralee that three years ago was for sale, and it was taken off the market, and I can't see but that it will be sold eventually.' The people [on the farm at the time] had a very settled way of life, you know; they were a bit reserved in themselves, but whether they were or they weren't, I made contact with them. I visited them, and I explained my position, that I was down on holidays, but that I was terribly interested in acquiring a farm of my own. And if ever the day came that they would consider selling, that maybe they could give me first refusal. I wasn't back to my job three days when I had a phone call. Would I like to come to Kerry? They'd like to talk to me."

Robert purchased the farm.

"I walked into a wilderness, an absolute wilderness, but I've no regrets. Betty and I, the first thing we did, the house wasn't livable, so we lived in a mobile home for ten years. Now I have a dairy herd of a hundred cows behind me. When I got started, I had thirteen hundred pounds in my hand, and that's all I had. And that's why I say if you've the commitment . . ."

And here Robert let the thought trail off, picking up with, "And that brought me to the 1970s and to the EEC, and, as I say, this efficiency and business kind of approach had arrived.

"I have two sons, and the eldest boy wasn't too interested in the farm. But luckily for me my youngest boy is, and that gave me the encouragement to keep going. And as you said, some people haven't the encouragement of their children, of somebody to take over the mantle of their farm. Go back thirty years in Ireland, and people would say, 'If God spares me, I built this place—I'm here for generations. And there it is going to stay, like it or leave it.' But that has changed. If you haven't an heir to the throne now, it doesn't cost the individual person a thought to just sell it, and that's the change.

"Luckily for me I've got a son, and he's been through college, and he has gone through a lot more college theoretic stuff than I ever had. But I suppose with my practical abilities, it's working fine so. But, you know, he knows that he's going to take over a marvelous asset. And I suppose I have a responsibility to my other two—I have a son and a daughter as well—and they have to, you know, get some of that surely too."

I thought back to the convention of splitting the in-coming daughter-in-law's dowry partially among the children who would "go traveling" in the past. But in modern Ireland Robert would be receiving no dowry to split among the other two offspring when the farmer son married. Whatever inheritance went to the non-farming son and daughter would have to come off the top. Focusing on the farm's future, I asked, "What will your son who stays on farming need to be successful in his own time, in the future?"

Robert hesitated just for an instant and replied, "He'd need to be focused. And he will need to . . . need to have a level head, I would say." Robert was being very deliberate here. I thought of Conrad Arensberg's admonition to stick to the present rather than asking about the future, but I wanted to know about the future. Robert elaborated, cautiously hopeful. "There's no point, if things are down for a year, getting depressed over it . . . and then saying, 'I'm going to try something else.' He'll stick to something. To my knowledge, it's the person who is in and out of something that has difficulties. But my young boy, if he keeps focused, if he watches capital expenses, you know, you don't 'go to town'—'go to town' is an expression I have—but just take your time, and keep just ahead of the posse at the same time, you know? I believe in keeping up . . . not with the Joneses, but keeping up with modern technologies and so on. And I'm happy with my young boy. He goes out to the young farmers' meetings and meets young people." Taking a deep breath, Robert continued, "He is aware of what I went through forty years ago."

The question about the future led Robert to talk about the past, about working toward his own future.

"And I wouldn't want anybody to go through that—although we were terribly, terribly happy. People have been saying to me, 'Robert, going back to the 50s and 60s in Ireland, were the people happy with all the manual work to do?' I say they were terribly happy." But he qualified any purely nostalgic interpretation of what he was describing regarding the old ways of doing things. "I have no doubt all this drudgery going back now—I can see and I refer to it now as 'drudgery,' the way that I'm [now] settled. You wouldn't think of it as such then—you were happy with your lot—but let's not go back to the thing! But again, I'm a believer that you reflect on the past, in the future."

In that past, "everybody supported one another, and there was that kind of support. And the woman of the house had a part to play, and she took pride in it, you know? But, now it's different. We have greater . . . how would I say it? I'm thinking of the lady folk now in the house—they aren't looked upon as 'Now the housekeeping's for you and that's it, full stop.' Thankfully, we have broadened our outlook, now, and I see women now and they're able to do as much as any man is able to do, and isn't it only right?" Robert had been doing yard work when I arrived, and his wife, Betty, had taken over seamlessly, the big tractor mower continuing to drone outside for most of the interview. I didn't ask Robert whether he helped with the housework, but I knew the history of this couple working side by side to tame the "wilderness" they had walked into and would wager Betty knew what there was to know about the running of this farm. No more taboo surrounded women handling the implements of the field.

There was a small lull, and I blankly introduced in the broadest possible terms one topic I hoped we would get to: "The EU, for you now, how is that working?"

The response was characteristically measured, thoughtful. "I think it has done well; I think it has done well. In the 70s when the EEC came on stream and the older farmers said, 'We're all going to be wiped out,' well, that hasn't been the case. The committed farmers stayed with it, like, and in all fairness I think that only for the EU the farming community would not be up as we are. And really, with technology and especially milk [farming] was the first to take the great plunge in marketing and so on. You know I think that only for the EU we'd not see the prosperity that I can see and you can surely see traveling around."

I asked at that point, thinking of the impact of regulations on farmers like the Gleasures who were milking fifty cows and feeling that they were on the edge, "But in milk—you say you milk one hundred cows—especially for dairymen, what size is the minimum size to be viable?"

"I would say around fifty."

"Will that change in the future?"

Robert answered quietly and reflectively, "Oh, it will go up, yes, 'twill go up. It was common practice ten years ago for a man to survive on thirty cows. But we should really be talking in quotas now, in milk quotas. In those days, going back twenty years ago, we had an average of six hundred gallons per cow. I mean, I have cows now in my herd that would be giving close to two thousand gallons. My average for the herd, a hundred cows, would be 1,500 gallons. And there's the technology—and I know the more I feed those cows and the more they're bred to generate more milk—so it's not the number—I shy away a little from that—you have a milk quota. And then [the question is] what would your quota need to be? and I would say now we're talking about sixty or seventy thousand gallons. And let that man have fifty cows to produce that, or let him have sixty cows to produce it. So if he had seventy thousand gallons and ran his business efficiently, [that would be the answer to your question]."

I asked about other modes of farming. "What is the most viable branch of farming to be in the future?"

"Well, I think the milk," said the committed dairyman. But there, "the big co-ops [the agri-corporations that buy, process, and market the products] are inclined to attract us to the New Zealand system."

I asked him to explain.

"The New Zealand system is a low-cost system. They produce milk from grass, full stop. No quotas whatsoever, and they have large numbers of cows. They acquire [a fairly low return] for their milk and are quite happy to produce it for that, while there is no way we could produce for that—you know, our costs—and that's the difference. In New Zealand they're big factory people, you know, they're producers, and they're going away from the family farm. And I'll go back to that again—the family farm, we have to protect it as best we can. And the best way to do that in the future in Ireland is milk. Everybody, you know, consumes milk, and if we produce with quality . . . and let me say one thing about the quality. I'm quite convinced I could go on my holidays, and the milk that I produced that morning, I could put it on the supermarket shelf, and I could come back in ten days, and that milk would still be perfect. An awful lot of emphasis has been put in Ireland over the last ten years to produce quality milk. And that's another area where my young lad needs to keep focus. You need to keep your fingers on quality. If you don't keep up with that, you could be down in the dumps over it; you could be penalized."

As competitive and dynamic as dairying might be, Robert was most confident about its future when compared to other kinds of farming in Ireland. Of dairy farming's chief rival, in terms of economic prominence, he said, "Beef, well, that's another day's work—but I think we've come to accept that all these mountains of beef have disappeared. Farmers can see [that] now. Going back a number of years ago—as long as they got an animal in calf, irrespective of what kind of animal was produced, there was some sale for it. But now they have been educated, and they know that you breed animals of quality that are going to be sold, and there's where the gains are, from here on. Of course, beef has a future, but not the same intensity as for milk."

And with regard to the shaggy sheep that dot the hills and mountains and make driving the narrow roads an exciting obstacle course for Irish drivers, Robert was less hopeful for the farmers that kept them. "I see probably a big change in the sheep end of it—now we're in the stage of decoupling, and the subsidies are going to disappear."

I took the opportunity to ask about the admission of the ten new members to the EU—it had occurred only in the past two weeks.

Robert's initial response was to think of the well-being of those nations, and he said he was sure that "they would experience the leap forward I suppose that we saw in the 70s. And that's the area now that we have to respect. We've been encouraged to modernize, and I think that now we're going to be left on our own." I asked if he meant that those were the countries now that were going to get the subsidies to bring them along, that Ireland's share of direct payments would dry up. "Oh yes," he said in a tired voice. I wondered if the weariness came more from the question or the long day just ending and the week of seeing to all the details of the Kingdom County Fair.

I asked if we were going past the time that he had to devote to our conversation. "Oh no, not a'tall. I'm up every morning at a quarter to six, and I'm busy all day. But don't ask me to be out and after my cows at seven o'clock or eight o'clock at night. And then I come in and can do anything I want, and that's why you saw me so active around the Kingdom County Fair—I have time for other things then."

OK, back to the EU then. I said, "So now Ireland will be able to stand on its own. Do you think it can?"

"I think so." He repeated it twice, as if he were trying out the idea. "I think so. I think that this country had the initiative when we joined, and I think they got the leadership. And the educational system encouraged the young people: I'm thinking now of Macra na Feirme and all the agricultural colleges—they had a boom time. For the past fifteen years or so you wouldn't dream of keeping your individual at home without getting them out to an agricultural college and getting them training. You wouldn't survive because, you know, your qualifications would [need to] be at a higher level to gain various subsidies and grants and so on."

I asked whether students receive actual instruction in agricultural college about EU grants and subsidies available to the farmer.

"Oh, you do, and they have structured programs on what's of benefit for you and you get—I can't think of the word right now—but you get continuous assessment and you're required to go back—a refresher—they continue to monitor your progress. And that gives a young lad encouragement then, and then he is eligible for it."

I asked, then, did he think the government was sufficiently favorably disposed toward farmers in Ireland, or should the government be doing more to support its farmers? Here, of course, I was thinking of bitter statements I had heard about the disappointment that government could not or would not do more.

"Well, I suppose being a farmer, Bill, we always think that we should get more and more and more. Sometimes I don't like our government, and then I think, well, we may be being a little too critical of them. Maybe sometimes we do gear ourselves for a goal, and then halfway through, the goalposts are changed. Maybe something's just come from Brussels, and then suddenly it appears that we're on the wrong track. We have to backpedal a bit. We were trying to blame the government for that, you know? I probably saw that going back maybe eight years or so. They had a policy where they would slaughter a lot of the male calves. That was something that I thought was going against what I was always brought up to. I shivered a little bit, and thankfully that's now behind us. Now we have this export, you know, and we export all calves and export all cattle and everything is, you know . . ." His thought trailed off. Robert might be getting a bit tired, I thought, something for which he might well be forgiven, having survived the week just passed.

I picked up the conversation and put the fine point on it, talking about those farmers in the newspapers who said they were going to be eliminated and nothing to do about it, and the government not willing to step in to save the Irish farm, not honoring the much-discussed "partnership" idea that it actively promoted. "You must hear that yourself from people around you?" I asked.

Robert responded in a low and grave voice. "I see it. Yes, I see it, Bill. I see that." I asked whether some of the frustration stemmed from the sense that it was the wider world changing, that there appeared to be frustration that there was no one to fight in order to save the small farm.

"Yes, I think that was the real challenge, maybe three years ago, and they've come now to accept that farming now can be a lonely life. I mean, there isn't the same comradeship, there isn't the same support from individual farmers and your neighbors as there was here going back just ten years ago—and I can see here, myself and my son, we'll be working here day after day and very seldom someone would come in—very seldom the neighbor would come in—except for a traveler who'd be selling something. But going back years gone by, there was a great old comradeship among everyone. And I think that that's where the frustration is actually.

"And apart from that, in those days going back twenty years ago, we had the department of agriculture, and it had an official dedicated to each community—we had a department official to cover maybe half of three townlands. And he was a qualified agricultural technician. His job was to visit every farm and support them and give them knowledge and advice, and if a young lad had been to agricultural college, he was able to relate very keenly to him. But, you see, all that changed, and all that stopped. And we don't have that anymore, and I think that more than anything is why farmers feel isolated. And the farmers now feel an awful isolation; they'll see nobody coming to give them advice and nobody coming to give them a bit of encouragement. And maybe their holding is fragmented, and they'll say, well, maybe I'm fifty, or I'm sixty, and what's it all for? And they lose the goal to keep going."

I asked again, considering all this, how's it going to be different in your son's time? I asked if farmers in the future would have to buy up more land, push neighbors still further away, to become more like the U.S. or New Zealand factory operation.

"There's a little bit of that, yes, there's a little bit of that. For my son, what gives me the enthusiasm and the happiness, I'm totally and utterly convinced that my son will have a living standard with what he has here, without going and needing to pressurize anyone else out of business — but I know where it's coming from, Bill, I know the question very well. Sadly, people tend to want more and more — to get bigger. I've a different view. To me we can only eat one lunch off the table, you know. And if we can respect other people's views and be happy with our lot — life is short enough, and I don't know what all this 'want more' is for, but maybe it's only human. There it is — I really don't know.

"I'm happy, and I'm lucky that I built up an enterprise here that my son — I'll be handing it down to him. That he will not have to go any further, you know. When I retire and when Betty retires, we need somewhere to go, and now I'm looking carefully at expenditure. I need to have something put aside for the day when I say, 'OK now, take it on from here. If you want my advice I will always be around.'"

A little alarmed, I said, "But you won't go anywhere — you'll stay here in the house?"

"Oh yes, I won't go anywhere."

I reminded him that in the old days there would be a west room in the house for the retiring couple — with one milk cow.

"Oh yes, but no longer," he said. "You'll have something more than that. Oh yes."

I thought it was the natural point to end the interview, so I turned off the tape, and we just chatted and had tea and cake. I thought about how Robert's life was a bridge between past and present. With the vast majority of farmers older than thirty-five, there were a lot of them who, like Robert, stood with one foot in the past and one in the dimly seen future. Farming to him was, as he said, a "way of life" that had been transformed into an enterprise requiring business acumen, a sixth sense for international market trends and future trade agreements, a firm grasp of the science of animal husbandry requiring advanced training that was continuously upgraded with continuing education credits, and a personal character that permitted an extraordinary capacity for hard work, commitment, and faith in a rational future. I wondered if the job description would be different for the successful beef farmer in Ireland. It wasn't.

Animal Science

I spent part of a morning and afternoon with Michael Bourke. He and his wife, Ina, raised cattle for market in North Cork. I asked him to give me a crash course in some of what I might need to know to do successful cattle farming in Ireland. I think I understood enough of what he said to report that the knowledge, hard work, commitment, and faith components of the work of the dairy farmer apply to the successful large cattle farmer as well.

Michael was about to feed his stock when I met him outside his enclosed feed lot. He said he first had to feed the cattle and then he would be right with me. I looked in on the two long rows of confinement pens running parallel to the other end of the enormous barn, the large open door at the opposite end appeared a smallish square of light in the far distance. I was in no hurry, but the thought did cross my mind that I would be standing around for some time while he fed that many cattle. Michael climbed onto a tractor that he had left idling at the end of the yard, and hauled a large, drum-shaped trailer onto the concrete floor that ran between the two rows of suddenly very animated cattle. He proceeded slowly down the line along one side of the building, and the churning drum deposited mixed feed in measured amounts in front of the cattle thrusting their heads forward for their breakfast. The feeding took little time.

The Bourkes farmed 137 acres of their own land and rented another three hundred within a twenty-mile radius of home. He finished cattle for the market and so specialized in buying weaned calves and turning them into animals ready for slaughter. The process took about eighteen months. This was a large operation. But it was also pretty much a one-man operation (it was Ina who said Michael did it all himself). The week before, he had sold sixty head for slaughter, and in a few days he would be selling another forty. It occurred to me that the number was equivalent to Robert Grove's entire herd of milk cows. With the decoupling policy on the horizon—the policy that would pay him a subsidy based on the average number of cattle he sold during the index years of 2000–2002—he would in future be paid whether or not he raised any stock in the current calendar year.

In order to make his operation continue to work financially, Michael had taken to heart the government's urgings that stockmen achieve efficiency and thereby viability by cutting their costs. To this end, Michael himself grew all the components of his feed mixture. Here was where my abbreviated lesson in the science of stock raising began. He exploited the different soils in the different parcels of the land that he rented to the best effect, growing the components: wholecrop wheat, wholecrop peas, urea-treated wheat for protein, and different types of grass silage. Raising his own feed also ensured that his cattle did not have any genetically modified soy in their feed or other GMOs (genetically modified organisms), which he preferred to avoid. (Many European consumers also prefer to avoid them.) He further reduced costs by doing all the crop work himself, hiring a contractor to help him only at harvest.

For the next lesson, I needed to know something of the science of what to feed and when to feed it. Cattle at twenty-two to twenty-six months need 13 percent protein in their diet, both degradable and undegradable bypass. To get the right formula, I should keep in mind that wholecrop wheat runs 9 to 10 percent protein, wholecrop peas 18 to 20 percent, and urea-treated wheat 16 to 18 percent protein. Feed the first two ingredients, which are forages on a fifty-fifty dry matter basis, and then balance the protein with urea wheat, which is a concentrate. As noted, if you have grown your own, you can avoid the use of the genetically modified soybean meal. Fiber comes directly from the two forages, which, when combined, slows the movement of food through the gut and helps the animal salivate, which results in a rumen-friendly pH. When two forages are fed, it increases cattle's intake by 10 percent over the feeding of one type of forage alone.

Younger cattle in the sixteen- to twenty-two-month range will need similar fiber and other components with the exception of protein, which needs to be elevated to the 16 to 17 percent range for bone growth and carcass development. Extra forage peas can be fed to achieve this goal.

When finishing cattle, you use the diet without grass silage in wintertime to achieve meat higher in color. It will shelve better, and the fat marbling results in better cooked flavor. In summertime, when finishing off grazing cattle, you supplement the diet with wheat to lighten the color of meat and improve the growth rate as well as the carcass grade. The latter is a standard measure having to do with conformation to established formula for several different grades of carcass. You want to achieve the highest grade because if you are selling a hundred cattle at a time, the grade makes a huge difference in your profit margin, and you don't want all your calculations and hard work to go for nothing. If you want a check on how you are doing (a kind of quality control measure), remember that the live weight gain for store cattle is .9 kilogram per day, and for finishing cattle it is 1.2 to 1.3 kilograms per day. I was trying to absorb all of this, but it seemed an awful lot. My idea of what was involved in the business of farming was rapidly shifting: this was as much applied life science as anything else. But Michael wasn't finished with my crash course in the basics yet.

None of this hands-on application of knowledge is a guarantee of business success if you don't keep a wary eye on the international markets. The EU may be a necessary management force in the international economy, but it is fickle and changes policy often. Michael believed that the real policy makers operate through the World Trade Organization, an organization which he and other Irish farmers suspected largely does the bidding of the United States and its agri-corporations. One needs a worldview, what scholars call a theory of political economy, some scheme of how things operate in the world, to give the marketplace some order, to inform your strategies for anticipating what will happen next. Anticipation, not reaction, is the key to success.

Michael thought that the near future held out mixed prospects to the Irish farmer, and there was a lot to consider, a lot to anticipate. There were the decoupled payments that would provide income to farmers whether or not they were producing, and that was such a strange slice of international reality that Michael reckoned he would just go on producing as he had done before. Having stock to sell in an uncertain world where people were paid to do little or nothing had to be better, at least for the short run, than having nothing to sell. The ten new members just admitted to the European Union, with their stagnant farm sectors in need of assistance and overhaul, would be able to more effectively make demands on the EU's limited resources than would Ireland. He expected that the subsidies to Irish farmers were not long for the world. Then there was the problem of Third World farmers and the big European agribusiness marketing corporations serving each other's needs. Farmers from Brazil, Argentina, Paraguay, and Uruguay competing for European market shares faced few regulations at home with regard to feeding their cattle growth hormones, using GMOs, and they had none of the European-mandated traceability of inputs and cattle movement regulations. Michael said that it was common knowledge among Irish farmers that the large agribusiness conglomerates were putting cheaply and dangerously produced South American–raised meat on Irish supermarket shelves. These measures were unfair and potentially disastrous for Irish farmers, who would soon be facing yet tighter competition from within Europe.

Taking all of this together, it was not hard to understand why so many were leaving the work of farming to a dwindling few. Standards were being raised, narrow profit margins demanded new attention to input costs, the required knowledge base was expanding exponentially, life and death policy decisions were being made for Irish farmers in remote capitals, and market conditions and competitive advantage were increasingly uncertain. Success in this business only required luck, incessant hard work, the talents of a professional gambler, and the nerves of a skydiver. I thought again of Séamisín putting out his potato sets year after year with only faith in some higher power determining success. Success for today's farmer meant something far different from what it had meant on Great Blasket in 1920 or in Luogh in the 1930s, yet there remained the one common measure: the historical thread of being able to pass on the farm.

Over lunch I asked whether Michael hoped his own son would follow him in the business he worked so hard to develop. Like Robert Groves, he had bought and built up his operation rather than inheriting it. He did hope that one of his offspring would carry on; they would have a real asset, a going operation. But he would not want them just to know farming. They would need to study a second trade as well, just because of the uncertainty of the future. Maybe, if worse came to worst, they could cut back to just the 137 acres he owned, drop the number of stock, and do it part-time. He said yes, that seemed to be a trend. But it was still something to hope for, that one of his children might know life on the land and value what he was able to pass on to them.

Michael said reflectively that farming and life in the countryside were different from what they had been in the past. He lamented the passing of the old times, some of which he remembered and some of which were related to him by his parent's generation. He was somewhat younger than the dairy farmers I had heard from, but the times he spoke of echoed the same themes, calling to mind the lives and communities described by Conrad Arensberg in the 1930s. People in the country used to cooperate more. These days one saw one's fellow farmers only at Mass, once a week, and then there was only the chance to say "hello." He didn't drink, so the pub was no source of social life for him. And the local creamery was shut down; that had been a gathering place that would give you a chance to get the local news. Also gone were the marts and the town market days—but he had heard that there was an effort to bring the market days back. He wouldn't mind. He would go and take a look at the calves for sale.

Now, when he happened to see the colors in a farmer's field lightening (due to mowing), he would drop everything and fly over to lend a hand, and his neighbors would do the same. But they each knew, with today's farm machinery, you could really do it all yourself. But still and all, it gave you a nice sense of tradition. Of course, the farms were so big that you could only see one or two farms over from your own place, down the road or across the way. There were no agreed upon dates or binding expectations of mutual sharing of work, no "cooring." You did it only by chance. Michael repeated the familiar theme, "It is different today, more rushed, and more lonely." There was no time for socializing, with two people working in every family. He thought that the old ways of community and sharing were going the way of the rest of the world, where everyone was just out for themselves.

Defining and Defying the Changes

So, in a way, even farmers and their farms have migrated, away from Ireland as an idea, an island in time. Just as the large electronic technology and chemistry multinationals have placed their footprint on the nation and kicked it forward, the food science and agri-marketing giants have given it another kick across the global marketplace and into the world's common future. I saw the products of this new science in the feed barn on Michael and Ina's farm and also saw them in the Kerry cousins of the Bourkes' cattle at the Kingdom County Fair. There, turned out mostly by farmers' teenaged offspring and other young farmers in white lab coats, were the modern breeds, large slabs of beef on the hoof, Charolais, Limousin, and Simmental cattle with sides like walls of steaks. There were Holstein-Friesian bullocks raised for beef, lean and squarely muscular. There were their young sisters, promising in their time to pump two thousand gallons of milk per year into their farmers' quotas.

This was the new face of Irish farming, which could hold its own with livestock raised anywhere in the world. The beasts were all the products of sophisticated formulas for carcass and bone development based on science. The science that farming has become was reflected in the white lab coats of the young well-schooled handlers, who, though ever fewer in number, understand practical things about macro and micro economics, soil chemistry, and bovine nutrition that would allow them to carry on informed conversations with PhD specialists in those fields. The scene at the fair's stock rings could have been from any-where in the globalized economy, which of course was precisely where it was taking place.

Irish farming, like Irish anything, must live and compete on the world stage if its products are to be consumed. Farmers realize this. As a result, they are dedicated to success, whatever science or art of ap-plied biology and economic speculation it may take. They have gotten bigger—or gotten out. In this light it is no surprise that their numbers were projected to dwindle by more than half in the ten years between 2000 and 2010, or that indications are that the actual trend is keep-ing pace with these gloomy projections. The numbers will continue to shrink after that. There is little room here for sentimental dwelling on what has been lost, except to acknowledge the loss and get on with it. Already, so many of the quaint little farmhouses strewn across the farm-lands of Ireland are the homes of commuters, artisans, and summer retreatists. No little farmers can survive in the new world order of the Kerry Group and other multinational agri-corps—except, perhaps, a certain kind of farmer.

The EU has not been unkind to the sheep farmer, for now, and they do receive subsidies for setting aside land and reducing the number of sheep they set loose over the mountains and passes. The small sheep farmers tend literally to live at the fringes of Ireland's development, back in the mountains and on the rough lands where no other livestock compete, except for a few cattle set out to graze among them. There are large sheep farmers, to be sure, in Ireland. But these are not the ones being discussed here. Instead we are talking about—they should forgive the expression—EU rural hustlers, who live just beyond the edge, who take advantage of what the affluent Irish economy leaves out for them in the way of jobs, in the way of land. At the same time they benefit from living where their family may always have lived, relatively little cash coming in but little going out, a little above the new suburban and exurban developments up in the hills, back behind the mountains, or out on the Atlantic fingers of land or on the islands. As long as there is an edge and beyond in Ireland, a beyond where there so far remains relatively little pressure on the land, such as it is, there will be the sheep farmer.

Inishbofin is less than five miles off the coast of Connemara. The fellow who works the boat that hauls mail, people, and other cargo to the island let me know that the EU was not working any miracles for anyone on either shore touched by his own work. He estimated the year-round population of the island at fewer than two hundred. I walked most of it in a couple of hours and finished my walk winding my way through scattered free-ranging sheep to the top of a low hill overlooking the harbor and most points on the island. The owner of the sheep was shearing with the old-style black-spring scissors joined only at the back of the handles. His dog herded me the last several yards in his direction, maybe figuring from the length of my beard—roughly the same color as the sheep—that I was next. The farmer was happy to talk as he worked. The four-year-old ewe sat on the farmer's feet, with her four legs splayed out in front and her back resting against his knees, as if on an easy chair. He held her in place easily with one hand grasping a curved horn. She looked back and forth to whichever of us was speaking. The dog, a classic black-and-white sheepdog, sat on my feet, demanding attention whenever the conversation distracted my good ear-scratching hand.

The island was a mix of change and things going on as they always had, the farmer said. The big changes for him were, first of all, the different breed of sheep that had appeared in recent years. They were sturdier, but still the sturdiest of all were the crossbred ones that took the best from the new and old locally adapted breeds. And the fishing was another change—he did both fishing and farming. The changes there weren't so good. It used to be when he was young that his lobster traps needed tending twice a day. "Now you could go out once a week, and the trip'd be wasted." Still, he kept his boat and his pots, out of habit as much as anything. He was critical of "the government," which was coming in now with schemes to reduce the amount of food and all produced by farmers to keep the prices up. "And there's people starving in the world. You'd think they could figure out a way to let us produce the food and they to get it to them!" Most of the farmers I talked to had said as much.

The world was full of puzzles. On the one hand, the population of the island had shrunk in his time. The number of children in school was down to a total of twenty, from eighty in his own time. But the schooling might be better now, as it was not much good in those days. It was wartime, and when the local teacher left, the government couldn't find anybody willing to be posted out teaching on an island to replace him. The priest took over, "but he couldn't control us, and consequently there were several years when no learning went on," he said.

We could hear distant sounds of hammers and power saws in the village below as we talked. "Yes, thank goodness for the building and the tourists, otherwise there'd be little for us. But the government is putting an end to the building, and the sale of land now. Says there's too much of it. I suppose that's all right. But if I wanted to sell that plot of land there for you to put a house on, we couldn't do it. It's all regulated now."

He thought the island a good place to live, having lived there all his life. But it was quiet. The tourists came back year after year, and the islanders were grateful for it. Some he knew had been coming back for forty years. "We don't understand it." He meant, with all the places in the world to go, why did people return to the modest place where he had spent all his life? Looking out from where we stood on the low rise over the harbor, we could see three of the four sides of the island, miles around, back to the Connemara coast and the mountains and across the smaller surf-battered islands to the Atlantic horizon in the opposite direction. "Yes, thank goodness for the tourists. Still, it's a quiet place in the winter, and lonely, with the wind driving the rain." That was a time to sit by the fire, and not much else. But there was TV, as well. It was the summer of 2003. Did I think Saddam Hussein was dead? Neither did he. "Nor that other fella, Bin Laden. No, I guess he's not either."

Inishbofin is one of the places at the fringe of the intense economic pressures Ireland has experienced. International politics, decades of tourism, and the influences of television have washed over the island. But nothing coming from the outside world had dislodged this sheepman or his way of living, and I couldn't imagine that anything would. But I didn't ask him if, on this island where the population had dwindled to only two hundred or so people, there were anyone to take over for him when he was done. Sometimes even those who have been out into the world find what they have left behind, a little farm emptied of romance by having spent one's childhood there, is still an attractive option.

Farmer Der of Iveragh was committed enough to the idea of the family farm to return to his father's in Kerry from a life of working in England and Australia when "family tragedy struck," ten years ago. Typical of the area's farmers, he raised a modest number of sheep on his land—fifty, give or take a few. He preferred the sturdy Scottish-type sheep to the other fancier varieties that were more fragile and required more care. He compared the breed to the old Kerry cow. When I said, "Ah, but you don't see them any more," he replied that he had acquired one just a few months ago and planned to breed her and sell the calves along with those of the four other cows he kept with his sheep. I thought that was hardly consistent with the new agricultural model of world market efficiency.

But Der had a different perspective on what constituted efficiency. He repeated that it was a time-proven fact that the ancient Kerry cow was a breed well suited to the local land, well able to fend for itself among the stones and stubble, able to find a living from land that would never sustain the big new racks of steak. You had to make the most of what you had. This was his theme, his slogan. Getting by on the edge with your wits, being your own man: that was the thing.

His was a small operation, indeed, and he did work off the farm here or there as it came up. It came up often enough—money came easier in Ireland these days but went just as easy, he said. Still, there were ways around the usual expenses for a local farmer. He kept a deal with a local butcher, exchanging sheep on the hoof for dressed mutton or pork. For an estimated outlay of €40 he would have enough in chops and stew to last his family three months, "when a good night in a pub could cost you €50."

The picture I got from Der made me think again of Arensberg's tale of Luogh in the 30s, in contrast to today's marketing science farm model. Der's was a farm of modest size, producing sheep and calves for sale, including whatever contribution would come from the old black Kerry cow. He bartered sheep for meat. He was satisfied with farming as a way of life. He had to work off the farm, of course. But I knew Gussie Russell in his time worked the quarries and sold turf to augment what he got from farming in the old days. Der was a man who prided himself on the independent way he looked at the world, and he wanted the world to look at him in that way, to see it in him.

So I asked how the EU had affected his sheep operation. He looked hard at me and said "Not one bit." He was one of the conspiratorial speakers, who alternately counted out the facts with a forefinger on my sleeve or stood sidelong and whispered them at close quarters. He said that business was important, you needed to pay attention to it, but there's more to farming—"and I'm not just being sentimental and giving the old farmer's line." Although I hadn't said much, he declared, "I know what you're getting at, but this is the way I see it," and I told him that's exactly what I wanted to hear, how he saw it. The EU had affected his operation and the way he did business "not at all or, maybe, 2 percent out of 100 percent." He said it added little to what he did, and nothing to what he earned. Regarding the costs of doing business, the price he got, the number of sheep he ran, and the way he lived his life, the EU had nothing to do with it. He didn't give a thought to reducing his stock or setting aside land. He farmed as he always had, as his father had. He was a man proud to own a Kerry cow, a symbol of the way a farmer ought to live in Kerry.

Certainly the world was changing. Der said, yes, the number of sheep farmers was going down constantly, but as sad as that was, it was due to the young people not being interested in that kind of life. If they weren't committed to it, then get out. He liked it fine for himself. He blessed the memory of his ma and da, and talked sadly about the loss of the old ways of his childhood, when, among other memories, "you slaughtered the pig on the kitchen table and put it all into the boiler hung from a crane over the hearth." In that historical context, bartering sheep for meat was a real change.

Others did not share Der's perspective on the impact of the EU on sheep farming and the small farmer. They were happy to cut their stock and set aside lands. But it was all the same, a matter of adapting what you did to hang onto what you had. You made your way along the edge of the growing economy, crafting a living from the environment, and if that environment included payments from a distant governing body in Brussels, then so be it, for however long it lasted. There was always a lot to know as a small farmer. In the old days it might include pulling fish from the sea. Today it might mean netting Euros from the continental treasury. For the family farmer big or small, as Robert Groves said, success was a matter of being quick-witted but careful, and staying just ahead of the posse. For the present, at least, if not for very long, there may be more than one way for the small farmer to do that.

CHAPTER 6

Parish Life: The Job of Keeping the Faith in Changing Times

Bad weather is to us . . . We said prayers for fine weather at all

Masses on Sunday, the seventh, and we hope, that people who

do not get it, as a result, might not associate our failure with

a lack of effective communication with the Almighty.

(Twohig, *Chronicus,* September 1997)

We heard, in the long ago, that angels smile when they hear

people talk of "passing the time." But is that not what everybody

is up to in this day and age—hurrying time instead of holding

it back by intense effort? Well, it's New Year's Day of next year,

and be grateful for it. Once it's gone time will, once again, have

you by the throat.

(Twohig, *Chronicus,* January 1, 2002)

Some time ago I was waiting at a traffic light in a city in the Midwest when a news item on the radio drew my attention. It was an interview with an Irish parish priest who had written a very detailed history on the circumstances leading up to the death of Michael Collins. I was fumbling around looking for something to write down his name with when the light changed, and that was the end of that. By the time I arrived home and unloaded the groceries, the details of the interview, including the names of the priest and the book, were gone.

In May 2001 I was on my way from Limerick to Bantry and stopped in Churchtown, County Cork, to have a look around. I was in the churchyard and thought about going into the church, but there were voices inside shouting to be heard over the noise of a vacuum cleaner. The front door was locked, and the only open entry was at the back, but rather than startling someone (I hate it when anybody sneaks up on me when I'm vacuuming), I let it go. I dawdled long enough in front of the church, however, that the vacuuming finished and the voices emerged in the form of the parish priest and a young woman. The priest was Father Patrick Twohig, the Collins scholar interviewed on the radio. The young woman was his all-around assistant and secretary, Louise Roche. She also ran the music school attached to Churchtown and the parish, a well-known and respected establishment in Irish music circles as it turned out. Father Twohig said he had spent some time in the United States and been in the capital at the time of the assassination of John Kennedy. Was I the Flanagan who wrote history? No, I wasn't. I wrote sociology and was fairly sure he had not heard of me. I recalled the radio interview to him and said I would read his book on Collins, *The Dark Secret of Beal-nablath* (I found it in a bookstore in Bantry a few days later). Well, nice to meet you, and I went on my way after I made a few notes.

As I began work on the present book, I thought of Father Twohig right away and called and asked if he would talk to me. Oh sure, people were doing that all the time, interested in the Black and Tans, the struggle for independence and the civil war times, Michael Collins. I explained that what I was interested in was his experience as parish priest in Church-town, in how life was going on and changing these days in a small parish in Ireland. "Oh, I thought you were a serious scholar," he said. After a minute he consented, without conceding the point that though my work might not be history, it could be serious all the same. I recall that in our first phone conversation I also told him I was not interested particularly in the scandals about priests and young children or in philosophical questions about the relevance of Catholicism in the current age, that sort of thing.

We met at his home just before Christmas 2002. He was eighty-two, and although he stood straight and had the dignified air of a man used to respect from those around him, he moved a little more slowly and stiffly than I remembered from our spring meeting just the year before. He showed my research and recording assistant, Mary Kate, and me into a sitting room warmed by a bed of glowing coals in an open fireplace, and we began easily with chat about his experience with the Kennedy funeral and about music, and then moved on from there to talk about the parish. Mary Kate set up the video and audio recording equipment. She had a way when we were working of settling into a soft chair with the video camera, sliding down and virtually disappearing into the background of Irish sitting rooms. A couple of times he turned to ask her whether she was bored with all the small talk. She was not, thanks. For her it was time travel. "Work away, Mary Katherine, I get this treatment all the time," he would say occasionally.

Father Pat came from a small parish in the West of Ireland, studied for the priesthood at Maynooth (deriving a strict loyalty to the institution and its classical principles), spent three years in West Africa and then two in the Washington, D.C., area, and returned to Ireland in 1964 to serve in various parishes. He has written a number of books about Irish history and culture, and his life and work span a crucial period of change during which he was able to devote his critical attention to the island from outside and in. He likes to recall the fact that he himself was arrested by the notorious Black and Tans when he was only four months old and in his father's arms. Actually, it was his father who was arrested, and he would be tried for his life for expected involvement in an ambush that had killed several troopers. I asked Father Pat whether he thought his father might have been involved. He said no, but his father knew "several of the lads" who had been, and had told his pupils not to come to school the day of the ambush, which clearly implied foreknowledge of the incident. A child had innocently repeated that to a trooper in response to some question or other, and it was only because Father Pat's father was a "fast talker" that he beat the charge.

Father Pat's interest in the way Ireland is changing is passionate and purposeful, and his viewpoint on change is filtered through his personality and his understanding of the purpose of human existence. He is dedicated to the business of preparing the soul, other people's and his own, for whatever is waiting on the other side. Writing or speaking, he is always deeply thoughtful, has a sharp and deadly aim as a humorist, and is habitually cranky, cynical, rebellious (he warned me about these traits from the start), and also, at the odd and unexpected moment, hopeful. Little of modern life escapes his critical eye and tongue as he surveys the world from his Churchtown vantage point.

I know more about Father Pat than about any of the other storytellers in this book. This is because when I visited him he presented me with his parish diaries, his *Chronicus* in two volumes, spanning the sixteen years of his Churchtown ministry. In these diaries he reflects openly, talking to himself and the unseen and unknown future reader, about every matter that touches on life and faith. He writes with the insights of a classical scholar, the dedication of a man whose job it is to help interpret the mysteries of eternal existence, and a wit reminiscent of John B. Keane taking on the character of one of his country subjects. Father Pat, the man of worldly experience, a music man who had played with popular bands in the United States, a Maynooth scholar, a historian and philosopher, has taken on the role of the Irish country priest very well. But his persona is not wholly of that environment, a fact that has often landed him in trouble with the bishop. Nevertheless, he remained committed during his priesthood to doing the job well. His cosmos includes the eternal existence of the soul, a view of existence in which we are all called to account for how well we did our job here, and he said that he did not want to come up a few souls short when it comes time to go over his record.

He mentioned the *Chronicus* to me on the phone the day I called from a local pub to set the interview time for that evening. After we had been talking for a while at his house, he got up stiffly from where he was sitting to tend the fire. He has had several hip operations. On the way back to his chair he picked up the two bound volumes from a little table. "Let me give these to you. It will save me moving again. You said you'd be interested. There's a lot of stuff in it." There was: sixteen years of running an Irish country parish at a time of declining attendance and vocations, slim revenues and rising costs, troubling and troublesome diocesan hierarchies and parish curates, and the most personal statements of unguarded reflection about almost everything having to do with faith, society, and the Church. When I visited with him again in July 2003, he entrusted me with more documents and narrative regarding the matter presently absorbing most of his energy, the heavy matter that marked the closing chapter of his priesthood and, perhaps, his long life. That matter comes in at the end of this story, as it did in his career.

I feel that I know this man with whom I have spent just a few hours as well as I know anyone. In his *Chronicus* he wrote reflectively, privately to himself. Yet there is also the clear sense, the hope, that these records might be read by others in the future. At our last meeting he gave me material with the expressed desire that I include it in the story of his life. Indeed, the story—his story as he reads and tells it—would otherwise be incomplete.

Following an itemized account of routine parish matters in June 1987, midway through his second year in Churchtown, Father Pat wonders on a page of his *Chronicus* what would become of his parish diary, invoking the name of the writer who has been his greatest literary influence.

Looking through the list above one wonders if the humdrum or run-of-the-mill is sufficient to grace such a title as "*Chronicus.*" . . . I am reminded that Evelyn Waugh, the 'flawed genius' of English literature this century, kept a scant diary throughout his life, sometimes worked an item from it into a short story and, occasionally, developed the short story into a major volume. He had, of course, a powerful memory. There is no reason to suppose . . . that I, or any future reader, would, or could, do anything similar for the present manuscript.

Life, taken day to day, often appears to lack pattern or drama. But sometimes it only takes a stranger entering a life from the outside to better see the story building.

Father Patrick J. Twohig was appointed parish priest of Churchtown-Liscarroll in November 1985 on his sixty-fifth birthday, an unusual stage of life to be starting a new job. He was immediately greeted at his door that first morning by a man on a bicycle who said politely, "Good morning, Father. Welcome to Churchtown. There's a woman dead up the road." Off he went to attend to the final earthly needs of Mrs. Murphy, and the routine of daily Churchtown parish life was underway.

Death quickly reveals the shape of life, not only the one just ended but also the ways that the local living are bound together. It is the most dramatic feature of existence in a small parish where the worth of what goes on day-to-day passes unnoticed and undervalued until it is ended for somebody close. Father Pat and the people of his parish would have repeated opportunities, of course, to reflect on this point during his years of service. In a time when the Church was struggling, it was difficult to lose members of the older generation who were the stalwart supporters of religious activities. It was difficult to sustain the loss of young people who died of sickness or suddenly by their own hand or in traffic accidents. Death in a village is magnified by the fact that the life lost, in a sense, belonged to the whole of the place.

Early in our fireside conversation Father Pat recalled the young man who went home after Vigil Mass and Holy Communion and hanged himself in the neighbor's shop. In the wider world we hear about these things, and they are lamentable. But in Churchtown, there he was at Mass, and then there he was hanging and lifeless, a particular young man known to all, on a particular day, in a familiar place, hanging, dead. Everyone has to make sense of it, personally experience the loss, face the impossible task of finding the words to comfort the living, prepare for the funeral—no one is exempt from the experience; the whole village is involved.

Ultimately, it is the job of the parish priest to find the words, to close the book, to close the ground over the dead. At the end of January 1991 Father Pat wrote of the month that "there were an unusual number of funerals. . . . The Parish Priest always regrets same, while realising that life goes on, regardless. If one were poetically inclined, Yeats's 'Ballad of Father Gilligan' could serve as slight consolation." In the first three stanzas of the ballad, the aged Father Gilligan struggles to pit faith against loss:

> The old priest Peter Gilligan
> Was weary night and day;
> For half his flock were in their beds,
> Or under green sods lay.
>
> Once, while he nodded on a chair
> At moth-hour of eve,
> Another poor man sent for him,
> And he began to grieve.
>
> 'I have no rest, nor joy, nor peace,
> For people die and die';
> And after cried he, 'God forgive!
> My body spake, not I!'

Father Gilligan falls asleep in his chair and sleeps through his parishioner's death, but the priest is consoled when he learns that God has sent an angel in his place to see after the man's needs before the end. From time to time Father Pat asked for that kind of help to get through the day-to-day business of running his parish and minding the souls.

The way in which death becomes an occasion for summarizing relationships and reaching closure is evident in Father Pat's tribute to Father Matthew Twomey of Liscarroll. The story also reminds us how lives are often surprisingly intertwined in Ireland, like vines in hedgerows at the edges of the fields. Neighboring Liscarroll is a separate township, but part of the same two-town parish that Father Pat administers as parish priest. Father Twomey was eighty when he died in August 1987, not quite two years after Father Pat took office as parish priest, Father Matt having retired from that very same Churchtown-Liscarroll post in 1977.

Coming from the same hometown, the two had known each other since Father Pat's childhood. Father Pat Twohig's own father, a school and catechism teacher, had taught Father Matt, and while the school had turned out many Christian Brothers and nuns, Father Twomey had been the senior Twohig's first priest, something the schoolmaster was proud of. So Father Pat's father had taught Father Matt in Father Pat's hometown (Kilnamartyra), and Father Pat had ultimately taken the parish job formerly held by Father Matt in Churchtown-Liscarroll, the job from which they both retired. The death of the older priest completes the circle of linkages, and "chance" seems a poor way of honoring the connections between the two lives.

Father Matt was ordained in Rome in 1930, went on to receive theological honors in the form of two doctorates, and was known as "Dr. Twomey" to all but his intimate friends within the diocese at large. In fact, Father Pat's own father had financially supported his star pupil, Father Matt, during his graduate studies. Despite the advanced degrees, to Father Pat, who knew him lifelong and followed his career closely, Father Matt "always remained just a country boy." Twomey was a maverick who had managed to achieve some notoriety in his time, and Father Pat admired that achievement as well as his more intellectual and spiritual ones. While the rewards of a clerical life are intrinsic to the job, and may come primarily in the hereafter, one might want a bit of comfort in the here and now, putting in seven days a week doing the Lord's work. Father Pat will tell you that a priest's living allowance has often made it hard for him to make ends meet. Matthew Twomey had apparently worked out a different deal regarding the material perks associated with a life of service while on the temporal plane.

He maintained a manorial-type dwelling at Castle McCarthy as his parish house, which he had carefully restored through his own hard work—with the increase in the property's value eventually benefiting the Church. The property allowed the country-boy parish priest to live a life conspicuously comfortable—something that often raises more than the eyebrows of the Church's critics. Another of Father Matt's achievements suggests that he probably paid little attention to diocesan gossip about the way he lived his life. According to Father Pat, Father Matt was "totally mad for greyhounds." Priests were forbidden by the bishop from having anything to do with greyhounds or with racing, a sport synonymous with gambling. It simply would not look right.

Father Matt had figured out a way around the prohibition. He owned a number of greyhounds during his priesthood but had others raise and train them. The subterfuge worked well enough, except for the one dog that won the championship Waterloo Cup. Father Matt assumed the rightful honor of acknowledgment as the dog's owner, and Bishop Roche was furious. So in addition to the local notoriety his material lifestyle drew to him, this sporting achievement in a nation full of dog-race enthusiasts had made the country squire quite famous at one point. What happened regarding the trouble with the bishop? That, according to Father Pat's notes, Twomey "laughed off until the day he died." Father Pat affectionately concludes his tribute to his friend, "And may God be good to Fr. Matt." It is a sure bet that there were many prayers and masses dedicated to softening whatever judgment might await the old sportsman.

For any Catholics who are literal believers, death is the transition between two contiguous stages of the same eternal life. Death is only a journey across a wide ocean. Once crossed, it is the unusual emigrant who returns, just as was the case for those going from Ireland to America or Australia in the old days. When people leave, you need to mark their departure in some way, say good-bye, wish them well. You continue to be concerned about their "living" conditions on the other side, once they pass through the judgment procedure. It is not as if they cease to exist simply because they have left the town or village. If you miss the *houly*, the send-off party, it is hard to reach closure. I learned about this long ago in another little parish in Cork, in Rylane, not so far from where the Fathers Pat and Matt grew up and went to school.

In the late 1970s I was on a country road on my way to Rylane to see Pat Joe and Nellie, kinfolk through marriage, when I saw a funeral cortege coming the other way from the village. I pulled off the narrow lane to let them pass. I was not close enough to most of the people of the village to feel comfortable joining the procession, but once it passed I went on ahead to the virtually emptied crossroad settlement to ask who was dead. I knew of some of the people there, in addition to the family I was coming to visit, but had heard no news of the death. I speculated about who might be the important villager who was gone. Pat Joe had a heart condition; there was the aged schoolmaster, a couple of publicans who did not get on well together but who were nice enough in their own right to each have a following, the ever-present possibility of a road or farm accident that I might not have heard about—no one I knew up there had a phone. When I got to Rylane the one employee of the shop who had been left behind in the village assured me that the dead person was no one I could have known—many of the villagers didn't really know him. He was known as "the Hermit" and had lived all his life at the back of a mountain, away from any road—his homestead hidden from direct sight from anywhere in the village. He came to town once in a great while for sugar, tea, and matches. Otherwise he kept to himself.

I spent the rest of the summer afternoon and early evening hanging about the empty village until Pat Joe and his family and the other mourners returned, having stopped off somewhere suitable to collectively examine the meaning of life and toast the departed soul. I eventually got around to asking how it was that the whole town had followed the casket of a hermit to a burial place several miles away—the "party excuse" aspect of the occasion would not do as a total explanation, since there had been some teetotalers in the train. It took Nellie and Pat Joe a minute to think about it: yes, he had been a recluse, you might go for years without seeing him, but he was always there, a human marker, part of what people who lived there knew about the place they lived in. You didn't see him, but you knew who and where he was. That was his importance. He held a place in the minds of the people, anchored the village, held one corner of it down. People could not let his passing go unmarked. You had to go to Mass with all the rest of the people and say good-bye to him as you would anyone else in the area, put him to rest in the ground, be reminded of your own soul, and speculate on the chances of getting a break in the hereafter. His death came as the end of something that belonged to those who had lived all their lives in the village, which was marked by his peculiar presence. Of course you had to go to his funeral.

Pat Joe died the following winter. I was away in the United States. When I got back to Cork, I took Nellie out to her husband's grave on the edge of Macroom, the big town, for a visit. The grave was just a bare place in the cemetery where the ground was closed over Pat Joe, nothing of him visible, no one else but us in the place, none of his friends and neighbors looking glum or telling stories. There was no closure but the gesture of the closed bare earth. I had missed the one chance to hear and see for myself how his life had given shape to those who had lived all of theirs around him. I had missed his death. No amount of standing about in the empty cemetery would change that.

Years later I was traveling west on the Macroom Road from Cork City to Kenmare. The traffic approaching Macroom from the east slowed to a crawl long before we got to the outskirts of the town. All through the streets the car didn't keep pace with the many pedestrians who all seemed to be heading in the same direction that we were. At the western edge of town, when we finally arrived, the cemetery was full of mourners, and they spilled out into the main road, forcing the opposing lines of traffic to alternate, using the one lane that was left passable. Who was dead this time? Was it a young person? An old patriot, a hero of the independence fight here in Michael Collins country? Was it a beloved teacher, priest, shopkeeper? I remembered the funeral of the Hermit in Rylane. It could have been anyone. Macroom is a big town, but not so large that with the usual country-Irish effort you couldn't know by reputation at least every other person who lived there, be able to place them, be placed by them. Everyone would have to turn out to mark the passing. The road immediately past the cemetery, the direction I was going, was wide open. I didn't stop to ask. I said a silent "hello" to Pat Joe, lying somewhere over there beneath the feet of the throng of mourners, and moved on. I would always have a more vivid image of the death of this stranger going into the ground that day than I did of Pat Joe's—having missed his death.

Father Pat comments in his journal, regarding death in the parish: "In a spirit of humility one tends to think of oneself as not being a loss to society when one has to go," but people's departures "leave a vacuum in the context of parish life." While some deaths are bound to leave a greater vacuum than others, each leaves an empty space of some measure, filled in by themed remembrances. Some losses have a practical dimension, as when the Father wrote in 1989 regarding the death of his sacristan, a kind of parish production manager whose duties are infinitely expandable relative to the unfathomable needs of the local church. Mrs. Fisher helped him get organized when he first arrived as the parish priest; she had been the agreeable and helpful presence that allowed him to land on his feet in the new job. Now he was on his own, and "some weeks later we have still not fully realised the enormity of what has happened to us in the community." The death of Mrs. Nora Mai Blake, the organist of the Liscarroll church, was another serious, even painful, loss. Apparently she was another peaceful soul who was able to bridge a perennial rift between the adult and youth choirs and produce a quality of music that the ever-critical Father Pat admired. "Suddenly, she was gone. From that day on there was only the occasional weird trumpetings of some young and some old enthusiasts, and, worse still, periodical piped music from some 'box' in the background, reminiscent of the most horrible of all religious institutions — an American funeral parlour." (Father Pat did not like changes around church services, especially when he didn't see how they improved things, and especially when they had to do with music.)

Death brings into focus the continuing crucial relevance of the priest in village life, whatever trends in Mass attendance might purport to show. When someone dies, no one asks, "Should we send for the priest?" It is always the first thought, the same as it was in Yeats's time. The universal recognition of the importance of this priestly function reminded Father Pat of the story told in the *Cork Examiner* by Sean Dunne some years ago. This is how Father Pat retells it:

There was this mountainy man in the Ballingeary region and he was dying. It was late at night, but they sent for the priest, down to the village. Time moved on and there was no sign of the priest arriving. Every now and then, the dying man, from his bed, sent someone out to look, but it was always the same story — no trace. Finally, come morning, he sent out again, but it was the same story again, so the old man threw back his head on the pillow and said — "Here, I'll chance it!" and died.

The natural association of the priest and the deathbed and graveside is just one of the many powerful reminders that, for the faithful of Irish parishes, the life of the soul is the real object of the business of living. The number of candles burning alongside the altar at Churchtown's St. Nicholas Church suggests that there remains a focus on the well-being of the spirits of those who have passed. But the well-being of the incarnate, preserving the lives of the living, especially young people in mortal peril, also draws the community together in a way that underlines the continuing relevance of faith during trying times. In January 1993 the Churchtown Shrine of St. Brigid was refurbished, and the effort included the installation of a newly cast statue of the saint. Actually, it was a statue of St. Theresa, which had to be modified for the purpose. The characteristic flowers in St. Theresa's hand were replaced by a model of the Churchtown church by the Cork artisan, who explained that no one had asked for a statue of St. Brigid in ages, and the casting mould had been broken.

The substitution was soon put to the test. In the first week of February Father Pat and parishioners held a nightly vigil for the recovery of a lad who was seriously ill in the hospital with leukemia. "The decades of the Rosary were suitably embellished with five prayers to St. Brigid from the Irish." However, the youngster succumbed on Ash Wednesday, an event open to interpretation for people of faith. Recovery from leukemia would truly have been a miracle, and the day was a propitious one for the life transition from body to soul. Today the shrine remains a powerful religious site for locals and pilgrims.

A MAN FROM MAYNOOTH

Father Pat's worldview is deeply colored by the vocation that took him to the Maynooth Seminary and the particular brand of Roman Catholic theology that prevailed at the time he studied there. For Father Pat there is the priesthood in general, and then there is the Maynooth priesthood: A Maynooth man knows his liturgy, his religion, the rules of the Church, and his mission. These do not change over time, there is not a lot of room for interpretation, and a priest carries on his work according to long-standing principles. The objective is to change people to bring them to the Church, not to change the Church in order to bring people into it. The objective may have become more difficult and less popular in these changing times, but in this view neither priests nor their superiors have the power to modify the principles of faith and practice to coincide with secular change. No mistake, this is a very conservative stance, one that is not held universally by either priests or parishioners today, and those who favor a more dynamic Church are frustrated with those who take this position. And Father Pat doesn't give a damn about that.

He is not blindly against change, nor is he particularly straightlaced in habits of thought or speech, but sees the changes taking place in the wider world as they are reflected in Churchtown as a mixed bag, both good and bad. You might have to pick through a lot of junk to find the good. The local development force, known corporately as "Boss Murphy" after an ancestor of the chief local mover, has changed the face of Churchtown in the past decade or so. The Boss Murphy name is carried on the local pub and hotel, and the company has built a considerable amount of new housing, which has brought in many outsiders to the town. Father Pat lends his unqualified support to the enterprise. In September 1999 he wrote, "Boss Murphy's new construction project for the village holds out great promise. . . . Already, many people about the place, including housewives, are benefiting with regard to jobs . . . Personally, I like the idea of progress around me, and am hoping for big things. . . . Someone said to me, 'He's going to buy up the whole place!' I said, 'Let him!' I always thought that there's too much lack of initiative in this country."

When the Murphy corporation executives came to town for a big, formal dress celebration, Father Pat and Louise were there for the occasion, and Louise played the piano as "no one else can"—transforming the occasion into a champagne-lubricated sing-along. I heard from people in town that on a more recent occasion Father Pat himself played ukulele and banjo while Louise played the piano at Boss Murphy's bar, when a scheduled guest artist couldn't make it. When I checked the story out with him, he said, "Oh yeah, poor fellow dropped dead or something. I guess we did OK. Louise was great, as usual."

Progress is good, but Father Pat believes two evils are ushered in by the prosperity attached to current changes in Ireland and everywhere: materialism and the single-minded quest to be amused in one's leisure, and these go hand in hand. When I asked him in particular how he saw childhood changing, he talked about the first of these, today's life-defining materialism. "The one thing that they have in common is that they have everything. And that, you might say, without being rigid, is not good for young people. It makes them . . . want more. So the business interests of the world are shoving all kinds of expensive toys on to them, and they must have it once they see it on television." And the same with parents. "The parents want more; they spend wildly." Then, slowly and severely, his eyes narrowing on the fire as if he had something particular in mind, he added, "without thinking." He looked up and added, in a lighter tone, "I have a man who would be quite near me. He'd been out of a job for years and years. They have a number of kids. And someone asked me where are the [here he gave the family name], and, 'Oh yes, they picked a holiday in Casablanca or'—where are the islands they all go to? Oh yes, 'the Canary Islands.' My God! How do they do it? They charge it, and they blow it wildly!"

"And the drink is increasing altogether. We had the great anti-drink campaigns back in the eighteenth and nineteenth centuries. Back then the drink was very cheap. Porter was one or two pennies. But they're back again. And I don't blame them, Bill: they're at a job, and the strain is terrible. What can a man do when he goes home, and sits there with the television, which is terrible anyway—yes, even with all the channels— they can't find anything worth looking at!

"The kids, then, get everything, and they take everything for granted. It becomes complicated with all of the 'scenery' they see on television. When they get to their later teens . . ." The thought trailed off and changed direction. "The boys so long ago . . . Well, we were afraid of girls, when I was young. You'd be afraid to approach these [nowadays]—but then it's come now so that girls want boys, and they want babies—to have dolls, is what they want, the completion of the Christmas doll thing. They like the idea of being a single mother, and they get paid by the government for doing it. And being in the style of things, to have a baby to show for it! Out of 'wedlock.' [laughing] I'd forgotten about that! What's wedlock? It's not such a lock, not such a lock."

He went on to talk about recent decades when there was a kind of prosperity for farmers, with their wives driving Mercedes and wearing furs. But that was a different sort of thing, he said, the farms and fisheries being Ireland's traditional economic foundations. It's all gone now, with the fish stocks depleted by foreign fishermen and the farmers dying off under the thumb of the EU. The decline of these employments was a great historical shift for Ireland, with traditional work left behind and people going into new kinds of work. "Now we've got the IDE, The Irish Industrial . . . [in a gesture, 'whatever'] who brought industry into the country. A lot of people were idle, they had no work, they were on the dole. And that's changed now because they've got jobs, industry's come in, and they've got jobs—and the wives got jobs now, which is fair enough, don't you think? But the children then are left on their own."

So while he welcomes prosperity, Father Pat raises many of the usual worries raised by other critics about attendant changes. At times he is perfectly glum regarding the impact of current changes on the state of the spirit. He fears that the "television-numbed brain of the general public" is too sedated to absorb worthwhile information, they are too immobilized to think critically and take action in their own best interest, and he worries that the same may be true for the condition of Catholicism (June

1998 diary entry). Back in March 1990 he was already expressing concern about the "lukewarm condition of modern practice" among Catholics. "Perhaps there is a necessary relativity in this modern age because of the advancing complexity of life and the massive population increase throughout the world."

The world-wise scholar might understand the reasons for it, but the parish priest, who was in the business of saving souls, worried that the many distractions of modern life left insufficient time and energy for spiritual effort. Even though he was pleased with the turnout for May Devotions in the year 2000, he wrote, "I remember the people loving this kind of liturgical activity in the past. Now they seem to love their own chosen activities, their freedoms, their spending of money, their pleasures. When I look deeper I detect an absurd shallowness of mind and a predominant stupidity. Even the 'best people' seem to be off-hand far too much. Is the Devil winning?"

And coming in for special consideration as a worldly distraction is the Irish passion for sport. Father Pat himself dedicated much personal effort to the creation of regulation pitches (fields) for hurling and football, wresting a choice piece of real estate from under the nose of the Boss Murphy enterprise for that purpose. Yet he eventually came to the conclusion that organized sport in Ireland is "probably now the greatest enemy of the Catholic Church in action. There are matches . . . for men, women, boys and girls, and those who were babies only the other day. Matches are substituted for Masses, even by well-meaning people. Saturday Vigil is regularly devastated, and during and between the Sunday morning Masses there is much sound of revelry in the background."

Change has arrived in the form of the global economy, and its cultural trappings have come to Churchtown and begun the process of economic and cultural homogenization there, no different from anywhere else. Previously, religion was the homogenizing force. In villages and towns the main street during Masses on Sunday mornings are still all but impassable, with cars parked in even more open defiance of parking restrictions than during the rest of the week, attesting to the continuing importance of the Church. But the influence of religion on people's lives has declined and is declining, and the rural parish priest is in the best position to gauge that, to feel it. Father Pat is troubled by the changes he sees. He worries about trends in teenaged parenthood, the suicide rate of young people, and a perceptible thinning out of religious influence. The world and its failings are on the doorstep of the little stone churches that dot the backcountry of Ireland. In 1996 Father Pat installed lock boxes in his parish churches to protect the candle shrine donations because of frequent break-ins. Within the Church itself there are problems of declining priestly vocations and the closing of seminaries, the aging of men in the priesthood. And then there are the sex scandals that have stigmatized the profession.

Father Pat had spent some time talking to me about the effects that the accusations of sexual misconduct were having on the priests and the priesthood. He said he knew men who were dismissed, ruined, cut off from their vocation and livelihood by mere accusation after decades of service. Old men were dying, abandoned by the Church, without the chance of defending themselves. These modern crises of the vocation are the broader issues that provide the context of operating day-to-day, the business of improving the condition of souls for the Man from Maynooth, a man sharp of mind, but physically in his declining years.

THE BUSINESS, DAY-TO-DAY

In his day-to-day operations as spiritual leader and business manager of his parish, Father Pat is an enigma. He hates change having to do with Church matters but is sometimes in the forefront. Actually, if he is seen in the role of the rebel that he is, someone who identifies strongly with the Irish Republican struggle for independence, the Ireland in which he has spent his intellectual life, his behavior is very consistent. He hates change for the sake of change; he doesn't like to make things easy for people, and that goes especially for men from whom he is expected to take orders. He is least of all interested in making things easy for his superiors in the Church hierarchy. Like any good (Irish) Republican, he doesn't believe you should compromise principle, because that would undo the moral satisfaction of victory. But sometimes you might have to make a minor adaptation in your methods in order to carry on the cause.

Over the years, his two favorite altar servers have been youth with developmental disabilities. One was a boy with Down syndrome in Washington, where Father Pat was assigned to an institution for young people with developmental disabilities. He loved the fact that the boy was so dedicated to getting it right—"it was complicated in those days, the change [in the Mass] hadn't taken place, and he got so he could do it himself, and he was so proud of himself, I feel very good about that. He was so attentive, the concentration was marvelous." He had another lad in Ireland, seriously challenged in understanding the usual academic subjects, but at Mass "his concentration was such that he was the best ever in my life."

As for male servers in general, they could be trouble. "You'd have to watch them, you know, blackguarding." So, in a small country parish, when the supply of interested and apt prospective altar servers ran thin in 1993, he took the logical, although unauthorized and to that time in Ireland unprecedented, step of introducing a girl server, "Louise Fitzgerald, with notable success. For September we introduced a second girl, Katie Doyle, also eminently suitable. We hope to handle this affair cautiously, but so far it seems quite acceptable," he wrote. By mid-1997, the girl servers outnumbered the boys in Churchtown, "but that does not bother anybody concerned, as the girls are so much more committed, efficient, and graceful. It is a delight to see such goodness and style in the service of the altar." When in 1994 the supply of men who sent round the collection baskets at Sunday Mass "had become quite erratic and undependable due to a superfluity of games of several kinds," Father Pat took the next logical step and introduced women collectors. "This departure also proved successful."

These are surely small matters as seen from the outside, but altering gender divisions that have stood for ages, divisions having to do with religious ritual, is a radical departure for those in traditional settings who are experiencing it for the first time. Father Pat risked putting off parishioners and being hit with negative sanctions from superiors, who were supposed to be consulted about all such matters. Why was the man who was opposed to change in the Church the first to try it out? Because it made sense under the circumstances, it broke no liturgical law, and because tactically it meant taking the high ground and digging in your troops, so that any critics, especially those in the Church hierarchy, would have to fight an uphill battle to effectively oppose it. Father Pat, the historian, was a student of successful guerilla warfare. And he loved to provoke Church authorities, while playing the innocent and humble servant.

On the other hand, knowing what I do of the man, I saw no point in raising the question of women in the priesthood with him. He likes women, admires them, has depended on women of skill and intelligence in his own life, but in his *Chronicus* he at times reveals a crusty generic mistrust of the opposite sex, especially at times when he has just had difficult dealings with them in the role of teachers, music examiners, graduate students looking for information he doesn't have, and parishioners telling him how he should do his job. He is at those times moved to make generalizations that would get him in trouble in progressive circles—in fact, in many circles.

The Man from Maynooth shows his colors when it comes to *substantive* change in religious practice. He opposes it. There are moves to make Catholicism more accessible to people, more convenient, to bring God to the people in more everyday surroundings. Nonsense. The Church is "The Church," and worship is worship. "Prayer meetings," which had become by the 1990s a popular mode of religious expression, are not part of the body of traditional liturgical practice and are, according to Father Pat, a bad idea. If people want to pray, or want to pray together, let them. But priests should not go out to them to distribute communion. Priests should not be transporting the sacrament in their pockets through crowded streets. The Lamb of God is the Lamb of God and should not be translated into such language as "this is Jesus, our Friend," as Father Pat has heard done. The practice "smacks of humanism," grumbles the priest, and "allowing priests to put their own words on matters of grave importance is, to my mind, an obvious road to chaos, nonsense, and even heresy." Also, he believes that the practice of having laypeople administer Holy Communion got out of hand with the authorized extension of this innovation to shut-ins, a "stupefying prospect" of having laypeople traipsing around, off on their own, carrying the sacrament.

And he is equally adamant when it comes to the relaxation of the requirements around the connection between confession and communion. His choice of metaphor is worth noting: "By way of judgment, if I may, it seems that the Church is capable of biting off more than it can chew with regard to domestic matters. A case in point is the Penitential Rite, which is now [January 1991] almost defunct. Authority will argue that it is up to the man concerned [i.e., the priest] to 'make things work,' but the men concerned in practice know that we cannot shove things down people's throats, particularly the Eucharist." A couple of years later (May 1993) he is still concerned, even more so. He complains that even old people, who should especially be concerned about their tenuous hold on their mortal status, no longer go to confession. "Why should the immediacy of confessing one's sins not be important for adequate preparation, but especially now when the Holy Eucharist Itself is reduced, by over-familiarity, almost to the commonplace? I have observed people who do not even go to Mass or otherwise practice their faith, or pay 'Dues,' go blithely to the altar rails on the occasion of family bereavement, as if it were their right and just a token."

Another of his pet irritations, this one involving changes handed down all the way from the top of the Church hierarchy, is the modification of the liturgical calendar, especially the shifting of saints' feast days from where they had stood for centuries to a more convenient date. Yet another is the scheduling of more masses or more convenient masses to accommodate people's busy schedules, with the most vexing of all modifications combining both changes, folding in feast days and regular masses so that parishioners get double credit for one attendance. For example, several years ago the Feast of the Epiphany fell on a Saturday, which meant a Friday, Saturday, and Sunday Vigil obligation, the Saturday obligation colliding with "the fact that some large towns (Charleville in our case) have introduced a Saturday evening Mass for the absolute laggards to enable them, as it were, to fulfill their [Sunday Mass] obligation." Father Pat did not like the idea that attendance on Saturday would do for both the Vigil and the Sunday Mass, or the Sunday Mass doing for both that and the Sunday Vigil. These things are not to be moved around; the way should not be smoothed for the faithful.

There is a principle that underlies his position in these matters, and he sticks to it. In May 1997 he wrote, "It is difficult to say. Perhaps this streamlining is necessary for the future but, as in the pruning of plants, one may go too far and start a die-back. This is a worrying matter. The old philosophy of letting people see to their own salvation seems more logical . . . and I must say that I personally favor such an approach. Salvation is for all, but they need to go after it. Otherwise . . . it is but one step to nothingness." Four months later, in September, not surprisingly, he had not changed his mind, and he gives us a little more of his philosophy of order and chaos, revealing a bit of the anarchist in the old Republican. "My own (private) opinion is that people may do as they please, seeing that they were born with free will, and if everything were to be thrown wide open, the world would right itself, out of sheer necessity, as it has done in the past. . . . You may say, 'but what about all the suffering?' What about it? The world goes on murdering and torturing itself and its inhabitants just the same!"

For the piece of the world that Father Pat holds some sway over, the part he is charged with administering, the old ways are proven, the old ways are best, rules are rules, and it is hard enough as it is to hold the line. "This is Jesus, your Friend," a Protestant sponsor at a Catholic baptism, a priest receiving Protestant communion, two other priests trying to bury a Protestant friend in a Catholic cemetery—these are the kinds of inroads into orthodox practice that Father Pat has worried over. Obviously, he has been no great sponsor of the ecumenical movement to bring the Christian churches closer together. His concern is that the Catholic Church is already on a slippery slope, far too close to becoming more like Protestantism in order to meet the competition, to market itself.

In response to the 1998 Annual Survey from diocese headquarters regarding activities to promote Christian ecumenism in his parish, Father Pat wrote the following reply:

Events of ecumenical interest in your parish since the 1998 Week of Prayer:
Whether it is a matter of regret, or not, the fact remains that there was no event of a specifically ecumenical nature in this parish over the past year. . . . I don't see this as a matter of grave concern as we did have some occurrences of a socio-religious nature. Our very successful annual plowing match in September attracted, as always, quite a few competitors from around the country who are of the Protestant persuasion. Our famous Donkey Day attracted . . . many Protestants . . . [and] Burton Park Guest House . . . attracts, every year, visitors from England, Wales, Scotland, Germany and the USA, most all of whom the proprietor, Mrs. Ryan-Purcell, cajoles into attending Mass and other Catholic functions. . . .

Ecumenical events planned for 1999:
Except for an expected recurrence of the above, I am afraid we will just have to wait and see. For myself, personally, I abhor any activities which tend to indicate a mere aping of Protestantism, or any other religion, and that greater care should be taken with regard to any drift into words or actions which to me are heretical.

Any other items of ecumenical interest for mention in the Annual Report: Otherwise, the Parish Priest of Churchtown-Liscarroll gets to kiss the very attractive wife and mother of the only Protestant family in the parish, which, incidentally, was regarded by the late lamented Bishop . . . as a mortal sin. In extenuation, the Gardiner family to whom I am referring, are wont to say that I and the old lady of the family, who still lives, are the only two Republicans left.

Patrick Twohig makes up his own mind about things. He supports or opposes a thing on the basis of what he sees to be its own flaws and merits. He gets along with the Catholic hierarchy, his curates, his parishioners, women, when what they do or say makes sense to him, when events appear to adhere to the principles of practice that he learned at Maynooth, when they make sense in terms of his philosophy of free will and self-determination, when they further the cause of the faith—on his terms. Otherwise, he can be cranky.

For example, he liked Pope John Paul's book *Crossing the Threshold of Hope.* "It is a book of healthy and clever straight-talking and enlightened thinking. If I may use a vulgarity of our time, the present Holy Father has an enormously up-market manner of 'cutting through the bullshit,' and I like him for it." But when it came to the pope's effort to present an accessible catechism to guide the faithful in their religious practice, Father Pat tossed it aside as unreadable and published his own (Twohig 2001), which reflected the author's scholarship as a historian. It places events in the history of Catholicism in the context of the parallel development of other world religions, and vice versa.

He thinks the Catholic hierarchy in Ireland could be more clever in meeting the needs of their priests. He objects to the experiments with meetings and seminars for the clergy that go nowhere, and to Church-sponsored retreats where men of the cloth are supposed to spend time together in order to bond more closely. "Disdain" may be too strong a term to describe Father Pat's attitude toward events organized to serve the needs of the clergy—perhaps "impatience" day-to-day, with disdain saved for special occasions, is more like it. Nevertheless, it is heartening to note that the aging priest has learned to take a certain amount of pleasure even from diocesan events that may have missed the intended goal of edification. The following is taken from a *Chronicus* entry from, let us say, the late 90s, in order to keep the identity of the participants no more than speculative.

> Meeting of the whole diocese . . . Two subjects — Sex Education in the Schools and Taxation: what an atrocious lot of "bull." I wish we sometimes got a chance to discuss matters relating to our priesthood.
>
> Weak microphone on table between Bishop and Canon, . . . They kept pulling it from each other and we couldn't hear a word. Then a woman joined them, sat down and started pulling the microphone also, but they kept pulling it back. What she represented I never got to know. Then [another high church official] took the floor to answer some question. . . . For sixty years I have been hopelessly trying to understand what he says . . . but he got loud guffaws for a series of grunts. Perhaps I don't speak the right language.

Another event meant to instruct and enlighten, a retreat for priests in the late 1990s, went poorly, according to Father Pat's assessment of it. The retreat master was not particularly effective, in his opinion, and ended awkwardly and abruptly, "when your man had apparently run out of material. I believe I could have kept the thing going myself; there are so many questions nowadays and so few answers." It wasn't like the old days, when a priest might look forward to these events, "when we tried to find our souls, having been crossing the hot and burning sands." There was one good joke that came out of the retreat, says Father Pat, although it was "slightly blasphemous." As retold by Father Pat the joke goes as follows: "Two fellows went on a shooting trip, one a blithe spirit, the other dour and gloomy. The blithe spirit brought along a dog that could walk on water. Boat out. First duck down, dog trotted across and collected it. Silence. Second duck down. Ditto. Blithe spirit said, did you notice the dog? 'Oh yeah. Bloody fucker can't even swim.'"

A part of Father Pat's yearly diocesan obligation is to attend the annual Chrism Mass at the Diocesan Cathedral in Cobh (the Queenstown departure point of millions), near Cork City. This came to be a particularly traumatic outing each year for him. Part of the Mass involved the blessing of oils, carried in large silver bowls by three elders of the church bureaucracy. "Every year I sweated as they stumbled up and down the steps and wondered what would have happened if disaster struck. I have seen [a particular bishop] send the chalice flying while emphasizing a point at a priest's funeral Mass, and I remember [when] a professor in Maynooth, at a time when there were no fuzzy edges in the Rubrics to work by, spilt the consecrated chalice all over his Roman chasuble! There are times when I simply don't know what to think about anything." He does know what he thinks about the humbling practice of washing the feet of others that is a part of the annual Mass at the Cathedral. He simply refuses to join in, can't face it, finds it "a thin superfluity." While others, from the pope to his own parish curates, annually perform the rite, Father Pat cuts out at that point in the ceremony.

The 1990 Mass at Cobh found him thinking about two young priests who had attended the year before. Many in attendance had found the pair's behavior offensive and troubling. They "talked, laughed, and mocked during the ceremony, even during the Consecretat of the Mass." Father Pat, who always had a young assistant or curate who served the Liscarroll half of his parish, had seldom had an easy relationship with the younger priests. In response to the behavior of the two at Cobh, he wrote, "It is a disturbing thought, and one which raises a question to my mind with regard to the training and general attitude of the young priests, who appear to be affected by the decadence of society in our time, rather more than the authorities realize, and far more than they themselves understand."

Of the young priests with whom Father Pat had direct dealings in one way or another in his own parish, there was often a tension, a doubt about their preparedness or dedication, or something in their style that went against the Maynooth grain. To be fair, there was general concern about the "new vocations" within the Church. The behavior of the two at Cobh is a good if extreme example of the problem that the Church had in exerting an effective influence over young priests, who knew they were a rare and valuable commodity, princes, within the organization. In 1993 he wrote, "The media say that the Church is not rising to its commitments, and the older clergy aver that the younger clergy are particularly uncontrollable, but are impossible to curb at the parochial level because of being in favor, with a view to the future benefit of the Church, with the higher Church authorities. If true, an impasse if ever there was one."

Repeatedly, Father Pat finds young priests only "semi-educated" in the faith, and with little attachment to a sense of duty, as in their practice of staying away in droves from the funerals of older priests. In the past, there was a clearly understood obligation to attend. He is fond of lamenting the reversal of the historical position of parish priest and curate in modern times. It was well understood, at least in the recent past, that in terms of the moral responsibility of the job,

> the people came first, second, and third, and the priest came nowhere, and that the Parish Priest's canonical *cura animarum* was a hanging offense if neglected. In the old days, this was always handled by the curate being at all times on duty, and the Parish Priest, never. Now the Parish Priest makes a phone call to his curate's house, receives an answer from a machine giving the number of a mobile phone, x-number of miles away, and when that number is dialed another machine discloses the fact that it is not activated at the moment. . . . So now, the Parish Priest is always on duty, the curate never.

In the early 1990s Father Pat looked forward to the day that changing circumstances might allow him once again to live like a curate.

Father Pat was dogged by questions of commitment in some of the young priests he met. One in particular, who said his first Mass in the local church, had troubled him from the beginning. At the large party, paid for out of the parish's resources (he wasn't very happy about that), that followed the celebrant's inaugural Mass, he observed the newly ordained priest walking about "among his peers of yesterday with a bottle of beer in one hand and a cigarette in the other. I said to myself, 'I give him one year.'" He fooled Father Pat. He remained in the priesthood for four years, marrying at that point. In the meantime, according to the Father, he had become "quite a celebrity." Father Pat worried, considering the fact that the young priest had performed many marriages, that he might never have been "validly ordained." On the other hand, whenever there were whispers about any of his own young curates, gossip about their moral suitability, Father Pat defended them vigorously as exemplary men of faith and good practice, even though he might have difficulty with them on other matters. Differences in age and style were probably bound to generate some degree of conflict, and, predictably, the potential grew as Father Pat aged and the age of new priests remained the same. This was accentuated because the era of his training and traditions became further removed from a Church struggling to meet the masses where they were in the New Ireland.

Of the many young priests who served as curates for Father Pat over the years, two stand out. They followed one another into the office toward the end of the parish priest's tenure, and the differences between the parish priest and his young curates shaped the closing years of his priesthood. Here is how he tells the story.

The first of the two was a man of action, "a man for our time," Father Pat remarks, but it is a mixed compliment, given what we know of Father Pat. At first the Father was optimistic, describing his new assistant as "smooth-talking, agreeable, obedient, 'laid-back,' with the ultimate in rapport where country people, especially youth, are concerned. That's my man! It makes life for an aging pastor, faced with the complexity of our time, so much more livable." Once he found his feet, the new curate was effective and undertook a program of "high-powered fund-raising to finance some totally new ideas," mostly associated with the restoration and development of the Liscarroll church. The stone walls were power-washed and flood-lit, the grounds improved, the interior redone, all in a very brief matter of time, considering the usual pace of these things and the lack of resources generally available for accomplishing them. The curate was innovative in fund-raising, sponsoring competitions and selling off on very favorable terms the old pews, which were being replaced. The curate even managed to generate an anonymous donation of €10,000, a huge amount in local terms, for the renovation of his boss's, Father Pat's, own church in Churchtown.

Astounding records of achievement are not set by people who are shy or cautious or by those who wait around for permission to try something new. In putting Liscarroll forward, the young curate put himself forward as well, and that ruffled some feathers around the town and in the diocese. There were local rumblings about where he was spending his time when away from the job, and a division developed among parishioners along the lines of his admirers and detractors. The issue came to a head over the erection of a particular monument. The project was reportedly undertaken without consultation or permission, with regard to either the parish priest or the bishop, both of whom would have been required to sign off on it. The monument was to give credit to the priest who had it erected, the curate himself. Within the town, some supported the whole project; others didn't like the details—especially the self-serving inscription etched in stone on the monument. When the issue was brought before Father Pat, he intervened, sending the workmen home to Mallow with double their expected wages, thus putting an end to the unauthorized project, as was his duty, in his interpretation. The division among parishioners flared into open conflict. A simple enough matter, but the conflict would persist, wearing away Father Pat's energy and legitimacy in this half of the parish, a perennial crisis, one that eventually would contribute to his resignation.

When a visit by the bishop to the parish took place as scheduled, the bishop was subject to the full blast of the fight. In a letter to Father Pat following the visit, the bishop attempted to restrain his indignity regarding the whole affair. After the usual formalities expressing thanks for the hospitality, and so forth, he comes to the point:

> As you know, this visit afforded me the opportunity to discuss certain matters which require attention in the Parish. In particular, I refer to works being carried out on Parish property without the knowledge or approval of the Parish Priest. I was very concerned to note that funding for such works and payment for them have been arranged in a manner which has by-passed the Parish accounts. . . . All such works should be approved by the Bishop and the necessary expenditure sanctioned by the Bishop. I am writing to Father _____ [the curate] in this regard.

The bishop was concerned about the politics of the situation getting out of hand, alleging that the curate had made matters worse through statements in private and during the liturgy that did not facilitate the prospect of reconciliation. Three years later, the division and political polarization still prevailed to the extent that there was the suggestion that *the bishop would not be welcome* on a visit he proposed to make to the town. It is the parish priest's job to reconcile differences within his parish. The fact that the division was the result of actions taken by his subordinate in a town that he did not directly practice in made no difference. The bishop repeatedly let Father Pat know, over the years that followed, that he expected the parish priest to heal the division, and Father Pat found the task sufficiently puzzling that he was able to make very little headway in accomplishing the goal. The issue put the priest and his bishop at odds, and the bishop became increasingly impatient with his aging parish priest.

When it came time for the curate to go, he did not go quietly, maintaining that he was still curate and in charge until he was given an alternate post within the diocese. It would be a few months before he was reassigned, a period characterized by confusion and deepening conflict. When the new curate finally arrived, Father Pat was instructed by the bishop to undertake some repairs to the priest's residence in Liscarroll. While the parish priest was responsible for paying for the work, the actual determination of the details of what turned out to be a major restoration job were in the hands of the new curate. According to Father Pat, it was the same old story regarding the high material expectations of spoiled youth. The new man "was determined to have everything he took a fancy to—it was how I found foreign religious orders when I lived with them. . . . The bursar had the purse strings and you got what you could, while you could, and to hell with the consequences. In this case . . . the bursar was the poor old P. P., and there were no strings. Come to think of it, there was no purse!"

So while the departing curate got him in trouble for the unorthodox manner in which he raised and spent money, his replacement was causing grief with only half the equation, the way he spent. And there was still the problem of the split in Liscarroll that the departing curate had not managed to take with him, Father Pat being implicated and reviled by one half of the people. The bishop was persona non grata to the other half. He had, in his attempt to heal the division from afar, countermanded Father Pat's cancellation of the work on the monument and ordered it completed. The action demonstrated to the dissatisfied half of the congregation that they had been right and had been wronged all along, while the other half were shown that their parish priest could not be expected to prevail on their behalf. No one was happy, Father Pat was in no position to make them happy, and the bishop lost no opportunity to remind him over time that making peace was the job of the parish priest.

MATTERS OF PRINCIPLE

From time to time over the years, Father Pat asked himself why he stayed on the job for so long. Sometimes he had no answer for himself when he raised the question in his parish diary. Sometimes, the answer was sheer cussedness and personal pride: "Sunday, the first of November, my seventy-eighth birthday, and I'm still parish priest, the oldest in the diocese, and proud of it. In good old senior-citizen style, I don't believe there's anybody who could take my place!" He told me that there was actually an underlying reason, a matter of principle, for having hung on so long: he had made a deal. He had wanted time off to write, to produce his histories, and he took five years away from the diocese and worked in Africa and the United States. While no one was holding such an agreement over his head, the deal that he made with himself was that he would pay back those five years to the diocese, a kind of verbal commitment made decades ago. As he reckoned it, the usual retirement age for priests is seventy-five. That meant that if he worked at it until he was eighty, he would have paid off the borrowed years.

So he hung on, through the daily duties and skirmishes, saying Mass, going out to the sick and dying, teaching music, finding the means to pay the parish's bills, fighting with the bishop when ends didn't meet. Once he complained to me that office help, clerks, made a better living than a priest did. In 1993 he wrote,

> The whole aspect of a priest's personal income looks very temerarious at the present time and I am not aware of any movement, official or otherwise, that is looking to the future. When, on occasion, I have queried certain financial aspects I have invariably gotten the advice, keep your head down and carry on the best that you can. I begin to wonder how long the ostrich has been around and has never apparently solved the problem. . . . At this moment I myself personally wish I had an old age pension and be free of financial as well as spiritual stress.

And, he says, the work wasn't easy. He resented the fact that "people in our time tend to see the priest's job, particularly the parish priest's, as a sinecure. I have found it not so! To maintain a twenty-four hour vigil, seven days a week, even sitting in an armchair, is not an easy prospect," and, he adds, "it is far from an armchair situation."

He especially did not welcome additional burdens that periodically showed up in the form of intrusions on his personal household, either with regard to domestic accommodation or budget. The most annoying of these intrusions were the church personnel whom he had to accommodate while they made special appeals or ran missions at his church.

What happens is this: The parish priest, suddenly and totally unexpectedly, receives a letter, or even a phone call, saying simply that father so-and-so will be with you next weekend—on the annual promotional visit, by permission of the Bishop, bed and breakfast to be provided. . . . Why I should have [this sort of thing] imposed on me, to the detriment of my domestic arrangements, which are considerable, I cannot say. . . . I fully realise the hospitality issue, and my own mere stewardship, but . . . these men seem to have an inveterate habit of not being able to talk or look after themselves without my complete and continuous support. Or worse, to talk interminably on the eternal subject of Sport, and 'What did you think of last Sunday's match?' Despite the fact that I have played most common games, and rather well, I simply abhor such conversational gambits, and suffer serious mental distress. (December 1992)

Nevertheless, day by day Father Pat carried on, giving his music lessons and exams and occasionally incurring the wrath of parents for this or that slight. He traveled to Cobh Cathedral for the annual Mass, kept his socks and shoes on during the washing of the feet, and quavered as men his age stumbled up and down the steps with the sacramental oils. He went on outings with his parishioners and choir to Knock Cathedral, where his brother Chris was assigned. (Father Chris had constant streams of pilgrims looking to make their confession there, while no one came to confession at Churchtown on Saturdays.) He accompanied the Mass servers, boys as well as girls, and youth choir members on annual outings to historical sites and amusement venues—he seemed to enjoy these—where there might be a sing-along on the bus ride home.

And he continued day-to-day to serve and love his parishioners, finding them maddening in turns. In 1997 he compared in his notes the Churchtown and Liscarroll halves of his parish. He wrote that the people of the two parishes were different, and "there's no use telling me it's my fault, even if my job depends on it. . . . It is historical. Liscarroll likes to be organized, somehow like I knew in the States," but getting the people of Churchtown to go along with anything new was futile, because "instruction in Churchtown falls on deaf ears." A case in point was the new collection boxes, metal safes installed at the rear of the church, so that people could insert their envelopes at any time of the week including Sunday. "It took some explaining off the altar, and rather more confusion than might be expected prevailed for some time, with the usual complaining of 'What do you want us to do?' The old psychology buff knew they would get the idea, and they did, but I must say, I had a lovely dog once, named 'Daisy,' who was much easier and quicker to train." Here I think it is important that we all remember that Father Pat is writing to himself at the time and simply having a little laugh to relieve the stress of the job. He loved his own Churchtown people. In comparing the two halves of the parish further on he says, "I much prefer the local people. . . . Liscarroll costs me a lot of money. They want to do things. They want everything."

At a couple of points he comments on the more progressive or ambitious nature of Liscarroll, which regularly made him uncomfortable. Concerning a particularly activist member of that township, he notes that she approached the bishop with her idea that a youth club be started in the church to introduce the children to the gospel message through such alternative devices as the arts, mime, dance, and drama. The parish priest was relieved on that occasion that the Bishop instructed the woman that all such innovative media activities be approved by Father Twohig. We only read of one example of this kind of experimentation, and that was in Churchtown. At the 2002 First Communion Mass "the little ones mimed the Our Father inside the [altar] rails to a calypso melody," an event he lets pass with the simple comment that it was a "new and interesting feature." Perhaps it was the fact that, in Churchtown, children miming prayers from the altar was not likely to mark a major trend, whereas in Liscarroll, Father Pat had always been uncomfortable with the people's readiness to put on a show.

For years, Irish towns have competed annually in a "Tops of the Town" competition, where amateur theater buffs join efforts to compete for selection as the best community act in Ireland. Liscarroll organized a "Tops of the Parish" night. Father Pat, who doesn't mind taking the spotlight as a musician himself, comments early in his tenure as parish priest that "it is good to see people making an effort on their own behalf at the community level." The Tops of the Parish event, however, was not what he had in mind. In his view the production was "over the top," and he was troubled by content that "would be shocking, to say the least, on television." There was sexual and violent content that bothered him, violating the community theme—and it especially bothered him that it was presented as a "parish" event. Popular culture was distancing itself from his sensibilities, from his Church, which could only bend so far to include without fatal compromise. As Father Pat filled out his end of the bargain, the seventy-five plus five years informal agreement he had made with himself, the world became increasingly distant from his cultural and religious rootedness.

His health became more compromised through his heart condition and repeated hip operations. In June 1996 he attended the Golden Jubilee Reunion of his graduating class at Maynooth. There were few there, only about half of those who were still alive, "and they were a sorry lot." It provided him with a time check, a mirror, and what he saw was sobering. Saddened, he "slunk away" before the celebration dinner, the image of a "proud and successful class disappearing like a wisp of smoke," and the specter of age and infirmity that was replacing it followed him out the door and all the way home.

After that reunion, there is determination in the tone of his parish diary, and year after year he strives to demonstrate that he is still able for the work. He sees to it that he attends every duty, every funeral of every priest that he can manage. But willpower alone is not enough to hold back the effects of age. One conscious marker of his ability to carry on came each year at the annual Corpus Christi procession, when in June he carried the Monstrance in procession. In 1997, a year after the trauma of the Golden Jubilee Reunion, he wrote that he carried it "with a limp but with great pride." But even then he wondered in his notes whether it was for the last time. In 1998 he was back to write again: "I carried the Monstrance despite three hip operations, a double by-pass, and a heart valve exchange." But, he added, "I wouldn't say that I was proud to do it— the usual comment. I was overawed and terrified." Still again, he was back at it the following year. "One has to give some semblance of suffering." In June 2000, his eightieth year, he simply mentions in his notes that the procession took place. There is no reference to whether he was able to attend, much less carry the heavy Monstrance. A month earlier, in May, he had observed that he was afraid to attend any events where there were large crowds: "My world-wide escapades have been reduced to a twist of the hip."

His physical capabilities were not the only indication that his active role in the Church might be coming to a close. All the way back in 1996, he had experienced a memory lapse during Mass. At that time, "big, red-haired, but gentle and serene Ann Marie Breen was acting

M.C., and was extremely good at the job, which was an invaluable assistance to the Priest, with a contrary memory, working on his own. At the Easter Vigil Mass I went blank after the choral 'Alleluia.' I urgently whispered, 'Ann Marie, what do I do next?' Loud and clear and authoritarian it came: 'G'over and read the Goshpel!' Which, as Eamon Kelly might say, I done." The memory problem did not go away.

And the pressure remained to solve the split in Liscarroll, with the bishop looking for progress. In 1998 Father Pat pondered the question of what to do with that lot, with the bishop expecting resolution and members of the congregation bearing a lingering ill will toward him. "How can one tell a Bishop that the act of stooping to lick their boots just gives them an opportunity to kick your ass!" Meanwhile, it emerged that the Liscarroll church, despite its earlier facelift, needed an enormous amount of very expensive structural repair, and a galaxy of local and national agencies had got involved in sponsorship. While help, especially financial, was welcome, the multilateral offers created a dizzying puzzle of ambitions, authority, and jurisdiction. The still-divided parishioners were called into the church by the curate for a meeting at which, very democratically, they could air their questions and preferences on the subject. They tore into each other and into Father Pat, who listened to their spluttering criticisms as his curate moved up and down the aisles with a microphone, U.S. TV talk show–style.

He was being pressured to resign; some pressure was subtle, some not so subtle. At the age of seventy-five he had submitted his resignation to the bishop, pro forma, as required, and pro forma, the bishop had declined, as expected, in this age of such a shortage of manpower. But with the Liscarroll mess carrying on, the bishop later changed his mind and wanted the parish priest to go. However, the one-year time limit that the bishop had had to accept Father Pat's earlier resignation had expired, and the priest was not about to write another one to please him—rather, just the opposite. The battle was on. Father Pat's goal was an extra five years on the job, to make it to his eightieth birthday. That was the deal he had made, the matter of principle. Despite failing health and memory, despite the politics at the local and diocesan levels, despite visits from well-intentioned friends in the Church and envoys who asked, "Pat, what the hell do you want the job for?" he stayed on. Sometimes he thought it was masochism, in the form of a trial by age that he had set for himself. But there was still the satisfaction in the work. Still the musical end of things. Still the mission for the man from Maynooth.

And there was the primary school, the children. In June 2000, four months before his eightieth birthday, he wrote in his diary of the children in the school next door to his residence on the occasion of the end-of-year school Mass: "It is an enduring experience for a hardened old sinner like myself to be briefly in the presence of angels. . . . I know that as grownups some of them will go to the Devil, but as they are ranged down there before my eyes with the teachers in nervous attendance, their restlessness and heedlessness, and even blackguarding, only makes me laugh. Their future activities are not my concern, and belong to another world."

Father Pat was committed to the young souls. He despaired of the slim chances that many of them would manage to lead pious lives in the future. But they were this world's only hope. As he struggled with everything else around him in his last years as parish priest, perhaps the brightest light that eased his mind and gave him a great deal of gratification was a musical group formed by three young women in his parish. He had, of course, known them for years as they were growing up, as had everyone in little Churchtown. One of them, Carmel Conroy, was the leading soloist in his church choir. Niamh O'Herlihy had written a song commissioned by Father Pat about the tragic school shooting in Dunblane, Scotland, one of those events that shocked the entire world. The third young woman was Niamh's sister, Anita. They called themselves "Nivita," had recorded a CD that was going well, and were just ready to launch a second when, in October 1999, as they were driving on a local country road, all three of them were killed, along with Carmel's baby daughter, in a collision with another Churchtown girl who was driving in the opposite direction.

Death again outlined the life of the parish, striking it an enormous, earth-shattering blow. The tragedy was nearly unbearable, incomprehensible in the small community, and the parish and town were reluctant to let them go. There were funeral masses, the Irish president called and asked Father Pat to convey her grief, more masses followed, and then a twenty-first birthday party and mass for Niamh were given the following spring. Father Pat's curate said that mass. The parish priest could not trust himself to get through it without weeping. He tried a short speech at the beginning, "but, unfortunately, broke down once again." The man responsible for consoling his flock could not console himself. The small community once again had to cope with death, but this was too much. After all that hope, when "they looked like having a Cranberries success" Father Pat wrote in his diary—all this at once—the village was bathed in tears for months.

In June 2001 Father Pat once again received a request from the bishop to give up his position as parish priest. He had passed his eightieth birthday the previous November. He reflected. "At eighty, it did not seem to me to be a necessity of life. . . . In today's dispensation it looks silly to be a parish priest at eighty. . . . I decided to go." The deal was that Father Pat would become curate at Churchtown, with the new parish priest taking up residence in the now nicely refurbished parish house in Liscarroll that Father Pat had "paid for." Father Pat would retain his present residence. The new man, in fact, turned out to be pretty good. Father Pat described him to me as a wise man who eventually pretty much patched up the Liscarroll squabble and, in addition, had drawn the Churchtown and Liscarroll halves of the parish closer together than they had been in the past. In passing, Father Pat mentioned that when he showed the new man some samples of the *Chronicus*, his new boss asked him to restrict record keeping in future to simple account keeping and lists of parish events, and Father Pat complied.

In fact the last entry in the *Chronicus* is for February 2002. With a few modifications of particulars with regard to identity, it reads as follows:

> Tuesday, 12 February: And here is a new one. An urn of ashes arrived by post from Manchester with a request that they be buried in a particular cemetery, down by the crossroad, which we did. We performed as much liturgy as we could manage with the understanding that the funeral Mass had been performed according to the new regulations at the crematorium. After the graveyard performance we made a little hole and pushed the essence of Tim Pat, late of Manchester, previously of Churchtown, down beside his mother as if it made an ounce of difference one way or another.
>
> Wednesday the thirteenth: Ash Wednesday. I had thought of using Tim Pat, but resisted the temptation. Anyway, we have new commercial black stuff which is fine.

Father Pat had finally attained the semiretirement that he had longed for. He had become curate in the modern church organization, where the responsibilities of the day-to-day had come to fall on the shoulders of the parish priest, as he had been fond of observing. The new man was a hands-on fellow who quickly showed that he had the necessary properties to do the job himself and to insulate his aging curate a bit from the cares of the never-ending duties.

Father Pat's tenure covered a lot of years. While he was leafing through Louise's recipe book one day, he came across a recipe for something called "Parochial Hopscotch." It read:

Take one lunatic
Build a beautiful home around him
Carefully watch him simmer for twenty-five years, and you have
The perfect Parish Priest.

Father Pat was amused. He wondered what the recipe for bishops might be.

In one of his last addresses to the young people of the parish, in June 2001, at a Mass intended to enhance their chances at exam time, he told them that "no matter what may be thought of them at this present time, and what they are undoubtedly heading into in the future with regard to neglect of religion and the evils that derive there from, just for now, they are simply growing children who are living in fear of what lies before them tomorrow. That is part of the sadness, even the suffering, of life, but what else is there?" It is not a particularly uplifting message. It makes it appear that life is a struggle and getting to heaven is no sure thing, even a long shot. But that is the world, according to the Man from Maynooth, and there is no getting around it. And that should be where the story of the parish priest who became curate ends, but it doesn't.

Father Pat had never liked the idea of the Church becoming an institution that tried to modify people's behavior through promoting institutional social reform—that is, by setting up programs to help people to do what they needed to do to live proper lives. His position is based on the free will argument—everybody has it, and as individuals they have the right to choose heaven or hell and what they will do with themselves on the journey. He opposed sex education in the schools and the Church making official pronouncements on abortion policy; he was against programs that were trying to save people from everything from "drugs, drink, smoking, warfare, health hazards, sexual extremes and aberrations, and the result thereof." He opposed, on the basis of the same principle, the Church's support for the Stay-Safe Campaign, directed at protecting children from sexual abuse, which he saw, again, as an issue concerning choices made by adults who are responsible for their own eternal condition—and the welfare of children in their trust.

When I first visited Father Pat in December 2002, he brought up the worldwide concerns about the sexual behavior of priests, in particular, the victimization of children. He focused on the consequences of the issue for priests themselves. "There is a lot of adverse publicity of course, but on our side of things, priests have gotten very much afraid. They've given up visiting the schools. Some of them have given up having altar help. They are deadly afraid because one word, and you're out of a job, you understand? The burden of proof is on the side of the defendant. There's a start of resistance among the clergy, there's been an upheaval by bishops, priests forming organizations. They're not going to take this anymore." We left the topic and went back to music.

Several days before my first interview with him, Father Pat had received two visitors, police detectives. The visit was a follow-up to a letter he had received from a Cork City solicitor that April. He was informed in that letter that the solicitor's client, a woman, had made serious allegations of sexual misconduct against him. The alleged events were said to have occurred more than thirty years ago, when she was a child. Father Pat denies the allegations in the strongest terms. When I visited in July 2003, the first time he had disclosed the matter of the charges to me, he gave me documents he had written in his defense, none of them a matter of official record, simply his version of the charges along with a step-by-step refutation of the alleged acts and the circumstances that were said to have made the acts possible. As we talked about the charges, he said he believed that there had been terrible crimes of abuse committed by priests, things that should not and could not go unpunished by the law. But he also believed that some of the charges being brought are unfounded, perhaps a matter of manufactured memories in the current climate that finds so many now looking suspiciously into their long-past childhood relationships with priests to see if there might have been something sinister. In the worst cases he believes that there is criminal motive, where people see such charges as a means for getting a cash settlement from a Church too fearful and beleaguered to defend itself, to defend its clergy.

As a result of the allegations Father Pat was forced to leave his position as Churchtown curate. The bishop's words were, "Pat, this time you have to go." His plans were to make his a test case, to stand up to the charges in court. To his mind there is a parallel with the case brought against his father in the old colonial days: guilty unless you can prove your innocence in surroundings where, politically, you are the underdog. As a sociologist, I am quite well aware that there are other ways to interpret the situation as seen from the outside, by the victims of abuse and their families. Of course, I am in no position to speculate about the charges, much less to come to a conclusion. This final episode in a man's life is presented here as it was presented to me, unfolding one chapter at a time, page by page in sixteen years of a parish *Chronicus* plus postscript that I have done little to characterize, except by way of identifying themes and stages. You and I have in the end an intimate portrait of a man of many parts who has been a parish priest in a changing Ireland and is now charged with a sexual crime. What can we say about the way that life is ending up? In tragedy, struggle, the whole of that life overshadowed by a dark cloud of suspicion. What are the events that produced that darkness, and what will be the outcome? The legal answer will be established in a Dublin court, if Pat Twohig has his way and his accuser has hers. The ultimate outcome of this story, to Father Pat's mind, comes not from the judgment of the court, but as he has told us repeatedly, in the final reckoning, where all are judged on the basis of how they have exercised what he sees as the human gift of free will.

CHAPTER 7

The New Irish

[Padhman, a fictional character, a surgeon from India working

in Dublin, is reflecting on how he is perceived by the Irish:]

When I discussed the lightness of her soufflé, Millie Gorman

realized I was normal. Eamon thought I was a regular guy when

we had that animated session about the chicanes at Monaco.

The hospital crowd must have deemed me normal, that night

on call, when I told them my dirty party piece. "An Indian, a

Pakistani, and a Bangladeshi walked into a pub . . ." They

thought I was great craic, even before I had finished the opening

line. It is incredible, thought Padhman, that it is my perceived

abnormality, my deviation from their idea of a defined norm for

someone like me, which makes me one of them, i.e., normal.

(Madhavan 2001)

At an Irish National School, Dublin schoolboys were preparing to pray.
They were washing their hands, face, and feet, getting ready to face
Mecca for one of their five daily prayers. In addition to the National
School, in which religious instruction is Islamic rather than Catholic,
the Dublin Islamic Center contains a library, retail shop, and restaurant. Dr. Nooh Al-Kaddo, the director, was happy to welcome non-
Islamic visitors. Originally from Iraq, he believed it was critical for
insiders and outsiders to reach for mutual understanding in the New
Ireland, where there were nineteen thousand Muslims by official census
count in 2002. "These days you hear about jihad, so the first question I
expect from people is 'what is holy war?' Then they ask about women:
'Why are they dressed in this way? Why are they covered?' They simply
want to know. I don't take insult, because when I see something I don't
understand, I ask too" (Ó Conghaile 2001).

Dr. Al-Kaddo appears to understand the delicacy of the public-
relations challenge faced by the growing and for the most part highly
visible Muslim population in every Irish town of any size: take the initiative, be open, educate, and try to pass quietly from being a cultural
novelty to an accepted ethnic presence. In particular, try to avoid the
intermediate stage of becoming a minority target of prejudice and discrimination, avoid the "social problem" label, avoid repeating the recent social history of immigration in so many other European states.

The Irish — in particular, the emigrated diaspora Irish — have at
best a mixed history when it comes to dealing with social and cultural

diversity. There is no point in splitting hairs over the question of which native European peoples historically have the best and worst record in their relations with people of color or "cultural others" wherever they may have encountered them around the world or at home. Generally speaking, the diaspora Irish have not appeared appreciably more or less enlightened than others of European extraction in this regard. We might want to forget certain episodes, like the New York Draft Riots of 1863 (not *all* of the whites in the mob were Irish), in order to make that claim, but other Europeans would have historical chapters, especially colonial chapters, that they would want to forget as well.

For the moment, the modern Ireland-Irish (exclusive of Ulster, where attacks on immigrants are common) might be counted something of an exception to the overt racism that makes the nationalist right-wing parties a renewed political menace elsewhere in Europe. However, it is still quite early in Ireland's experiment with multiculturalism. It is quite possible to read the history of Ireland's official policy toward non-Western peoples and its treatment of its own Traveler minority population as little different from the less enlightened impulses of European governance. The government's current stance with regard to immigration and asylum issues has, not surprisingly, "mirrored responses throughout 'fortress Europe' and in other western countries" (Fanning 2002, 1). Ireland will share a European future that is bound to include increasing numbers of newcomers from around the world, and it would be going out on a limb to predict that culturally and racially different immigrants will in future be treated any differently in Ireland than in other Western European nations. Why should the Irish be any different?

Nevertheless, Ireland *is* somewhat different from its neighbors historically, in important ways that might produce a somewhat different immigrant experience there. For an extended period the Irish themselves were considered a race apart from the rest of Europe. And in contrast to other European nations, the Irish homeland was still a colony of a foreign power for the first two decades of the twentieth century. Now that Ireland has become a target of immigration—only in the very earliest stages of a multiethnic transformation—the question of what kind of reception newcomers are getting at the moment is an important one.

In my first two years in Ireland, now a quarter century ago, homeland Irish liked to claim that they had a certain sophistication regarding the treatment of racial and cultural others. In the 1970s I was sometimes asked what all the fuss over race was about in the United States, since the Irish themselves were free of such problems at home. My usual response had three parts. There was no population of cultural others, let alone of people of color, in Ireland worth speaking of at the time. The vast majority of Africans, Asians, and other visitors were understood to be just passing through as students and trainees. As paying guests they were not a likely target for discrimination. Finally, if one wanted to look for a long-standing record of prejudice and discrimination in Ireland, one need look no further than popular attitudes and behavior with regard to Ireland's Travelers, the "Tinkers" as they were called in the past. I had the feeling the latter comment was seen by some as a low blow.

Yet it is true that by and large the Ireland Irish have an earned reputation as a friendly, outgoing people, eager to look after the stranger. Television and print news features indicate an Irish interest in people and issues everywhere in the world, including the less developed nations. This may be a combined result of Irish Catholic missionary traditions, with sons and daughters heading off to remote locations as priests, brothers, and nuns; the just-mentioned recent status of the country as a colony itself; and the fact that wherever you look in the world there are bound to be some descendants of those Irish who emigrated in search of work. But in recent years, global events have decided to test the capacity for tolerance of the Irish at home. As a result of the 1990s economic boom, Ireland joined fully with the other European nations as a magnet for immigration. As elsewhere, some of this immigration is legal, some not; some newcomers arrive with much-needed technical training and skills, and some don't; some flowed immediately into employment and entrepreneurial positions in the labor-starved economy of late, and some have not. And some of the latter have been restrained by the law from doing so.

As elsewhere, the inflow of new people has resulted in some well-publicized acts of intolerance against newcomers. Hate crimes directed at immigrants and visitors of color have occurred. Many native Irish react in horror at reports of these incidents and are quick to distance themselves from acts of intolerance at every opportunity. Efforts by minor political figures to play the anti-foreigner and race cards have met with resistance and quick condemnation by a chorus of critics poised to strike back at any hint of foreign or racial profiling in public statements or proposed policies. But taken together, the well-publicized incidents of foreigner bashing, on the one hand, and the emergence of vigilant attitudes and organizations directed at preventing the abuse of immigrants and asylum seekers, on the other, raise questions about just what the balance is. At issue is whether the native Irish, who are having to learn about tolerance and true multiculturalism in a hurry, will on average behave any better toward growing numbers of newcomers than their European counterparts. The troubling question has to do with the near future: How will the Irish react when the number of strangers in their midst reaches some critical mass of increased visibility that promises society-wide cultural and political transformation? Was Ireland approaching some tipping point by 2005, when the proportion of New Irish exceeded 10 percent of the total population?

The immigrant perception is that not all Irish people are sophisticated regarding matters of prejudice and discrimination toward newcomers, but that many have been making a real effort, enough to lead to the conclusion that Ireland is a notch above other places in Europe in welcoming the newly arrived. The situation remains fluid today. At present the medium- and long-term future of the Irish economy is something of a question, with new competitive locations attractive to electronics industries and other technologies popping up all over the globe. So it is still unclear what sort of welcome the future holds in store for the New Irish. The newcomers themselves think about this and worry a little, especially with regard to how their children will be treated. Nevertheless, they have come to stay.

STILL A SMALL ISLAND

Early in the new century it was estimated that as many as 500,000 illegal immigrants make their way into Europe each year, while an additional 400,000 apply for asylum. In 2002 a survey found that 14 percent of Europeans wanted no more immigrants of any kind to their particular country; an additional 25 percent were "ambivalent" (*Irish Times,* June 6, 2002). Anti-immigration politicians have enjoyed a popular resurgence in much of Europe since the late 1990s, drawing votes in France, Germany, Netherlands, Denmark, and elsewhere. Lawmakers in individual European states have moved to more restrictive immigration policies since the mid 90s, and the European Commission of the EU has followed suit in a series of recent conventions and agreements.

The EU has vigorously advanced the principle that a common policy is needed for all member states, including a single set of measures for evaluating asylum seekers. A series of conferences in recent years has defined various categories of legal migrants, developed criteria for admission to asylum-seeker status, and agreed on provisions for classifying temporary admission status for students and workers. In 2002 a comprehensive plan was adopted for combating illegal immigration and for establishing procedures to return people illegally entering EU nations to their country of origin. In June 2003 an EU Commission adopted common guidelines for assisting legal immigrants with employment and integration. In late 2005 and early 2006 the EU Commission in a series of conferences was attempting to develop a policy that would assist poorer nations where illegal migration originates with programs of prevention and repatriation. The aim has been to develop a uniform set of regulations across all of Europe for standardized treatment of all types of immigration from a perspective that understands widespread shifts in population as a natural if unwieldy consequence of globalization. Ireland is one of a few EU nations that does not automatically adopt each new regulation coming from Brussels regarding immigration policy, but generally supports the development of international standards for Europe. These regulations, coming top-down as they have and in quick succession, have left national enforcement agencies and common citizens scratching their heads at times, trying to find the logic in some policies that on the ground may appear counterintuitive.

In Ireland one hears over and over the comment "Why is the government spending my taxes accommodating asylum seekers in hotels and mobile homes rather than letting them go to work, get settled, and pay their own way?" In the heat of the moment it is difficult to effectively make the point that it makes perfect sense on the global level for a tiny country not to hold out a bigger carrot (certain employment) to a fluid pool of millions of people scouring the globe for an accommodating place to live and find work. One would have to follow that initial response with, "It's bad enough that you Irish already have the reputation for being a little more friendly and humane toward struggling foreigners than do other Europeans. Putting them to work and paying them a decent wage would be altogether foolhardy."

With its 4.1 million people in 2005, Ireland represented little more than a pinpoint of population among the six billion inhabitants of the world. To the estimated *millions* of people in the world who are on the move in a given year—some driven by economic desperation and lethal politics at home, others simply looking for a decent livelihood and a stable life—a little country with a reputation for prosperity looks pretty good. If you are not lucky enough to come from one of the European Union states from which Ireland allows open labor migration, but have the skills or can obtain the requisite entry permits, it makes sense to seek legal entry. If legal admission appears doubtful, you might slip in quietly, overstay your visa, hope for the best. Or you might enter and apply for asylum because in your homeland you fear for your life and the lives of your family members, or you think maybe there is a reason to do so, or you don't really have a reason to fear for your life at home but would like a chance to try out the refugee argument on an asylum commission. Given what is at stake, these are all reasonable strategies for seeking entry to the EU in general and Ireland in particular for people facing difficult lives elsewhere. Cross-border traffic in Europe includes the hapless clients of ruthless human smugglers, enterprising drug dealers, and desperados on the run but, mostly, just millions of people with and without papers looking for a better life. And there it is, the tiny Celtic Tiger, burning bright in the North Atlantic. And so also an "immigration problem" has the potential to take shape in the minds of the natives of a place known for the best part of two centuries for exporting rather than importing people looking for that better life.

The 2002 census listed a total of 150,000 people as having legally immigrated since 1996, making up 5.8 percent of the population. But between 2004 and 2006 arrived 150,000 new immigrants from Eastern Europe alone, and suddenly more than 10 percent of the 4.1 million people in the Republic were immigrants. In 2002 19,000 Muslims were living in Ireland, four times as many as the number in 1991. They are a part of the New Ireland, and, in concert with other immigrant communities, they will help shape the cultural future. Their experience in coming to Ireland, their sense of the kind of reception they have received there, and the layering of personal emotions as Ireland becomes home for them and their children form one among the many stories that help to define Ireland today. As is the case with any immigrant group, the newcomers become more and more like the natives as Ireland becomes home.

When I mentioned the figure of nineteen thousand New Irish Muslims to Khalid Sallabi, the young imam of the Galway Mosque, he shrugged a little—he wasn't impressed. He said that maybe some immigrants are not so eager to respond to an official document asking them to give an account of themselves. He added that they would not necessarily be concerned about the Irish government, but that people from some parts of the world find it makes more sense to remain not so visible when officials of any government agency ask questions. It was his guess that the census figures for the number of Muslims in Ireland could be somewhat below the actual population. I was visiting Imam Sallabi because I was interested in meeting some of the New Irish he knew. He was very generous with his time and arranged visits with several immigrants living in the city. We agreed to meet first at the Galway Community Center after the Friday midday prayer: the daily mosque itself was not large enough to accommodate all of the faithful for the week's main prayer, so Friday prayer was at Galway's municipal community center.

As I stood outside waiting for Imam Sallabi, dozens of men and boys came out of the generic public building that could have been adapted to any function involving a large gathering. Hundreds of men were exiting other doors leading out from the large gymnasium-style hall. They spoke the languages of Malaysia, Pakistan, Libya, India, Kuwait, Nigeria, Saudi Arabia, Tunisia, Algeria, Turkey, the Sudan, Iraq, and Iran. They also spoke English to communicate across ethnic memberships: their English greetings to each other were warm, sometimes reverent, sometimes joking. There were lots of smiles and laughter. I spoke to one of the middle-aged men and said that I had an appointment to meet the imam. "Go inside. Go inside. Don't worry," he said, ushering me in enthusiastically. I was escorted into the gym, stopping to leave my shoes in the hallway with dozens of other pairs of shoes, sneakers, boots, flip-flops. I was greeted amiably by other men. My gray beard matched many in the building: "Salaam Alaikem," a man in a longer gray beard saluted me. "Salaam," I responded, not quite able to get the rest out. "Salaam, Salaam" came more greetings, and I responded.

I was trying to make out which of the capped and gowned figures scattered among the others in Western dress might be the imam. A young man was pointed out to me, and I was led over to greet him.

His untucked, soft, gray, loose-fitting shirt and pants were worn under a knitted white gown, open at the front, otherwise somewhat similar to a Catholic priest's cassock. A white knitted skullcap covered his short hair; a thin line of beard was trimmed neat. He had a soft voice and handshake. For a minute it appeared odd to me that this angular young guy was the religious leader of this room full of lingering elders who did not have to race back to a Friday job after a prayer break. But his manner set him apart, added stature. His eyes were quick, scholarly, a little grave even when he smiled. His gestures were those of a man used to giving directions, organizing things. But for all of that he was hardly imposing.

He announced that we were expected for lunch at the house of Dr. J, a physician at the University Hospital. He would ride with me so I would not get lost in the Friday afternoon Galway City traffic. Resmiye, who was helping me with recordings and such, would ride with Dr. J, who had also been at the Friday prayer. We were barely out of the car park when our conversation turned to the current U.S. military action in Iraq. The imam held that the unilateral move by the U.S. administration with few allies at it side appeared a bad strategy if the effort was intended to reduce terrorist attacks on the United States. We agreed that no matter how big a problem Saddam Hussein was, creating martyrs among the Iraqi military and civilian population was bound to have long-term implications for U.S. security. It was a grim conversation to begin our discussion, but the alternative was to dance around the topic for the rest of the long day we would spend together. We laughed because we had both decided individually beforehand that we would avoid the topic, and now we were relieved to have it behind us, finding that we were in agreement. Trust was no small matter in determining how that day would go: imam or not, he was a Libyan national sponsoring a visit by a U.S. citizen who would be asking other Libyans, Algerians, and Pakistanis questions about topics that included their patterns of association. Before my visit he had been questioned about why an American was coming to Ireland to talk to Muslims from the Middle East. And while I was there, there were some pointed jokes—"Now, did you say you were CIA, or is it FBI?"

Dr. J's house was a semidetached in an older, close-in Galway suburb. The sitting room featured both Western and Eastern furnishings: upholstered living room furniture and long cushions on the floor, the former for sitting, the latter for dining. A lamb dish was served in a large bowl set in the middle of a red and white checkered tablecloth. According to custom, everyone ate in common from the one bowl using their own tablespoon. There was also salad and potatoes stuffed with minced beef. Bowls of fruit and sweets followed for dessert. Also according to custom, the host's wife remained in the staging area, the kitchen, behind the scene, all during the meal. The food was excellent, and we all sent our compliments back to the "government," the physician's wife, who, following conventional practice, never appeared and whose name was not mentioned.

Eight people were present at various stages during the meal, and Resmiye was the only woman. Her status as a physician, along with her Westernized style and experience, gave her a certain legitimacy in the gathering of men, some of whom were also physicians. The fact that she was a woman from the Middle East, who could exchange regional anecdotes and discuss regional differences in language, did not necessarily add to her acceptability in the male circle. Everyone, including Resmiye, graciously negotiated any cultural contradiction. Later, at another house, the imam did say, as we waited for someone to answer the doorbell, a little uncomfortably perhaps but with subtle humor, that Resmiye "might have to stay with the women" in the kitchen. She didn't, as it turned out. Imported Middle Eastern customs were softening in Galway City. But when Resmiye had asked the men at dinner about how Islamic women found working outside the home in Ireland, there was a subtle shifting of sitting positions followed by some very general comments about "women doctors" finding it just fine, perhaps indicating that the topic did not come up much in these circles. Resmiye let go of the question, and conversation was directed at her background: she was from the Middle East but from Turkey, the most secular nation in the region; she wore no head covering, was in Western dress, spoke to men as their equal.

"Ah, so you are from Turkey. What part?" The question, on the face of it, was just about geography, but there was more to it. Being from eastern Turkey or any small mountain or seacoast village could indicate at least some probability of Muslim belief or practice.

"Izmir." The answer indicated Turkey's godless geographic extreme. Not even Istanbul had the same reputation for secularism, partying, and Western influence as did Izmir. In fact, Resmiye was a true and militant daughter of Kemal Attaturk's de-Islamicized vision of a secular

Turkish nation. I hoped the conversation would turn away from blunt questions about religious politics. It did. The imam stuck to geography and travelogue.

"Oh yes, that is a very beautiful area." He described some of the islands in the Aegean. Earlier he had talked of how friendly he found the people of Mexico. He had spent time in the Pacific, described the shadier side of street-life in Bangkok, had seen something of Europe. I could see confusion spreading across Resmiye's expression.

"So you have traveled quite a bit! How is that? That is so much against my impression of an imam." I knew very well her impression of Turkish imams, and a worldly religious leader did not at all square with that understanding. "In Turkey, imams just stay put; they don't travel. Are all imams like you, open to other cultures, traveling all over?" Khalid's response did not help her to resolve the mismatch of her impression and the man before her.

"I play a lot of sport. I am a sportsman. Some of the people in Libya, they know me as a sportsman."

Resmiye's eyes were wide. What was this? A soccer imam? "That is very unusual for Turkey," she said flatly. "Are you unusual?

"Well, you could say that," Khalid responded.

Resmiye laughed. "OK, so not all imams in Libya play sports then!" Her sense of reality was restored, a little.

Ahmet, another guest and physician, arrived, and we started to eat. Ahmet assured us that the imam was indeed a very good soccer player. Two more arrivals, both young men from Algeria pursuing PhDs in computer science, came in and seated themselves. I asked if they played soccer too, and everyone laughed. They were all soccer players except for our host, Dr. J. "But you have heard: *he* is the real soccer player!" the newcomers said, pointing to their imam. "He is a professional." Is he tough? I asked them. "Is he tough? Oh my God!" Everyone laughed including Khalid, as they often referred to him by his first name, their religious leader, the "very tough" tackler. They were all easy with each other, like a big family of brothers, like the men coming out of the mosque earlier.

Suddenly, surrounded by these men, sitting on the floor with the taste of deliciously spiced Middle Eastern dishes, I felt a little confused about where I was. These people were at home in this space, and I had been allowed to slip behind the scenes of Islamic private life. I glanced out the window and was reassured that, yes, this is a living room in a Galway neighborhood of stucco semidetached housing like a thousand similar neighborhoods in Irish cities. I asked the Algerian students how long they had been in Ireland. About two years, said one.

"Oim hair aboat six yairs," said the other.

"You have an Irish accent!" Resmiye declared. He did, and we were all firmly back in Galway.

We talked more soccer. Please come to see them play on Sunday if we can; they can use the supporters. Also to see how roughly they are treated on the field by their imam—bring our video camera to document it! He was the midfielder, the general, the play maker. For intrasquad practice matches they would arrive half an hour early to choose sides, arguing over which side got Khalid. In addition to being the star player, he of course was the ultimate voice of authority on all debated plays. Whichever side got him for the practice game was the same as deciding beforehand which side would win. Soccer is an important feature of transplanted Islamic culture in Galway. At Friday's main prayer, after the sermon, games and practice dates and places are announced for both the boys' and men's matches on Sunday, along with other announcements. It struck me that alternating holy day and sports days this way contrasted with the frustration faced by Catholic priests whose Sunday masses must compete with the recreational schedules of their more sporting male parishioners on the Christian Sabbath.

Resmiye and I were assured that Imam Sallabi was not recruited to Galway on the basis of his talent and reputation in sports. He competed directly with other applicants and was selected largely on the basis of his knowledge of the Qur'an and his ability to apply the lessons to the worldly questions and problems faced by parishioners. The selection committee had been thoroughly impressed with the young man's wisdom. And while the men in the room teased and joked very easily with the imam, he had a gentle command of them at the same time. Ahmet, who appeared in some ways closest to Khalid, said he would often jokingly ask for a synopsis of the upcoming Friday sermon. He explained, "Because I tell him, 'Khalid, sometimes, you know, I may be a little busy; you can give it to me now.' But he never gives it to me!"

I asked the imam what today's topic had been. It was about preparing for the day of judgment. While everyone is anxious on that day, there are seven types of mortals who will not be. Today they had discussed the

Just Ruler, the first type who is truly saved. The lesson is that we are all rulers of ourselves and that we cannot leave things up to those who are above us. Just as we scrutinize our own thoughts and actions for goodness, we must pay critical attention to the mighty, because it is only by this means that leaders themselves will be led by their followers to be just.

"We say that the Just Ruler comes from the Just People. Don't give up. You have to do your duty and that's it. And I will have to keep thinking about 'What is the right? What is the wrong?' . . . So you keep doing good, and you can't do wrong. To keep our front clean and our back clean. This is our philosophy." The two of us in the room hearing the message for the first time thought that it was indeed a wise teaching. We asked what were the other six types, in addition to the Just Ruler, who would be sure to gain heaven. "Ah, for that you will have to stay with us for the next six weeks," Khalid said. Ahmet shrugged, palms up, as if to say, "See—what did I tell you?"

The imam spoke of his philosophy of teaching. In the Islamic world there is a tendency toward formality that he was not comfortable with. His inspiration came from a famous Qur'anic scholar from Iraq; when you saw him among his students, you wouldn't be able to tell which was the teacher. "That scholar, he was of a very open mind, you could say. He would debate with his students. He would sit down, and they would debate from sunrise to maybe one o'clock, maybe two. His students would grow up and come to their own conclusions. His critics might say, 'But they could be wrong.' But he could in this way make them as good a scholar as he is, to make their own decisions."

Khalid seemed to follow the formula faithfully. Except for his ceremonial vestments he was only slightly set apart from the other men in the room, mostly by his command of their attention when he spoke. But when he declined the offer of fresh fruit following the main course, Ahmet directed him to eat a "unit of fruit—you have just eaten meat," and he complied. Ahmet said, "Yes, on matters of diet, we doctors are the boss. You are the boss of everything else."

The imam explained to me later that an imam is simply a facilitator of good practice, a guide rather than a leader. He said that, as their imam, he had to meet the members of his community where they were in terms of faith and practice; he recognized from the start that Islamic practice in a Western environment like Galway City was different from what it had been in Libya or elsewhere in the Middle East. People would come to the imam with their questions, and his job was to respond with answers they could use in Galway and yet be true to the faith. Over time, with maturity and reflection, studying the Qur'an, each individual comes to know in his or her heart what salvation requires. He was not in a position to be their judge, "thank God." Further, it was part of the work of the imam to encourage the development of a community of faith (called *umma*) that included many guides who could stand in for the imam in answering questions that would lead people to a recognition of the Right and the Wrong. With the faithful leading the faithful, in a community of equals, the imam is simply the midfielder, passing the ball when it comes his way. In Galway, Ireland, the ball might have a different spin on it from what it had back in Libya, but you had to play it as it came to you, adjust your game.

These were the issues I wanted to talk about: What in particular were the adjustments to Irish society and culture? We had spent the whole meal getting to know each other. I had earlier attempted to draw the conversation toward the adjustment questions, not remembering that bluntly asking strangers to bare their feelings about personal issues was a strictly Western habit. In the Middle East and elsewhere in the civil world, you take the time to get to know each other before you talk business. Then, once you have established some familiarity, know who your correspondent is, have created at least a joking relationship, *then* you can talk about whatever business brings you together. In a room full of people from nations often at odds with each other, that can take a couple of hours and a good meal, graciously provided according to the custom of the Libyan host, thoroughly appreciated by the American guest. Resmiye, from U.S.-allied Turkey, provided the perfect intermediary, announcing she and her country were adamantly opposed to the U.S.-sponsored embargoes against Libya. We were ready, after compliments once more went back to the government in the kitchen, to get down to business.

Here and there throughout the meal there had been hints that among the Western nations, Ireland was a reasonably snug harbor for Muslims. Was my impression correct? Oh yes, came the general agreement, very good, quite nice. Some of them had experience in other countries; how did Ireland compare? They had heard that the Irish were more accepting and tolerant than the people of other nations before they left home. "The Irish people are friendly, more kindly than the British," said one of the Algerian graduate students, and more than the French, agreed the other. That is why everyone decided to come here, added one of the doctors. There was also general agreement on the next point: that with the Irish, it depends on how you treat them, respect being returned with respect. Maybe the Americans, and especially the Canadians, had the most experience and sophistication with multiculturalism and were less likely than the Irish to ask immediately, "So where do you come from?" This is the easiest place for Middle Easterners to live, said the Algerian with the Irish-English accent: he had lived in France for two years, and Ireland compared favorably. Ireland had been "so far, very nice, you know?"

Regarding establishing friendships with the Irish, the answer that I would grow used to hearing from expats was offered by Ahmet, "You know, this is 2003, and nobody has time. Like my friends sitting here, I don't see them, only on Friday, and *we are friends*. But [gesturing] he's busy with his work, and he's busy with his work . . . and the same with the Irish. In the neighborhood, their kiddies play with my kiddies, and when you go out it's 'Hi. How are you? Nice weather. What's your plan? . . . Are you going on holiday? Where?' And where they're going, etc. If they have the time."

I asked whether the native Irish were generally flexible and accommodating to Muslim practice. We had noticed that some of those attending the main prayer on Friday arrived quite late, parked their car anywhere, and ran into the community center to arrive in time to be credited for attending at least part of the week's main prayer. Afterwards, several clearly had to hurry back to work. But many other working-age men had strolled out of the mosque and socialized leisurely with friends, in no hurry, apparently with the day or at least the afternoon free to meet their day-long religious obligations. Had employers learned to schedule around the Friday holy day for their Islamic employees?

They thought employers were generally flexible. They understood the situation, and Muslim employees typically were allowed to make up the time for Friday on other days of the week. And they themselves had found that fellow employees and colleagues at work were quite good about making accommodations and showing respect for religious practice. During fast days, when people go on break together and Muslims cannot eat, people out of respect will not eat in front of them. "And here sometimes, like with Dr. J here, people won't eat in front of him when he is fasting, and some people, they will fast one day with him." Another said he had also experienced a similar respectfulness. When people bring food to work to share and realize it is a fast day, they will apologize for not thinking of that beforehand. And during Ramadan, a period of dawn-to-dusk fasting, Muslims may be given a free break at four p.m. so they can eat something, "because people understand this."

For kids in schools it is hard to fast when all their friends are eating at midday, but some will do it just for the challenge. Fasting varies by age. Imam Sallabi offered that he was good about fasting when he was quite young, and of course scrupulously followed the required practice at present, but when he was a young man of twenty-one or twenty-two, that was a different story. "Sometimes I would just fast half a day, or I would fast the first day, then go to a party! But here, when the kids go to school, they can't fast." And so, as their imam, he meets them where they are, under these conditions of Western cultural influence.

In fact, the Irish national schools reportedly have been extraordinarily welcoming and enthusiastic about the growing diversity of their students. Beyond the question of accepting cultural difference, they celebrate it. Ahmet told us that at the end of the school year in his child's school, where "there were fifteen different nationalities — from the Middle East, the Philippines, Russia, Asia, Nigeria, Libya — fifteen different nationalities — they had a small party. They [the Irish native parents and teachers] liked it, and they asked us to wear our traditional costumes, they made photos of the different traditions, and the different foods — sweets from each country — and there is one kid from each place that made a small talk about their country, like my daughter, and Dr. J's, too. And another made some notes about Russia, and some notes about South Africa. It's really a fantastic day. They took a lot of pictures. And everyone was very happy. It was very nice, really. And the teachers are very good. They know the kids can't speak English, and they are very patient with them. And they have special classes, and they take them from the class to the English class. And [they] even respect their religion and will sometimes give a lecture about their religion. And about religion class, they ask about your religion at the beginning, and your children do not have to attend the religion class."

This part of the immigrant experience conveyed the impression that, at least in some quarters, the native Irish are admirable multiculturalists. But there is at least one area of leisure culture that will require considerable intercultural accommodation. Speaking for the rest, who nod thoughtfully in agreement, the more recently arrived Algerian computer specialist says, "You know, the culture *is* different," and immediately I think I know what he's speaking of. "Sometime, you couldn't do what they do. . . . Some situations are tolerable, some differences. If all go to a lecture together, some are vegetarian; some are drinking wine; I don't eat pork. And you respect me; I respect you. But not to go to a pub, that kind of thing . . . When they stay together, they like to drink, you know? And this kind of thing, it is not allowed to stay in a place of drinking, to drink. This kind of thing limits relationships."

A serious cultural difference, to be sure. But since the taboo had to do with a leisure trait of the host culture, this appeared to be something that could be managed. After all, the Irish are not drinking all of their leisure time. And the Irish are aware of the sensibility of moderation or abstinence; actually, that awareness has existed for some time, especially among the middle and professional classes. If other forms of cultural and religious pluralism were possible in the world, then perhaps a single society might be able to contain religious drinkers and religious non-drinkers.

I wasn't hearing tales of clash and struggle here, instead a little about mutual adjustment, and that was nice, but it was making the sociologist in me uneasy. So I restated in the most general terms what I was hearing: everything is good; the Irish are reasonably accommodating. I said I was not looking for trouble necessarily, but I did want to hear all sides of the story, wherever there are other sides. Resmiye added, somewhat more pointedly, "What about after September 11?" One of the first things that was said, when we and the group were getting to know one another, when it was learned that I came from quite close to New York City, was that they all hoped I had not known anyone who had been killed or injured. They said they would have been very sorry if I did.

One of the doctors present said that the Irish may be a little scared, wary, when dealing with apparent Easterners. He had recently felt particularly scrutinized at the airport, as his family was leaving for the Middle East. That was natural enough: he didn't blame the officials, didn't consider it discrimination. But the special attention—it was hard to pinpoint just what it was. It was more a feeling than something you actually could point to on the part of the officials—but it was real enough to frighten his wife and his young son, Ali. Then the officials noticed that little Ali was carrying a gun, a toy gun. The special attention immediately became unmistakable.

The inspector said, "'Gentleman! You know I have to take this gun.'

"I told him, 'It's just a toy.'

"He told me, 'I don't care. You know what I mean!' I know he means after September 11. He told me, 'I'll destroy it.' And my son was crying."

But another in the room quickly added that the same thing had happened to his uncle's child ten years ago in the United Kingdom. He thought that they would probably have to do the same with toy guns carried to the airport by native Irish kids. We all agreed that that was very probable.

But they also had concerns about prejudice and mistreatment that went beyond behavior at airports and among security and customs personnel. This was especially keenly felt with regard to people who did not follow the appropriate expectations regarding how Muslim women should be addressed and treated. The degree of shelter afforded to women by Islamic cultures is well known. In Dr. J's house, in the private domestic realm, the woman of the house was shielded from view. When Islamic women are out in public places, their covered appearance may draw the attention and even remarks from male passersby. But we were assured that inappropriateness and public affronts came only from people of "very, very, very low personage." Such a definition of those who display rude manners exempts most Irish natives, and the group attributed good will and respect to the everyday Irish they met.

Yes, our host told us, for some people you meet, not officials or people in the schools, but others, there are sometimes open affronts. In a soccer match against native Irish they had heard the taunt, "Why are you staying here in my country? Why don't you go home?" Sometimes they said they saw behavior, especially against Africans, from people who wanted to make trouble. "But you see this in every country." A chorus of agreement followed the comment.

Nevertheless, under circumstances in which even a few people are hostile, there emerges a nagging feeling of suspicion, which can sometimes get in the way. There is always room for suspecting hostility in what is being said to you, as a foreigner, and it can sometimes lead to misunderstanding and overreaction in particular situations. One of the students said, "I remember a Syrian guy, a doctor [applying for a hospital post], so his professor asks him, 'What is your future plan?' So the

Syrian guy, he misunderstands the question, and he says, 'Look! I'm staying here! This is my country, if anybody likes it or not!' So the prof says, 'Sorry. Sorry. Don't misunderstand!' And he gives him the job! The professor meant, 'What are your long-term plans?' but, people understand the question as 'Are you going to stay here and compete with us for jobs?'"

Another noted that maybe there is some hostility because immigrants currently include a lot of medical doctors whose higher salaries help to drive up the costs of housing. And direct competition between skilled immigrants and natives means it is harder for native Irish to obtain certain kinds of work. One of the doctors present responded that he thought that in any direct competition between him and a native, he could pretty well guess who would get the job. "But I think this is right. Every country should take the priority for their people first. I think that if I were the prime minister, I would get in trouble for this, you know, if my people aren't working. Then, if I have extra, I'll give it to an Algerian, Turkish, or Russian."

The imam's silent thoughtfulness on this point drew attention even before he spoke, as he slowly leaned forward. "Yes, this is quite understandable. You know, it is acceptable for all mentalities. But we are talking about the *legality* of this one [i.e., this practice]. That is totally wrong. We have [a] constitution. It says [counting on his fingers], we have one, two, three, all equal. So how can you make it different [in practice]?" It was becoming increasingly clear that Khalid was shifting attention to the United States. "It's easy, yes. By nature we find it easy to understand, but if we want to talk about something noble, and some nations can stick to their constitution, then this is wrong. . . . Sure, you can say this is our mentality, and we find it everywhere. . . . But we are talking about a constitution. The constitution says this one [i.e., all are equally considered]; I would like to see it."

His voice had changed; his tone was sharp. All of us were focused on his words now: "Or don't say you have this one. And you have to change it! . . . It started in America, itself. Yes, the law in general is OK. It sounds nice, but you can't see it now! It is losing its justice. And that is why a lot of people are leaving America, especially if you are talking about the Middle East, especially Muslims. We used to 'live there' because of freedom and equality, but we can't see it there anymore! So my point, I think, that as Ahmet says, this is normal, you can't blame them, but we'd like to say that this is not perfect. If you have a constitution, and you say this is against the constitution, then *change* your constitution."

The computer specialist from Algeria who had spent only two years in Ireland protested, "But Khalid, if every country does this, then nobody has a job."

Khalid repeated the point: "If you say, 'I am the only country with such a constitution,' then you have to make it work, otherwise, admit that your practices are no fairer than anyone else's." He had the last word, making his point in a way that both supported the ideals of the United States while chiding it for what he saw as its disappointing record.

The atmosphere was softened by a redirection of the conversation to the issue of racism in general, and we could all easily agree that we were against it. Dr. J noted that there was an increase in the formation of activist anti-racist groups in Ireland, observing that while this was a welcomed sentiment it must also mean that there was a growing concern among natives about racism here. Some of these human rights groups expressed concerns that the growing numbers of immigrants were reaching a visible critical mass that might draw attention and hostility. The concern became more acute after the attacks in the United States on September 11, 2001. But the men at dinner had not personally experienced any increase in hostility during their time in Ireland.

Admittedly, this was not a representative cross-section of Irish Muslims or even of the Galway Islamic community. Not at all—this was lunch with a group of friends who had let us into their usual Friday gathering this week. These people were not in the trenches slogging it out with the working-class and poor natives, competing for entry-level, on-the-job training positions in factories and restaurants. These were men who could afford to avoid certain areas of the city, who had jobs (not restaurant work) that allowed them to make sure they were off the street after a certain hour when the threat of attack increased ("maybe ten o'clock," they said). They were aware that bad things happened in "bad places," especially places where there was excessive drinking, but they had no reason to go there. It could be dangerous or unpleasant for your wife to be out at night. They told us that after the attack on the World Trade Center and the other U.S. targets, an Afghani taxi driver in an English city was beaten so severely that he is a quadriplegic today. But they had heard of no misplaced reprisals nearly so serious in Ireland. With regard to specifically anti-Islamic reprisals, Dr. J observed, "Here in

Ireland, at least in Galway, maybe I can't generalize, but here we don't hear anything like this. Maybe they carry something inside, but we don't hear any story that they are attacking anybody."

The future of intergroup relationships in Ireland will in no small part be determined by world events and hostilities, and shaped further by the way the story of immigration is reported in the news. As everywhere, the sensational story, playing on stereotype, often crowds onto center stage: the Nigerian caught financing his entry to Ireland by trafficking drugs; someone arrested at the border with a fake passport; the truckload of illegals arriving by ferry. The imam thought that news corporations would play a key role in determining the direction of intergroup relations. They could choose to report the positive or negative, and so far he thought the job they had done was generally alright, but he had some concerns. He had been active in establishing open discussions and collaborations with the Catholic clergy on cultural differences and peaceful integration, but he was worried as to whether some of his clerical counterparts would continue to pursue a conciliatory atmosphere in the future. The imam is acutely aware that news interests and religious interests together can do much to shape public opinion, and they will, one way or the other. That is why it is so important for the Muslims and other groups to become open to each other, to let members of all groups know what they are about. He is guarded, but hopeful that there is something about Irish history that will promote a unique understanding and accommodation between Muslims and Christians there.

"The Irish have suffered a lot. Yes, today they are pro-U.S. and pro-British, but the Irish people have suffered, as in famine years. . . . That's why you see the Irish—they are very close to the Palestinian side. Why? Because they have the same feeling. This is very important. . . . In general, the public opinion is supporting the Muslims because they [the Irish] used to suffer a lot. They used to know oppression, that this is wrong. And, yes, you will find some people here in Ireland, even outside your mosque, saying 'you go home,' something like that." But you need to keep your eye on the big picture.

Khalid believed that the Irish were in a position to take on their historic role, one that reflects the experience of their recent past, to be a voice of reason and mediation between the rest of the West and the Middle East. As such this makes Ireland a reasonable place for Muslims to put down roots. The key to the future would be determined by what kind of press immigrants would get, what would be the spin that the news media and the Church would place on the growing numbers of Islamic immigrants. For now, the strategy is to open the religious culture to plain view by all interested parties, countering any preconceived images of Islam in the Western mind. That is what afforded Resmiye and me the opportunity to slip so quickly into a private living room for a feast on the Muslim holy day. Before we left the house, Resmiye had found an opportunity to slip behind one more fold of the curtain that separated the Islamic private sphere from Galway public life. She burst in and greeted and thanked the government in the kitchen.

It had been a very agreeable visit, but it was time to move on to our next stop. We thanked everyone for their cooperation and Dr. J for his and his wife's hospitality. All agreed they would show up at my house in the States for dinner one day soon. As we walked to the car, several kids ran to the imam, still in his ceremonial vestments, with a soccer ball. Some appeared to be from the Middle East, while some were clearly natives; all spoke and shouted with the same Galway accent. Khalid took off with the ball, with all the kids running after him toward the end of the cul de sac. He dribbled it in the air on his shiny pointed black shoe, flipped it for them to head back to him. We got in the car and headed for the next house, and he talked about the stranger elements of Bangkok street culture that he had witnessed on his visit there. Resmiye was still trying to work out what kind of imam this was.

GROWING UP MUSLIM IN GALWAY

"If you're looking for racism, there wasn't any." The statement came early in a conversation with a young man, a physician, whose family we visited in their Galway City home. He was more than curious about the purpose of my visit, what it was I was looking for, what I was going to do with whatever I might learn about Muslims in Ireland. I should not have been caught off guard by his wariness: he was worldly-wise and appropriately protective in his role as the eldest male in a family that was well-known within the Galway Muslim community. His father, an important man in that circle, was dead. His parents had emigrated from Pakistan in the 70s, and he and a younger brother and sister had been born and raised in Ireland.

I explained that the purpose of my visit was to learn about his experiences growing up, that I arrived with no preconceived notions about those experiences, and that he was in charge of whatever he might want to talk about in that regard. He was satisfied, and he began his narrative.

He had gone to the national schools in the 1980s, the only "Pakistani-type kid" in Galway at the time, so far as he knew. "It was fine, you know; everything was fine. Other kids were curious; teachers were curious; there wasn't as much exposure as there is today. They used to ask me to say a prayer in class; everyone thought it was cool — they always wanted to know more and more. There were questions about customs and religion, Ramadan and stuff like that. They seemed pretty interested about all that goes on. 'Why can't you do this and that?' This continued until secondary school. By then there were a few more [like me] filtering in. You know, school was fun. I never had any problems."

Different but equal, no particular problems, an object of curiosity but not in any negative way — this was a happy story of cross-cultural appreciation. It was true that the coach of the hurling team couldn't pronounce his name, so he just Anglicized it, but it was all good-natured, and he had fond memories of the coach. The fact that he played hurling in national school — "everyone thought that was a riot." He had been pretty good at the sport but gave it up in secondary school when talented kids from all over the country made it difficult to compete successfully for a slot on the team. And just as it was natural to take up an Irish sport, it was natural that he pick up the Irish language as a required academic subject at school. Being a good student, he of course excelled. "You had no excuse if you were born here." Other kids who arrived later, at age eight or ten, could get exemptions.

Religion was no real problem. It was an academic subject. "I grew up with priests. A lot of the teachers in our school were priests. I actually went to Lourdes with them. It was a three-week or four-week annual trip for the Catholic schools. They used to do a week in Lourdes, and then they'd travel around France. There was a young priest — he was also my geography teacher — and we used always to have discussions, you know. He'd feel great about bringing me to Lourdes. He'd always want my insight."

"The place is filled with hope. A lot of people came. As soon as they stepped off the plane, they were happy. I was happy to help them to do whatever they wanted to do. That was fine." He was struck that "some of it was very commercial," with shops selling trinkets and things around the shrine. I mentioned the similar commercial development near the shrine at Knock in Mayo, and as we compared notes and reactions, our talk went on easily after the guarded beginning.

In secondary school he came up against the drink culture. "The alcohol thing was big. Once you got into secondary school people were amazed if you didn't drink or smoke. You just explain to them that you can't drink. This only figured later in school, and then college. But there were always good guys, and it never was a big factor." Did it get in the way as he got older? Never. His friends had a house party for his twentieth birthday, but the rule was no alcohol. It was a huge gathering with people spilling out of the doors. He knew that a lot of Irish families kept alcohol in the house; in fact, he couldn't think of one that didn't. On the other hand, some of the young Catholic Irish he knew had taken the pledge against drinking and prided themselves in sticking to it.

The younger brother arrived at that point in the conversation, entering the cool and dark sitting room and greeting everyone. Coming from the Friday prayer, he wore a long formal shirt-jacket reaching to his knees, the Pakistani variant of the long shirt that Khalid wore under his knitted vest. He had a softer manner than his brother. He had graduated in law the previous spring and was still looking for an appropriate position. I joked that every Irish mother would love to have a doctor, a lawyer, and—I hesitated a second for effect—a priest in the family. No priest? They gently corrected me, saying that there were no priests in Islam. I started to explain the joke, but dropped it. Joking across cultures is difficult, let alone joking across religions on the weekly holy day. No more Irish-Catholic culture jokes in the Islamic community. I asked instead how the younger brother had found growing up in Galway. He answered in a word.

"Difficult."

"What was the difficult part?" I asked.

"School. Where there might be eight or nine children in the school who are identifiably different today, when we were going to school, he [indicating his brother] was the only other one. So you feel different. As you get older, you realize you can't do what they are doing. You just see that you have to get over it. Over the years you get more and more marginalized, and you realize that your group of friends is getting smaller and smaller. When you get to college, you meet more people, but in college so many of the activities are alcohol related."

There it was. Growing up in the same family and attending the same schools, these two bright and handsome brothers had had very different experiences. I was sorry that their sister wasn't home (she was away studying) for a further comparison of schoolday notes. Once again, here was a reminder that the same set of experiences produced different reactions, different stories, from two different individuals. I turned to the doctor and asked him to reflect again about whether his circle of friends seemed to shrink, as was the case for his younger brother.

"No, but I don't know. My friends were weird, though. They were pretty much like me. Everything was football or movies." Certainly there had been numerous other avenues of youthful sociability as well for young Muslims and other native Irish to share in Galway. It may simply be that the doctor found more than enough spice in the permissible options, while the interests of the lawyer grew beyond those options. How had their mother managed?

Their mother had sat quietly in a corner of the room since our arrival, between Resmiye, who had gone to sit beside her on a low stool, and the imam. She had come to Ireland as a young bride in 1977 without a word of English or knowledge of the culture. Her husband had died while her children were young. He had been instrumental in establishing the first mosque in the city in 1979. They had run the shop next door for years after the textile plant, where he was an engineer, had closed. The doctor said of his father, "He was very popular, you know. When he died, there was a line stretching all the way down the street with people coming into our house. I remember that."

I asked the mother how it had been, raising the kids on her own: Was it easy enough to keep them in line, to keep them well-behaved?

"Oh, yes, it was."

I commented, "What can she say? The doctor is sitting here."

She answered evenly, "He was very, very good. But it's very difficult in this place. You have to tell them not to do this thing, not to do that thing." In response to my questions she would direct her responses to Resmiye rather than to me.

Resmiye asked, "So they all followed their culture and never became mainstream Irish?"

"No, no, no. They all passed through phases, though. They all knew their limits. And their friends were very comforting; they know they're Muslims."

I asked what it was like for her in the beginning, just starting out. She continued to direct her comments to Resmiye, modestly refraining from speaking directly to the male stranger in her house. "Oh, different, you know. There were only ten or twenty Pakistanis here, and I was young. I had no children. . . ." She spoke in a measured way, with a slight quiver in her voice. This question-and-answer business with strangers in her sitting room was highly unusual, but the imam had requested the audience on my behalf. "People were very good—the ordinary people, the Irish. And my English wasn't good. And I was very quiet."

She was proud of her husband's role in establishing the mosque. "Today, everyone knows the mosque—taxi drivers, whoever, they know where it is."

The imam himself then asked how she kept her identity, living alone in this country. She was deliberate and spoke with a reflective dignity, as if only the absolute truth was worthy of breath. She had maintained her sense of who and what she was "by playing violin, keeping fasting, being very modest. And we had the shop, you know." Her social circle had expanded over the years. Today she had many friends, "all sorts— Pakistanis, Indians, Sikhs—and Irish. Christians."

For all the members of the family, living in Ireland offered a challenge, but also an environment where their Muslim identity could crystallize and be reconfirmed by plural religious and cultural contacts. Small everyday things reminded them of who they were; the need to make an effort reflected their cultural distinction like a mirror, defined the difference in an ongoing fashion. For example, the brothers agreed that dietary restrictions on meats not slaughtered according to religious requirements (*hallal* meats) made eating out a nuisance. "When we grew up, it was always fish, fish, fish. At graduation we wanted to eat out, so we had to find a seafood restaurant. You can't eat *anything* at McDonald's. When we would carry out, it was the fishburger—that's it." Fish, every time, at the international house of the burger. A mirror, a reminder.

Both remembered Ramadan as a challenge when they were kids. They could go to friends' birthday parties during the month, but the friends' mothers had to fix them a goody bag to take home for after sundown. But in school, fasting might be played to advantage. "Sometimes we'd get up so early in the morning to eat during fast days, we'd get tired and start to fall asleep, so they'd send us home." Once a smart lad figured that out, it could make all-day attendance optional at times. "You could use it," said the lawyer innocently. The mother, perhaps hearing the candid admission for the first time, added that sometimes the family found daylight fasts in the summer very hard in Ireland's northern latitude, where it stays light for so many hours. At one point they fasted from two a.m. until ten p.m. They would have the evening meal and wake the children at one-thirty for cereal or something, then all go back to bed and resume the fast in the morning. Resmiye and I voiced sympathetic expressions. But the boys' mother said, "The Lord gives us the strength."

A recent trip to Karachi was an eye-opener, something of a culture shock for the young Islamic Irishmen. One thing that was easier there was the observation of the weekly holy day: with everybody doing pretty much the same thing, you could just go with the flow, whereas Friday practice in Ireland could be "a bit uphill." But something they could not get used to in Pakistan was having servants around to do everything for you.

"A person has to move," said the doctor.

"You just eat and eat and eat," said the lawyer.

"People do get used to having servants," said the mother.

"Weren't you just a little tempted to bring one back?" asked the sociologist.

"No. Whenever we need something we make the younger brother do it," said the doctor, and they all laughed.

Before we left, his mother *did* ask the younger brother to do something. She asked him to take down a photo that was sitting on top of the china cabinet across from me. I had glanced at the handsome couple in it from time to time. It was her engagement photo. Her husband-to-be gazed assuredly at the camera lens; the eyes of his bride-to-be were cast down in modesty. It was the style at the time, she said. Things had changed today.

The doctor agreed. The trip to Pakistan had been revealing with regard to their own strict Galway-Islamic upbringing. "Everything we had been brought up to learn wasn't really happening over there."

"Yes, I had brought them up being very strict with them, but then they got over there and saw TV and Karachi."

An immigrant Irish paradox: it had proved effective for a single mother to raise her children within the traditional values of Pakistani Islamic culture while they played hurling and spoke Irish in party-prone Galway City. She might have had a more difficult time raising them in a changing Pakistan. She had raised good Galway Islamic boys.

"We're an anomaly," said the doctor.

Irish-Muslims present an interesting case of an immigrant culture that is dedicated formally to the goal of cultural preservation. The requirements of Islam obligate the faithful to set up communities based on religious practice. Multiple markers routinely symbolize the community's integrity: strict divisions based on gender, restrictions regarding diet, a weekly holy day different from that of the host society, multiple daily prayers, and community-based education. These will continue to set Muslims apart as communities of preservation in whatever Western nation they might settle, Ireland included.

Some of this impulse for the preservation of who one is, based on the culture of where one is from, is found in all immigrant experiences. Ethnic preservation is evident in all of the world's major cities in the distinctive neighborhoods that give city life one of its most attractive features, the diversity of its population. But for the members of most immigrant groups, there is also another impulse that has brought them to a foreign shore: the drive to get ahead, to make something of themselves personally, while they adopt the more attractive features of the host culture. The interesting factor regarding the Muslims I spoke to in Galway is that all of them were pursuing advanced professional career goals, following the immigrant dream on a track that would lead to relative affluence for themselves and their children. At the same time, they were committed to preserving religious conventions rooted in a different time and place. To a large extent the impulse of adaptation is the dilemma of Islam, and this is true even in the traditional homeplaces of the Muslim immigrants, where Western material culture with its worldly allure has arrived on the doorstep of the Eastern holy houses they have left behind. In the new lands of the emigrants, the job of keeping the faith and related cultural practices in the descending generations may prove quite difficult in the midst of material temptation. Time will tell.

Many other immigrant cultures have come to Ireland with fewer restrictions on the ways that their members may participate in the host society. Tight communities of identity, like the Islamic community that must hold itself apart, will put their cultural mark on Irish society in the future. The less culturally restricted immigrants, for whom decisions about immersing oneself in the host culture are a matter of personal choice, will also leave their mark by becoming active members and agents of change from within the host culture.

INDO-IRISHWOMEN TAKE A HAND IN SHAPING A NEW IRELAND

Among the New Irish there is a substantial and growing Indian-Irish, or Indo-Irish community. Naishadh (Nash) and Anita arrived in Ireland from Bombay in 1993, when the Irish economy was just taking off. Nash came to practice medicine and Anita to pursue further education in business and law. The couple landed on their feet, buying a home in Galway on favorable terms, bought another a little while later, and found that they liked Ireland enough to consider it a permanent home. When the first of their two boys was born, Anita decided to stay home full-time, since no Indian extended family was present to fall back on. She is an extremely energetic person, an overwhelmingly dynamic presence in any crowd, not someone who sits back to see what life will offer. She became active in Galway and Dublin charities, meeting Irish people from every walk of life. When I met with them in their first house (they were freshening up the place to let it), she had just returned from a week away in Dublin helping to host the Special Olympics.

Anita and Nash are an equally balanced pair of opposites. Nash is soft-spoken but firm in his opinions and arguments. Anita is vigorously assertive and drives home whatever she has to say with rapid-fire verbal conviction. Something of her style comes across in the following story, in which she told me about her hope to establish an extensive public garden spot in Ireland and to import plant species that are rare to Europe but may do well in the wet Irish climate. As she says, her idea is to save one or a few tracts of farmland from non-agricultural commercial development.

"So I've always been interested in greenery and conservation, that sort of thing, and Ireland is a dream in that sense because it's not called the Emerald Isle for nothing, you know?" She laughed quickly to move on in the same breath: "So with the weather that's the only benefit because as far as the rest of it goes, we're complaining all the time," waiving away the weather, "so I actually approached the government to find out if there was some way I could get involved in a conservation scheme — it was very interesting because they said it'd be only the Irish farmers that would be allowed to do that — so I asked, if I wanted to become a farmer, how would I do it? And the answer was you'd have to have held land for a period of time, that you'd actually had to have tilled and generated a certain amount of income from it, quite a small income."

While this would have sounded like a dead end to most, Anita pushed on without hesitation.

"So basically now what I've done is we have kind of picked up some land in Cavan and Roscommon and places like that, and we started participating in one of these schemes, the one called the Woodlands Conservation Scheme. So basically what that is: You promise, no matter how tempted you are, that you'll never rezone your land for industrial or residential or any other kind of commercial purpose. And that you will keep it under green cover, and the government will help you with saplings and that sort of thing.

"But it's interesting because the people you deal with there are completely different from you, having come from a big city like we did, Bombay. So one of the things that we did was we applied for permission to develop a tropical park, a tropical garden, if you like. We are applying for permission to bring the tropical plants . . . to get permission to bring rare bamboo and jasmine, stuff that can be gathered from the Far East. . . . But that again is a long term project, one of the things that I'm working with."

She said that it was her impression that while many Irish farmers are truly struggling, the big landholders, of which there are a few in every community, are not badly off — except for the isolated living, which would in no way suit her. I asked what kind of reception she gets when she shows up at their door, an Indian woman looking to buy farmland?

"Initially, I face a lot of suspicion. It's just not knowing what this person is all about: Why does she want the land? You know, what does she want to do? But once I'm able to chill out with them and say, 'Look, I don't know what to do. You tell me.' And that sort of thing, basically, I just let them lead me: 'You're the guys that know everything,' and I'm just there. . . . You know, any time you approach a new project and come into contact with new people, you're very guarded. But I think that's temporary, because I think by nature the Irish are an easygoing folk. They're trusting and gregarious. But, yes, guarded would be their first reaction."

As Anita talked, I could easily picture the guardedness of the big country landholder dissolving under the steady stream of her assured and good-natured chat. I could see the tall, terribly attractive, worldly woman asking them for help, getting them to do what she needed them to do—transfer their wealth of experience to the fledgling and charming landholder and neighbor, offer to introduce her to county officials, put in a good word. I remember being drawn irresistibly to the image of Anita running for office in a few years. She knew many influential people through her work with Irish charities, and I was sure she had impressed them with her sharpness and drive. In the space of one meeting we were friends, and she invited Resmiye and me for dinner the following weekend. I asked if she and Nash knew of other Indo-Irish friends of mine, Cauvery and Prakash Madhavan. They knew of them, might have met them, but weren't sure.

I had met Cauvery and Prakash the previous December. I had stayed with them then at Straffan, outside Dublin. When I had e-mailed Cauvery to ask if she would talk with me about her life in Ireland, she insisted that Mary Kate, who was traveling with me on that trip, and I not stay in some hotel or B and B. I initially contacted Cauvery after reading her first novel, *Paddy Indian*. In it she tells the story of a surgeon from India who emigrates to Ireland and becomes involved with his chief surgeon's daughter. The book provides insight into the sophisticated foreigner being caught in the subtle throes of culture shock, making compassionate sense of the Indian immigrant experience in Ireland. When I discovered that Cauvery herself had immigrated in 1987 with her surgeon husband, raising questions about the links between biography and fictional storytelling in my mind, I knew I had to talk with her.

Their more or less permanent arrival as immigrants in 1987 makes Prakash and Cauvery old-timers among the New Irish. Cauvery says that when she came to Ireland, you would "turn around on the street" if you saw a person of color in the crowd—"I've done it myself." But things have changed. "Just look around you, at the number of different faces and accents that there are in Ireland today. It's a world apart from what was out there five years ago. Today you could step out onto Grafton Street and be transported to any city in the world. You couldn't say that eight years ago."

Cauvery became an avid participant-observer during the period of rapid economic and social change in Ireland. In *Paddy Indian* there is very little reflection of friction between the newcomers from India and the native-born Irish. The book focuses much more on the dilemma of whether to become uprooted from one's culture, to abscond with oneself, a self that parents consider a jewel in their personal store of wealth in the world. That is the part of her work of fiction that reflects something like the Madhavans' tentative putting down of roots in the Irish soil. Cauvery admitted to one other piece of drollery as being a touch autobiographical. In the background of *Paddy Indian* there is a hopelessly happy Indian couple who love to cook and eat and have a good time. The husband is the envy of the bachelor surgeon, who continuously reminds his close friend that he is "a lucky bastard." As she drew the parallel between the happy couple and their own situation, Cauvery laughed and looked at Prakash.

Given their years of experience in the country, Cauvery's close and nuanced observations of Irish life, and the fact that she and Prakash are raising three kids who were born and have lived all of their young lives in Ireland, I was very interested in the Madhavans' story. By and large, their experiences in Ireland have been very positive. As professionals, people whose personal bearing reflects the dignity and social standing of their families of origin, and as thoroughly pleasant and outgoing cosmopolitans, they would have been insulated somewhat from some of the daily insults that could be experienced by people of color anywhere in the West. And yet their personal experiences are framed by the wider social question: Just how are people of color, of any social standing, perceived and accepted by other members of society? Cauvery and Prakash brought the gift of extraordinary perceptiveness and openness to this question.

Cauvery reflected: "If I say, 'No, I haven't found any racist attitudes; I haven't had any racist incidents,' people just think you're being nice. I'm not being nice, and I may be unusual, but I haven't." It wasn't until some time in 1999, when the news media was full of reports about a surge in the influx of immigrants and asylum seekers, that she even thought much about herself as a foreigner. She was suddenly a member of a publicly stigmatized category of persons, and it affected her public behavior. Since the increase in attention that made foreigners a social issue, she would not go out unless she was "decently dressed. Before, I might go out is some old track suit and go about the shops and couldn't care less. But I never do that now. And I always make sure that the kids are decently dressed. And that is actually quite sad. Because nobody's ever said anything. Nobody's ever turned round and said, 'Oh, look at her. . . . You look like a refugee!'" She worried self-consciously for a moment about what this might reflect about how she herself perceives the refugee image and why she might want to distance herself and her children from being perceived as such. She concluded that it was true, her own self-image in public had been affected by perceived public concerns about foreigners, and in the odd instance this even affected her behavior toward native-born Irish people.

She recalled the time when her mother was visiting and they had been standing in line at a cinema multiplex. "There were huge lines of impatient and cross people, and for some reason I got it into my head that someone might pass a negative remark, and I was feeling very protective of my mother, and I was ready to shoot back that 'Well, my husband saves Irish lives!' Or, 'I'm as Irish as you are!' But a half dozen people spoke to me, and all they said was 'Isn't it dreadful that we have to wait so long?' and that sort of thing. And everyone was being friendly, and there I was feeling so foolish in my own head. I was so ready! You become paranoid."

But this did not stem from anything Cauvery or members of her family experienced personally. Nevertheless, there is the general impression, a projection of the common knowledge, that personal affronts based on perceptions of racial difference do occur in Irish cities. People, strangers, have come up to her after this or that nasty hate-based assault was reported in the news and said, "Isn't it awful that a few are creating such a bad impression of the rest of us?" An interesting social reality is being created by how quickly things are changing in Ireland. The reality is balanced, on the one side, by a general perception of the emergence of racial tensions, and on the other, by the efforts of some individuals to distance themselves from those tensions. It is a reality that dances on flickering glimpses in public, too brief to do much more than raise questions about what is going on. Was that a look? Was that a slight?

One of the first things Cauvery and Prakash talked about were the kinds of stories featured in news reporting. Cauvery was quite animated by the topic. She thought there was a tendency toward the sensational in the press that potentially reinforced an atmosphere that people were trying to distance themselves from. A favorite story, repeated monthly it seemed, was about crowding in the hospitals, particularly in maternity wards, and the bottom line had to do with the high proportion of non-native births in the country. "When you read it, you say to yourself, God, certainly 60 percent—here I'm just making up some sensational figure—of the women in these wards can't be refugees! But when you think of the word they're using, 'non-nationals,' you associate it with foreigners as immigrants and asylum seekers, that sort of thing. Ireland is full of people from elsewhere, the Yankee sector, etc. It just means non-native, not refugees—they could be Australian or English or other Europeans, or Americans. Sure, we're all here legitimately! Are we not allowed to have babies? It's such a silly way of reporting it ... even if we say they're accounting for 20 percent of all births, people are shocked. It appears that people are coming to Ireland to have babies here and get permanent resident status. . . . The number of asylum seekers and refugees among the non-nationals is miniscule."

Prakash added that the picture is not made clearer by the fact that, although it is true that the numbers remain proportionately small, some visitors do time their arrival in the country to coincide with the birth of a child. Legislation was pending (and later passed) at the time of this interview to withdraw the legitimating claim to residency offered by the birth of a child.

But while public opinion might be soured at some point by the "social problem" nature of the immigration story, and although there were periodic reminders that race was an issue, the Madhavans found much in their personal experience that indicated open acceptance of them and their children. They had always found it easy to make friends in the Irish cities in which they had lived over the years. Until recently they had made no special effort to associate with people from India, even though Prakash knew of several colleagues from Madras and from his medical school cohort living in Ireland. Given the press of his work, they had little time to seek out Indo-Irish friends—and little reason, since they had always found a rich social life among native colleagues and neighbors. Recently they had made the move to Straffan, a village in the

Dublin suburbs. After deciding on the move, Cauvery did have second thoughts. As far as she knew—and this turned out to be the case—they would be the only immigrant family of color in the village. What kind of reception would they, and especially the children, receive? The kids and the parents were especially nervous about the children having to start anew in a strange school. It was 2001, and the new influx of immigrants and the public concerns surrounding it were in full swing.

Before her family moved in, Cauvery spent a couple of days at the new house cleaning it up. She stopped at one of the shops nearby at lunchtime for a candy bar and a bag of crisps. The proprietor, a woman, asked if she was moved in yet—apparently the news of the Indian family's arrival in town had made all the rounds. "No, not yet, just cleaning."

"And you're alone, up there all day? Just wait a minute." And she left Cauvery alone in the shop. She came back with freshly made sandwiches on a plate, hot soup, and apple tart and insisted that Cauvery stay there in the shop until she had it all eaten.

"And I was, well actually, I was so filthy in my old clothes, and the next person that came in the shop—I actually hid behind this huge display, because I felt like I looked like this poor person who had knocked at the door and had asked for a bit of something to eat, begged a meal, that sort of thing. It was brilliant!"

Yet she remained a little apprehensive, maybe more than a little, regarding the move to the new community. How would her kids be received at school? She drove them to school on the first day and left them standing in line waiting to go in. For a moment she was nearly overcome with anxiety, about having wrenched them out of their old school, where they had been quite comfortable, and plopped them down in the lap of the unknown. She thought, "What have we done to them?" As she left, her head was lowered, trying to hide a few stray tears, "and as I looked up, there were four women, and they were my four neighbors, and they were saying, 'Oh, c'mon now, they'll be fine. Wait 'til you come pick them up, and you'll see their smiling faces. Come on and have a cup of tea.' And that's how I met my four neighbors. I'd never met them before, and all they knew was that there was a foreign couple moving into this house, and they spotted me in the school, the only dark-skinned Irish at the school." A year later the kids told me they were quite fond of their new school and their lives in the community.

The Madhavans all were delighted with their new home, their neighbors, the village in which they lived, Ireland. I asked again about the other side of things. I wasn't looking for trouble, etc., but wanted the whole picture, and Prakash and Cauvery did not have to reach far for it.

Prakash answered first: "Well, I suppose that the truth of the matter is that for me to have got the job I've got [a hospital consultancy position] is the exception rather than the rule. I would say I was the first non-Irish-born person to have gotten a position [equivalent to this] in a teaching hospital in Dublin. It's to do with the colleagues I've got. They don't conform to the old-boy network, things like that. But there are plenty of stories of people who have been well-trained, etc., who have been messed about by the system. Other people have had bad experiences. Yes, it's there *all* the time, in different kinds of ways. There isn't overt racism around, but it's the very subtle things that people say and do and imply when they tell you certain things. For me it's blatantly obvious what they are trying to tell a 'black person.' It hasn't happened to me, but I can see it happening all around me." When I asked if this had increased in, say, the last five years with expanding immigration, he said just the opposite appeared to be the case.

"There is now more of a willingness to accept—the Irish establishment realizes that there aren't enough people around, home grown, that can do the job, so you have to look outside. So that's a sea change. For that to filter down, it's going to take another generation. . . . Part and parcel of being an immigrant is having to put up with attitudes that see you taking a job from a native, but I'm willing to put up with that, because that's just a part of human nature. For me, if people say, 'you're in a job that an Irishman didn't get,' I say, 'Well, yes, and I'm proud of it.'"

Cauvery broke in to say, not without a hint of admiration, "But not everybody can be so cut and dried about it. You can say, 'Yes, that's the way it is. . . . That's your nature . . . you know."

"Well, yes, I suppose I am an aggressive son of a gun."

Cauvery reminded him of one incident in which a female patient at the hospital refused to be seen by him, and he told the nurse, "Fine, let her wait for someone else." But in the general case, he admits that the cumulative affect of slights, real or suspected, can build up.

Cauvery spoke of a recent gathering of Indian MDs working in Ireland in which she was troubled by the line the conversation took at some points, although she recognized the kinds of experiences that it was rooted in. "As I was sitting talking to them, I found it very jarring a number of times when somebody said, 'Oh, you know we fellows . . .' meaning 'when it comes to us Indians in Ireland.' . . . Maybe for us it's been somehow different, and thank God it's been." For others seeking to settle professionally, there is a dilemma. "I see them being almost stuck," she said, "unable to go back because they want to give their children opportunity."

Yet, even in Prakash's case, he had his doubts about the chances for advancement—certainly not about himself or his skills or training—but about the selection process. He was passed over for the first post he had been encouraged by colleagues to apply for, in fact, but determinedly sought and received the second. And once on the job he has seen to it, through continuously sustained effort, that no one could be seen as more deserving of the position. The widespread perception of discrimination in promotion is followed naturally by concerns once an immigrant attains an elevated rank. If you are Prakash, it is all business as usual; you just work harder and watch your back.

Cauvery has found within the social sphere of neighboring a much less competitive course of assimilation. "I have not had to be an outstanding neighbor to have my neighbors like me," she said jokingly. But she and Prakash both realized that not all immigrants share their comfortable social circumstances. She said, "There are parts of Dublin where there is a more ghettoized foreign community. And all of the things that you hear in the media seem to come out there." She reflected that it might have as much to do with education and ability to speak the language, which she does with an accent much more Dublin than Madras, than it does with being foreign or less economically well-off. But here she second-guessed herself midstream and said, "There are certain parts of Dublin that I wouldn't go into myself. There are parts of Dublin the internationals would not go into, say, after half-eleven. Ah, they'd be nervous, and that's something that's happened only in the last two years."

She reflected for another moment and added, "And if I said that to any of my neighbors, they'd only laugh at me. They'd tell me that I'm paranoid. They don't see it, and they don't feel it. Having said that now, neither have I. Certainly, though, you hear this on the TV and radio: 'Chinese student slashed by mob,' or 'Nigerian man stabbed to death.'

And perfect strangers will come up to *me* and say, 'Isn't it dreadful what they're doing to them?' or 'Isn't it dreadful what happened to that Chinese man?' It's almost like they're feeling guilty for the rest, or for a small minority. They wouldn't know now that I've lived in Ireland for years, or that I know exactly what they're talking about."

RAISING THE NEXT GENERATION OF NEW IRISH

The two Indo-Irish families share many experiences. Chief among them is that they are raising children who have only been to India to visit, like the Pakistani lawyer and doctor brothers in Galway. What it has been like to raise second-generation New Irish immigrants has been a "mixed" experience, said Anita. For her two boys, "the obvious advantage is the fact that you can take a lot of things for granted [in Ireland]. The fact that it's so much safer, society is so much more open." And, according to Anita, a person with a very positive outlook on life in general, there has actually been an advantage to having darker skin. "When we were in India, we admired fair skins, and when you come here, everybody is so jealous of your color. Everybody says 'I wish I could be that brown.' And so our kids have a great advantage. In the school play, that sort of thing, everybody says that these kids have to be in there because they're so good-looking."

The disadvantage from Anita's perspective? She answered that "the disadvantage has nothing to do with the fact that it's Ireland, just that it's *such* a small place. I never missed my family, selfishly, until I had kids. But you really miss these things, others to teach them our language, to teach them our culture. . . . We've said that we made the conscious decision to live in Ireland so we wouldn't try to make them *that* Indian, you know, *as* Indian as we might like them to be. So they speak better Irish than they speak our language; they know more about Irish music than they do about ours. . . . If you ask my kids, as far as they're concerned, they're Irish, and India's this exotic holiday destination that they go to once in a while to get spoiled rotten by their grandparents."

Cauvery and Prakash related similar tales of living in a house full of Irish children. Prakash said of his three children that "all they know is Ireland, and they are by birth and everything else as Irish as the man next door." The parents were satisfied with the national school system, where they believed the education their kids were receiving was on a par with what they would get in India. Cauvery qualified this observation: mathematics and sciences might be two or three times as demanding in Madras, but that was not necessarily better. "Life in Madras would be far more stressful. Every year from age four on, the kids would have to pass an exam to move on." In Ireland they would have a far better chance of attending an EU university, their parents' goal for them.

Cauvery and Prakash carried around pictures from India in their heads, of city streets teeming with people with advanced degrees. A simple university education would not be enough, wherever their kids might end up. The oldest would start in a private school the following year. Prakash said of that, "It's going to cost us an arm and a leg, but, as we say, the most important thing is to give them a proper education. After that, they may twiddle their thumbs, but that's on their heads. We will have given them a proper start in life." And Ireland, strategically, is part of that proper start.

The cultural aspect of their children's training is an issue that has emerged gradually. The Madhavans had never quite determined to stay in Ireland until recently, following Prakash's advancement. Up to that point they were always "eighteen months from going home" in their minds. They had always figured that the kids would have plenty of opportunity to "become Indian" once they got back to India. "We thought we'd go back; they'd get all the Indian culture they needed into them. But from the moment we knew we were going to stay, we actually have made a concerted effort." They pledged to each other that "from now on" they were going to all the cultural events at the Indian embassy, become more active in the Indo-Irish Society that observes Indian festivals, and look up and attend events at the India Club. Their kids might be growing up Irish, but they would know something of where they (that is, their parents) were from.

The results were mixed, apparently. While the family stuck to its plan "to sort of go for—well, everything Indian," the kids of course remained thoroughly steeped in and identified themselves with the host society environment. When I stayed with them in their summerhouse in west Cork, six months after my first visit, the kids talked, bickered, and played like any Irish kids I had ever known. The oldest, teenaged Sagari, was a vigilant monitor of her mother's use of Irish colloquialisms, ready to pounce on any slight misstep. When it was time for Maya, the youngest daughter, to join her older brother and sister in dressing up for Halloween for the first time, she said, "Oh great, I'm going to dress up to be an Indian [that is, someone from India]." Clearly, she was Irish the rest of the year.

The fact that kids born in Ireland are Irish, wherever the parents may have come from, is self-evident, simply stated, but in everyday experience that fact may at times be overlooked. It may catch the unwary off guard and be absolutely mystifying. Multiculturalism is still a new enough phenomenon in Ireland that, despite the intent to get it right, natives and visitors unused to it can behave in silly ways. Anita's two boys were approached by a group of tourists at a Galway shopping center recently, "and one of the ladies kept on asking the kids 'Where are you from?'" And her son "kept saying, 'Newcastle,' you know, and she was thinking Newcastle in the U.K., and he kept on saying, 'No, Newcastle down the road, by the hospital,' and she kept on saying, 'Yes, but where are you *from?*' And this went on for *five or ten minutes!* And I could hear, but I waited to see, and those guys couldn't understand, and they were saying 'Newcastle, *Galway!*' 'But *where are you from originally?*' So finally I said, 'Look, what the kids are trying to say is that they're Irish, as far as they're concerned.'"

Anita and Nash had at one point determined to speak Hindi at home, but once the kids went to school, they would always respond to their parents in English. Then matters got worse. The kids learned Irish. Now that they were sufficiently fluent so that they could communicate with each other, said Anita, "they have secrets from Nash and I! Well, I've sworn I'm going to learn Irish this year."

The kids were of the age that they had begun to follow Irish pop music. Anita related the following story: "In January we were in London for this course that Nash was doing. And we were walking on Oxford Street, passing every culture you can imagine. And there's this song that Sinead O'Connor sings in Irish [and Anita repeats a line] which is quite a big hit, and my younger one is belting this at the top of his lungs. And there are these two men, and they must have been of Irish stock or whatever, and they turned to look, completely surprised. And one of the guys comes back and says, 'Like where are you from — are you from around here?' Obviously, in the U.K. you've got all kinds, but a person looking like *that* and singing Irish! 'How come you're singing in Irish? Do they teach that in school?' And I said, 'No, we're visiting from Galway.

We're Irish.' So that's the way it is with them, and we haven't consciously tried to change that, because, as Nash was saying, we made the decision to come to this country—they didn't choose that. They were born and brought up here, and they consider themselves Irish, and I think it's important for them to be able to do that as much as they can. . . . I feel it's important for them to feel that they belong completely. And apparently they do. So hopefully, that won't change."

What both sets of Indo-Irish parents were hopeful of was that the mild slights and rebuffs that they have faced would not become more pronounced in the years ahead as their children make their way in the New Ireland. They would do everything possible to give their kids a proper start in life. But so much of what lies in store for the next generation is really beyond the control of immigrant parents to Ireland, especially people of color. The future is in the hands of the native Irish and depends on how prepared they are—how prepared they will be—to welcome and respect newcomers and their native Irish offspring.

It is early days yet. Widespread immigration is still a novel phenomenon. You can hear every reaction imaginable from Irish people today on the topic. Many remain distracted by the asylum seeker issue, and spontaneous narratives on the immigration topic usually stray in that direction. I have heard a dozen times: "We don't mind all these people coming in, welcome to them, if they want to work and get ahead. But it's these ones sneaking in, and they don't want to work, or the government won't let them for whatever reason—and they're put up in hotels or caravans, and I'm paying for them with the taxes that are killing me. That's what we don't want here!"

At the extreme, at least a few among the natives indulge themselves in xenophobic paranoia. I have endured, in the interest of my work, narratives based on worn-out tales of international Jewish conspiracies, now extended ironically to include all Middle Easterners, from a sullen few men nursing their pints at the local. But, for the moment, the high-minded people of good will still set the tone, and the circles that my New Irish friends travel in allow them to feel at ease and at home in their adopted country. Still, they are aware that there are times and places they ought to avoid, that the level of acceptance they enjoy is in part a function of their economic and professional status. We are all aware that the stories told by kitchen workers and laborers would be somewhat different. And we all look warily to the future.

So much of the future of interracial and intercultural relations in Ireland appears to depend on maintaining indefinitely the era of Irish economic ascendancy in Europe. So much depends on whether the native Irish have within them some mysterious quality that will allow them to continue to absorb numbers of highly visible immigrants who will find their way to Ireland in the future. And there are the questions of how the news media will choose to frame the immigrant story, which immigrant stories the media will choose to feature, whether small-minded politicians will appeal to mistrust and disappointment that may grow among the natives, and how the natives will treat such appeals.

Meanwhile, the newcomers are coming to stay, just as elsewhere in Europe and the wider world, where millions every year shift among nations. One of the paradoxes of globalization is that it is producing novel forms of culture, cultural hybridization, at the same time that it works to homogenize the world into a single consumer culture. Imam Sallabi meets his multinational congregation where they are, as the Irish version of Islam emerges and takes shape, a brand-new addition to a culturally diverse world. The roots of the Irish imams and the people they serve go down into the rich soil of the island. Anita, a city woman from Bombay, becomes an Irish farmer to preserve green space by transforming farm and woodlands into subtropical gardens, where bamboo and jasmine will grow alongside native holly and heather. Cauvery Madhavan's novel about an immigrant Indian surgeon who is not her surgeon-husband artfully interprets the intersection of Ireland's current historical transformations and the lives of newly arrived immigrants like herself becoming Indo-Irish or Paddy Indians. As such the New Irish become key participants and interpreters of the contemporary "What is Ireland?" puzzle.

The former land of emigration has now become the place where immigrants will help us understand the natives. We add their stories to the mix. Ireland is a place of traditions carried on the eye and in the ear of people around the world; it is a clever place of dramatic economic advancement that is not clearly of its own making or clearly to the benefit of many of its own people; it is not a place at all because it exists in the mind or in the heart, and it cannot be located on a map; but it *is* a place to the people who come there from somewhere else to stay and who find they have arrived home once they get there.

CHAPTER 8

Global Ireland and Places Called Home

Anyhow, exile's no longer exile, however far away we may be;

let us be in the dip of the deepest valley, or skylined on the highest

hill, we can return now to a native land in less time than it takes a

devotee to say a fervent prayer. And as for an Irish exile, Ireland

has a long arm, which, though it may not be able to drag him

back, never lets go.

(O'Casey [1957] 1994)

Ireland's televised match with Germany was about to get underway early in the 2002 World Cup. Minutes before the game began, the streets of Kilkenny were full of people. It was more or less a normal business day, except for the undercurrent of anticipation that grew stronger as game time approached: people worked, walked, talked, smoked faster. Then, at the stroke of the hour, there was near silence on the narrow public ways. Very few pedestrians, virtually no vehicle traffic. Little by little a muffled clamor built from inside the public houses, sounding from the street like crowds of people trapped in giant drums somewhere nearby. There were hastily penned notes taped to the front doors of closed shops: "Closed for the game." "Open for normal hours after the match." "World Cup, sorry."

A few places stayed open: the internet café, a bookstore, an alternative culture imports shop. The young woman behind the counter of the imports shop asked if she could help me. I told her I was looking for a birthday present, and she seemed happy enough to enter into the spirit of the event, saying what she would like if it were her birthday. Her accent was Australian, and I asked what brought her to Ireland. Her people were originally from here, having emigrated more than a century ago, and she was the first to come back, to try to get a sense of the place. She had always felt a strong connection. I asked if working in the shop helped her to do that, to meet lots of Irish coming through the door each day, to work alongside young natives. No. The only way she could connect with what she had come to find was to be by herself. She had a friend with a small place along the west coast, and she was able to stay there on her own when the friend was away. In that solitude she found the real Ireland—where all was quiet, no modern human intrusions, just the sea and the wind. She could take herself back to the place her family had left, centuries before they had left it.

We found a suitable present, and as I was about to leave, I commented on how quiet the big town had become. "Yes," she said, and wondered why that was. "The World Cup," I said. "What's that?" I explained that Ireland was playing Germany in an international soccer match. "Oh, I don't care a thing about sports," she said. The Ireland she was looking for, the Ireland she had found, was different from the one that the rest of Kilkenny wildly celebrated later that afternoon, as Ireland scored in injury time to tie the heavily favored Germans 1 to 1. Many of the businesses never reopened after the game; many workers never made it back to the shops or construction sites. The tying goal was as good as a victory, as I was told many times that afternoon. The celebrations poured out of the bars and into the streets. The young Irish-Australian woman in the shop, who had brought such a different sense of where to find Ireland with her when she came, would have found little of what she would consider authentic Ireland on these streets. She had found her homeland by reaching back through a particular solitude to a time beyond memory or history, and this noisy human clutter would not distract her from it.

The placelessness of the Irish homeland is a wonderfully accommodating device that allows Irish people to be at home in their Ireland as a personal matter of fact. It allows the distant descendants of emigrants and newly arriving immigrants alike to lay claim to what is theirs with the surety of natives: the genuineness of their sense of themselves defies challenge. Jane, who had never been to Ireland, lay claim to her Irish roots in no uncertain terms at a dinner gathering one night in the U.S. Midwest. She thumped the table and declared herself to be one of the "black Irish, the most beautiful people in the world!" Since she spoke with her usual conviction, no one in the party asked for a definition or for qualification—she was a striking and active woman of seventy-five who typically commanded agreement from those around her when she spoke this way. I called on her at her daughter's house the next day to hear more about her Irish connections over a cup of tea. The picture that emerged had to do with a soft sense of attachment that provided Jane with an important piece of her identity based on half-seen, half-sensed fragments of genealogy, sentiment, and personal conviction. There was a link between what she remembered of her childhood and her father, and something that had caught her eye in a photo some friends had taken in Ireland in recent years, where the sky and land often appeared "dark and brooding." She liked that; it suited her as a portrait of a personal homeplace.

Her father, who gave the family its Irish name (Glavin), was a tantalizing mystery for her. He had been "a very locked up, silent man." She got nothing solid from him about what being Irish might mean, but as a little girl she had been proud of the name she had through him. From childhood onward she had to make up the substance of her connection to Ireland, the place she later recognized in the pictures — the connection that had evolved from her relationship to her central Irishman, her dark and brooding father. All she knew of him was that he had at one time lived in a boarding house, kept a pet cockroach, and had friends who had a pair of parrots that they taught to say "naughty" things. When still very young she had tended her father while he died slowly. She remembered how he got up and washed his face and combed his hair just before he laid down to wait for the last time. So *this* was what a dying Irishman might do at the end.

When I asked if she could say any more about her father's ties to Ireland, she said that she could fill pages, but somehow little else found its way onto my tape, aside from the fact that "he loved that Galway song." She added little else to the memory of her father, whose Irish name she was sad to give up when she married her German husband and lost that public badge of who she was. What is it that makes this story so perfectly recognizable? Is it the need to understand our attachment to primary origins, an attachment that depends upon a few fragments of memory in some instances? Perhaps it is the glimpse of a homeland in drab colors, mirroring the fading portrait of a father with an Irish name who might or might not have been able to say more about the place his people had come from, himself generations removed from the immigrant saga. Only bits of biography fill in questions about a place beyond memory, with a pet roach and naughty parrots standing in for wee people or brave rebels draped in the tricolor.

Here deeply personal meanings authenticate a person's claim to her origins. How many Irish-Americans will hear this claim and say, "Yes, that's it; I've the name, and if that's not enough, I have the memory of the scrape of the chair across the floor, the smell of cigarette smoke off the sleeve of his jacket, the newspaper crumpled on the floor by his feet as he dozed in the living room on Sunday; yes, that's it; that's my link"? They will say, "My childhood was real and personal, and that's the proof of who I am, and it may be a bit complicated about why that makes me Irish, but there was that Galway song." Maybe the homeland was more the Bronx or Boston or Detroit than Ireland itself, but there is no denying that the hometown was a real place where the real Irish came from.

In her life Jane had joined no Irish organization, had no particularly Irish friends (there was that one who had masses said for people, that sort of thing), did not surround herself with Irish things (but she had a Claddagh ring somewhere and liked Riverdance very much, and of course her son loved *The Quiet Man*), and although she had never been to Ireland, she thought it would be nice, someday. She did not in any way pursue Irishness. She was just Irish, always had been, always would be; that was just *it*, she said. "It's within myself. But, see, I always felt very alone. I'm very much of a loner. And my Irishness was just part of my special me that I didn't share with anybody. I didn't go talking about myself. You don't learn anything that way." Our conversation had provoked her to action, though: when her daughter came into the room she announced, "Karen, Bill has convinced me we should go to Ireland!" Actually, the idea of a trip, as such, had barely entered the conversation; the need for a trip had emerged on its own. But if she does go, I think I can guess something about the Ireland she would bring back to her homeland, and I wonder whether she will come back with the same Ireland intact when she returns to the United States.

At times people who are open and hungry for the experience of home, who are clever like Jane and able to sift through many layers of experience, find that multiple Irelands exist in the world in addition to the ones they carry in their head. They are, at least for a time, disconcerted by new ways to look at the place. My friend Mary Kate, who traveled and worked with me in Ireland, was still sorting out her attachment to home months after she returned to the United States.

MARY KATE'S NOT IRISH

When Mary Kate came with me to Ireland to help with video and audio recording, it was her second time there, the first being a flying visit of a few days. We visited a branch of her family in Mayo after we had stopped with Cauvery and Prakash Madhavan in Dublin for a couple of days. Cauvery, who has strong ties of identity with Ireland, asked Mary if she had deepened her experience of herself as Irish as a result of the trip. Mary, not answering quite directly, said that she was born in the States and that her great grandparents were the ones who came over. She had heard about the family farm and was looking forward to the visit very much. Then Cauvery, who had emigrated from India to live in Ireland in 1987, described the area in Mayo where the farm is to Mary, the red-haired and freckled descendant of the farmers. "It's beautiful. Killala, particularly, is just so beautiful," Cauvery said with whispered feeling. "All of Ballina, so beautiful." Cauvery loves all of the natural areas of Ireland without exception, but she does think Killala exceptional.

On our way to Killala the next day, we stayed overnight in a small town in Roscommon. It was Saturday evening, and we walked down to a bar, where we got talking to the local people sitting on either side of us. Mary got stuck talking most of the time to Lewis (not his real name), a local man of middle age who had apparently started drinking a good while before we arrived. From time to time I thought that maybe I should rescue her, but she is able to take care of herself and seemed to be enjoying the conversation well enough.

After we left the packed pub, Mary Kate made an emphatic declaration: "I'm not Irish! I don't feel Irish. I'm the all-American girl from Illinois. I'm a Midwest American. That's how I feel over here; that's who I am." It challenged my preconception of how Mary would react to the Ireland written all over her face. I asked what provoked her, and whether there was room for some sort of dual identity, a this *and* that, rather than a this *or* that. She stuck to the revelation, saying she knew who she was at the core, at heart, and that's what mattered—and that if it was good enough for her, it should be good enough for me. "You know who you are," I said. But I thought to myself, I will get another chance to revisit the identity question soon enough. How will she react to being "home" on the family farm? I looked forward to a reverse epiphany.

Killala was described to us as a half hour's drive from the little town with the pub, and it only took us two. In driving rain we missed the "you can't miss it" marker, a bridge off to one side that would indicate a crucial right turn. Mary was navigator, but as she was only too ready to point out, I also had two eyes in my head and presumably had also been watching the road. Eventually, after three stops for directions and one wrong house ("Sorry for disturbing your Sunday dinner"; "No problem"), we were there. She had never met the relatives, but they greeted both of us like the long-lost kin (in Mary's case) and countrymen (at the moment in doubt for her) they took us for. As far as kinship, a potentially strong bond between these people was separated by generations from the time of emigration. With the aging of the Irish branch of the family, a strategy for the passing on of the land had only just recently been worked out on the Ireland side of the family, with some previous discussion of whether Mary's brother might re-emigrate after generations to take over the farm. On the U.S. side, there was not much depth or breadth to the existing pool of Freeston relatives, so the Irish kin were a family treasure.

Now, here we were on the farm, and we sat before a cut-peat fire on Killala Bay near the north coast of Mayo, with rain lashing the windows, surrounded by people — most of whom were middle aged and who spoke with country accents — in a sitting room decorated to the highest comfy standards. Her people were *so* delighted to meet Mary for the first time, and she was clearly deeply touched by the welcome. I watched the non-Irish-American. She looked perfectly at home among these people, laughed and joked easily with them, almost as if she had stopped for her usual Sunday visit. This was a long distance from any Chicago suburb I had ever known.

The talk was about local history and economy, and places and events in America. Our hosts were able to tell us a great deal about Ireland, and it appeared that there was little we could tell them about the United States that they had not already heard or read. The conversations were animated, several going on simultaneously. Mary and I sat on kitchen chairs that had been set for us in the middle of the living room, side by side. The five relations were arrayed in a half-circle before and around us to either side, young cousin Angela to Mary's left and Uncle Vincent to my right. The arrangement actually worked rather well, with the two women more or less on Mary's side of the room, and the three men on mine. Occasionally a question or point was made across gender lines, and as the voices rose to be heard above the cross-talk, things might get a bit jumbled, especially with the complication of foreign accents — Mary spoke Midwestern and I a kind of East Coast New York–ese. Tea and sandwiches along with two kinds of cakes were served, and Mary and I were encouraged to eat. The sandwiches and tea were welcome on a cold and rainy late December evening.

After sandwiches and a couple of drinks, and after the men in the room each felt obliged to voluntarily deny ever having made *poteen*, talk turned to the prospects for war between Iraq and whatever coalition the current U.S. leadership had managed to pull together. Each person in the room marveled that the answer to the question of whether there would be war rested in the hands of the U.S. president. Their concern went beyond the issue of general competency to a conviction that Bush and his henchmen were committed to accessing and administering Iraqi oil reserves on terms favorable to the West and multinational corporate interests. Neither Mary nor I was disposed to disagree. In our travels and visits, and a certain amount of pub time, we had met one or two native Irish who thought well of the sitting U.S. president. But to put this in some perspective, we had met and talked to *a lot* of people. Most might bring up the Bush competency question gingerly at first, but once they learned that they were among political comrades, they fired away with enthusiasm.

Mary Kate's kin were no exception to the rule. "Gangsters" was how Vincent referred to Bush and company. These people were not the kind to be wishy-washy about political issues. Looking at leftist-feminist Mary Kate again, I thought I saw a further family resemblance. With regard to Irish national politics, while it wasn't clear to us whether quite everyone in the room agreed, there were expressions of genuine political delight among older family members over the fact that a number of Sinn Fein candidates for national office had got in at the spring elections. Fianna Fail was the rich man's party, and Fine Gael not much better. It was time Irish politicians, honest and otherwise, who represented the dominant parties heard the message: there was another choice.

When someone in the room declared Gerry Adams a good and honorable man who kept his word and an eye on the interests of the common people, there was no debate. When the talk turned back to geopolitics, it struck me that these people might live in as remote a region as you are likely to find in Europe, but they were well informed, earnestly engaged by the issues of the day, and, for our money, clear in their assessments. As night fell and the dark closed around us sitting by the fire within sight of the coast, we resisted the inevitable — the need to take our leave for the long drive to our next destination through fog and rain. But we did have a distance to go. They came out into the wind and wet to say their good-byes, and I as well as Mary was pressed to say that there was at least a chance that she or I would be back. I thought Mary was the one more likely to follow through.

Mary Kate was full of the glow of the welcome she had received as we drove south through the thick wet darkness. Her people had accepted and liked her, didn't want us to go, wanted us to return, valued their connection to the long-lost cousin. Mary was clearly and openly touched. So I asked her as she was still caught in the mesh of sentimental leave-taking, when she was off balance. "Mary, are you Irish?" It was a harder question now than the evening before. She grinned. She was not ready to give in: "I'm an American from the USA. Nothing can or will change that. That's where I'm from; that's who I am. But I'm an American with family members in Ireland who I care about a lot."

"OK." I thought I probably wouldn't bring it up again.

I didn't. She did. But it was not until September, nine months later. We were sitting on my back porch and talking about her new graduate program in women's studies. By then, her recent experience in Ireland had had time to percolate through her layers of cultural identity. She interrupted something she was saying mid-sentence and changed the subject. "You know, since I've been back, I know that I'm really Irish. I tell everyone that I am now. I tell them I've been home twice, and the last time I really got to know some of the people. I feel such a strong attachment to the place. That's where my people are from; that's where they still farm, in a beautiful place." Killala is the beautiful place that Cauvery knew and described to her in Dublin, not the place she went home to, but the home she came back from. Now, in her own words, she says that she "can't wait to go home again."

WHEN HOMELAND IS NOT HOME

A person could search the country a long time and not find a better symbol of contemporary Ireland than Cauvery telling Mary Kate about the place that Mary Kate eventually called home. Cauvery is trans-patriated; Mary Kate, for the moment, was still a visitor. Of course Cauvery would know much more than Mary about Ireland because Cauvery is Irish and Mary Kate is only recently from there. When Cauvery goes home, it is to Dublin. She has become a visitor to Madras; she is only from there. This is more than a matter of playing with words. People often undertake journeys in which they discover absolute home for the first time. The immigrant main character in Cauvery's first novel, *Paddy Indian*, recognizes that, over time, he is saying and doing things that appear odd for an Indian. The same things make him seem perfectly at home as an Irishman.

Cauvery is much more comfortable raising her kids in a Dublin suburb than she could be in Madras. A few years ago the Madhavans brought two Irish families to India. Cauvery was the unofficial tour guide and interpreter of local culture, and she prescribed a dress code for the young women, her daughter included. T-shirts and modest shorts were OK, but no spaghetti strap tops and no radical short shorts. "When we got there, they were mad at me because the shops were full of spaghetti strap tops and short shorts. The world has completely changed," Cauvery said later. Cauvery can hold forth in detail about goings on in Dublin and elsewhere in Ireland, but she needs a refresher for going back to Madras. When she gets magazines from India, "it's shocking the changes in the morality of fashions."

Some matters of culture are well established and not a matter of fad or personal whim; the proper wearing of a sari is one of them. A *sari* is meant to cover a woman and, no matter what kind of blouse or whatever she might wear it with, to go over a woman's chest and cover both breasts. Any lapse in that convention was considered *really* immodest in the Indian culture she left behind, and it remains so in the Indian-Irish subculture in and around Dublin today. One variation that Cauvery finds quite troubling is the accessorized use of the sari, particularly in combination with a bikini. She showed me a photo in a popular Indian magazine. If you live in India, you might get used to the change gradually, but to return after years and see something that never existed when you left is too jarring. As Cauvery commented, "No doubt that TV has changed it; that MTV has changed it. MTV was available in India probably before it was available here in Ireland."

The Madhavans are sophisticated cosmopolitans at home with all dimensions of the cultural diversity of contemporary Dublin. In Madras, it is a different story. They cannot be at home with the very same things there. In Europe, Cauvery is delighted by change, flows with it, lives it. But her India is the one she knows best, the one she left some years ago. She lives the dynamics of change in the one place and is rudely confronted by change in the other. This describes the universal condition of the immigrant culture traveler: the national become ethnic. The meaning of "home" drifts between the two poles, origin and established residence, requiring continuous negotiation. Cauvery said, "For years when we first arrived here, when we were going back to India, we used to say that we were going 'home.' Then, someplace along the line after the children were born, I'd say to Prakash when we were going back to India, 'Is that home?'"

The fact that the question of home has a somewhat different answer for Cauvery and Prakash demonstrates how much home is an individual matter that has little to do with the place where your key fits the door. "There's a clear distinction," said Prakash. "Where you're 'from'—and no matter how many years I may live in this part of the world—that part of me will never change. [Madras] is my home—that is my 'home' home, if you see what I mean."

Cauvery explained: "You see, Prakash wants to spend six months in India and six months here, and I want to spend six months in Dublin and six months in West Cork! Then we'd meet in Dublin every six months."

Prakash said his feelings had nothing to do with being comfortable in Ireland culturally, or anything else of that nature. When he says he would like to spend more time in Madras, it is something that Cauvery cannot understand. "She can't see why I'd want to do that. And I can't see why she wouldn't want to do that. It's all about, I suppose, the memories and what you have there and what you don't have here, the friends you have there—that sort of thing. It's a number of little, little pieces that make up that feeling for you. . . . I think that where you come from, there's an invisible link, an invisible rope, a bond that will always tether you to your country of origin, no matter where you are. It's nice to go back; I like to take my children back and show them this is where I did that, and that's where I did that, and this is where I was messing about, and that's where I met Mom."

Cauvery added, "We've had a number of discussions about it, and we're winding each other up over it. Deciding, when you're an immigrant, on what you're going to call home—well, I dwell on that a lot."

Prakash began once more to attempt to frame a nuanced distinction: "I have no doubt in saying that *this* is where I feel most comfortable, this is where my work is, this is where my life is. . . ." At this precise moment one of the older Madhavan children broke in breathlessly to announce that the family's little Irish horse had once again broken through the fence and joined the neighbor's mare in the next field. The children were instructed to bring the horse home. Prakash planned to go to the hardware and home improvement shop the next day to get materials to mend the fence to keep the horse in and preserve peace among the neighbors. The surgeon and country squire might have strong ties to Madras, but he had a wife who was known to shed tears of joy coming back from India when her plane touched down in Dublin, three kids who craved beef and sausage rolls, and a little horse with a yen for the mare next door in their Dublin suburb. Yes, day-to-day, his life truly was here.

As for Cauvery, she is truly at home in cosmopolitan Dublin, and since she is a writer of popular fiction, this has implications for Madras, her place of origin. An Indian reviewer of her first two novels marveled at how this "girl from Madras is writing comfortably about Amsterdam's red light district and other such adventures, offering good old Madrasis a culture shock. Maybe there's a new Madras girl who has been emerging out there over the last twenty years whom I've not known and who knows all about canoodling beneath club cupolas in this staid city, to judge by what I've been reading in her first book, *Paddy Indian*, set in the Ireland she now lives in. Earthily Irish as Joyce's Blooms, Cauvery Madhavan's two books could be a pointer to Madras authors in the days ahead catching up with the more explicit world of English writing" (Muthiah 2003).

So Cauvery is revealed to be a secret agent of change along the lines of MTV. Shocking—not in Dublin but in staid *Madras*. I am certainly not saying that next she will try the sari/bikini combination. But her mom told me that modesty and tradition used to dictate that she herself would leave Madras in her traditional sari and only change to Western clothing en route to her daughter's house in Dublin. This has not been true for the past few years. She leaves Madras now wearing the

Western clothes in which she arrives in Ireland. One wonders what subtle influences her Dublin daughter has been working on her. The conversation among the three generations of the family slipped easily from India to Ireland and back, filling the cultural spaces in between that are without geography. I listened to Cauvery and her daughter, Sagari, debate the appropriate usage of current Dublin slang. I wanted to turn to Padhman, "Paddy Indian" in Cauvery's novel, to see if he agreed that the scene made life in this household "very normal" in the New Ireland, which Cauvery is helping to make home for the people who can appreciate it—both natives and new arrivals.

ART AS HOME

Peter Potter.   It wasn't his name, and he hadn't changed it, but other people did. Peter Potter came to Ireland from Germany via Belgium because the island was more open and he could get away from people. It is not that he dislikes people; he just likes them on his own terms. To some extent he has managed to get away, down a winding wooded lane, below rocky ridges, up a path through a tangle of vines, in a small cottage with low doors and windows full of the pottery and ceramic sheep and little people-like figures that he makes. Peter had his name "Mittlestrass" changed for him because everyone here called him Peter Potter. Pottery was what he did, and "Mittlestrass" did not roll easily off the West Cork tongue. If you go to look for him, there are a few small signs reading "Potter" that with years of twisting wind and weathering only generally point the way. The people of Glengarriff know where to find him, and their directions are more animated than the little signs, but only slightly more precise. Turn here, turn there, another turn, then turn, follow the fork, and you can't miss it. If you get that far, Peter's last sign pointing through a hedge of vines will appear misplaced; there couldn't be anything up the cow path. But that is where Peter lives and works. Don't look for a car or tractor. He walks wherever he needs to go, unless it is to Dublin to visit friends or go to a Stones concert. Then he takes the train.

Peter is squarely built and ambles like a bear. His graying hair is long and a little wild for the city, but this is not the city. He has a broad face, especially when he smiles. He looks like someone who lives in the woods and makes little figures of clay or children's toys or casts spells. He is *of* the chosen space in the world where he lives, as if he were molded himself from the local clay, a landmark in a place where several immigrants gather to make things and lives, and he is in Ireland to stay, at home, no day-to-day decision, no moving on from here. "Where would I go?" he asks. "This is a good place." The community could use a little more ethnic and racial diversity to suit him, nothing that a few Asian or African additions couldn't cure, but a good place. He does get a little depressed by the weather, but everyone does. He can always retreat to his potter's wheel or fashion a tribe of his ceramic elflings on bad weather days. He usually likes the rain outside as he works by a fire and listens to his collection of pirated CDs swapped back and forth with some other transplanted Germans who live in the area. "Why so many Germans here? As many reasons as there are Germans here. But to some extent they all came for the freedom to do their work, to do their art."

The chief features of Peter's house, once you are inside, are music and pictures. His cottage is a gallery of photos, and he enjoys placing them in outrageous juxtaposition, the political discontinuities creating a unique aesthetic: Margaret Thatcher clustered with Keith Richard and Saddam Hussein, sharing a narrow space between windows and doors with Buddhist religious icons. Peter gave me a copy of my favorite, a photo of the American president morphed into an Osama Bin Laden beard, turban, and robe. Whatever your politics, you have to appreciate the intense cognitive tension caused by the resulting image, flawlessly contrived.

Hundreds of CDs are stacked around the sound system. He likes blues but is a huge fan of the Rolling Stones. A poster-sized banner of them hangs over his work area. He is especially a fan of Keith Richard—lots of photos of leathery-feathery Keith. For this fan of the Stones, appreciation goes beyond music. For him their lives are theater: Richard is the pimp and Jagger the prostitute. They are cartoons that keep him amused; they create art despite themselves in a kind of Andy Warhol self-parody. In that playful world a German migrant artisan from the European counterculture of the 60s becomes a forest-dwelling imp, a dancing bear, a gregarious recluse, a congruent inhabitant. When I came in, he was listening to Muddy Waters and the Stones in concert together. That combination pretty much characterizes the height of popular culture for him. He left it on while he made us a pot of tea.

Whenever the Stones play Dublin, he goes up for the concert. They would be back there in September or October, and of course he would go, although he had seen them a hundred times, he said—which might or might not have been an exaggeration. His brother had been in Hamburg when the Beatles played there every night, and the brother said that they were "kind of" a good band but not as good as some of the others that played the same club. He liked the story because it represented something of the role of chance in shaping lives. The Beatles understood the theater of the created self and had made the world their own. We talked about the 60s like old veterans of the same battles, about what it was like to be aging characters from that era, how we both identified with expired popular music figures, and how, when we lost a lifelong companion like George Harrison, the departure took a piece of our own biographies with it—the colors in our picture of the world faded a little; the antic movement slowed a bit; the cast diminished.

He found the Irish friendly enough to suit him. He said even though he was European, and to other Europeans all nations have stereotypes associated with their national character, he did not have any indelibly preconceived impression of what the Irish would be like—how they would behave toward him—when he immigrated. He said that like anywhere in the world he expected to find "good people and assholes," and the anticipation was borne out. For the most part he had found the local Irish open and accepting of his foreign presence. He himself loved cultural diversity. He thought that what was happening in Ireland by way of immigration was great but a little slow in coming. It was making Ireland all that much more livable. He said that Germany had more right-wingers, and "young people who are violent, unreflecting idiots," and you might have the same bigots in Ireland. But for the most part they would be sullen, isolated individuals who mumble into their beer. They don't bother anybody, and that was fine, part of the diversity. He welcomed those people as an inevitable part of the mix, but avoided them, and they did not take the trouble to come out to visit him.

He cheerfully accepted the name that the people of West Cork have given him, and he was quite happy signing his pottery with "Peter Potter." It fit with a world where you could invent yourself and your invention became a piece of the community, where the German potter Peter Potter helped to give the region around Glengarriff its true character, its authentic richness as part of the Irish countryside. Peter had an "Irish" name, a name very much in keeping with how people were named in the past. He would not have children, so there would be no little Potters to carry on after him, but if he did have kids at this stage, he would be hard pressed to choose whether they would carry his old German name or his new Irish one. Whichever he chose would make little difference to his children as they grew up in Glengarriff, except that teachers might have a slightly more difficult time with one than the other.

Peter turned out his people and sheep in some quantity, and they were sold around Ireland in craft shops, so he did not trouble to draw people to his workshop. As we talked, he worked, crafting the herd of sheep before us on the table, first naked or shorn; then, using an extruder that looked like it might be designed to produce angel-hair spaghetti, he put long shaggy coats on them. You would want to use the tool to create the same effect if you were sculpting a bust of Peter. We had a good talk: a little of it was about Ireland; a lot of it was about the 60s, dope, pacifism—comparing notes. We toasted with a cup of tea the memory of his grandmother who was part of the resistance during the Nazi era—not so dangerous, she had told him, because the Nazis were such morons.

What Peter liked about his life was that it was simple, that he didn't have to spend much money to live, and that he was perfectly free to do as he pleased. You could still live like that there if you didn't require too much. But this corner of Ireland had changed a lot in the past twenty years, he said sadly. He quickly added that it was a good thing because many people today were economically better off, and that was fine. But it was too bad that the old people he knew were dying off—the whole generation who lived simply and knew things and could tell stories about the area, the history, and the lore, people of good memory who were good company. I thought of the old-timers who had shared their stories with me: the beekeeper, Gussie Russell, Adam Gleasure, Father Pat. Gussie was gone in 2004, Adam in the spring of 2006. How much longer? Peter had taken the time over the course of twenty years to learn and know the things the old people knew, and they were important to him because this was the place he had chosen to live; the place that gave him the freedom to be who he wanted, to invent himself; the place that was home.

It is possible to still see the simplicity of what Ireland was like twenty years ago and longer, how much it has changed, by comparing Peter's life to the lives of the new generation of Irish who have more. His cottage is "unimproved." The place would be recognizable—if not all of the sounds that come from it—to many of the old-timers whose passing he laments. The remarkable thing here is that it is the German who came to change his life who is preserving something of the past in the way he lives, but even more so in the things of local memory that he knows. We joked that we were the new old generation that would be dying off, so we had better hurry up and get our stories told. I told him that I would see about telling his story and try to get back for his birthday in the spring. Who knows how many we have left.

The weavers.   Robert and Yvonne O'Flynn choose to call what they do full-time farming. They can because, although they are weavers who depend on that income to live, they do grow their own basket-making materials, along with chickens, geese, turkeys, ducks, and goats for sale, as well as their own vegetables. They have developed a customer base for their organic produce by word of mouth, and they attract customers for the woven goods through some very modest signs (not unlike Peter's) that allowed me to get lost three times between the main road and the entrance to their farmyard.

Robert is from England, Yvonne from the Netherlands. They each came to Ireland twenty years ago and met here. He was a self-described "refugee from Thatcher's England," and she came to a place that offered a more rural and natural environment, a more integrated and independent lifestyle. Most of the time they were happy with their choice to live in Ireland. They said the occasional questioning that occurs to them was not so much a matter of being in Ireland as it was being in the human condition. You can always think of reasons for being somewhere else, doing something else, wherever you are and whatever you are doing. Their success at living modestly did provide a source of financial inertia that prevented them from simply pulling up stakes and moving on. The balance between low income and low outgo suited them. They did not have much money, but they did not need much. "We eat well," said Yvonne. They agreed that if they had a million Euros, it would present a nuisance. They would have to face the choice of whether to stay or leave the life they had and all the right living and healthy things it embodied for something else. There was not much chance that they would face the dilemma.

Yvonne shuddered as she said that she would hate working for someone else. Robert reported a daily routine that would have set both Marx and Gandhi (*and* Peter Potter) nodding approvingly. On a typical day he would make a basket or two in the morning, then work outside doing farming in the afternoon. If he felt like it, he might make another basket in the evening. If it rained, they worked around the weather that the day offered. Their lives were fit easily to the weather and the seasons. Their big two months for the basket trade, July and August, were just underway, and they wove as we talked to augment the substantial store of baskets and other woven things laid by on the floor of the old stone barn where they worked. He was starting a large basket; she was working on a child's chair with a woven back and seat. When the basket trade season wound down, they would look to the harvest and sale of what they raised. During winter they would begin work on items for next summer's craft trade.

The buildings were old, the farmyard green but well worn. I hoped that the two people here would stay and stay, having found what so many dream of finding. If it worked for them, then in a way it would validate the dream for the rest of us who never put the dream to the test but see through Robert and Yvonne that it might have worked.

There are good signs of them staying put, some domestic, some international. "Having children keeps you from moving around a lot," said Robert. The ones still living at home were happy with their lives in West Cork. And the weavers had found a viable if modest farming niche in European agri-economics: under new EU regulations they would be subsidized for reducing the number of their livestock, enhancing their ability to keep on with their full-time farming scheme. I cheered them on, feeling a little like an itinerant propagandist for a back-to-the-land movement, striking a little blow for the sake of all the dreamers. People who like baskets can do their bit—Willow Basketry, Kealkil, can be found online more easily than it can off the main road—but maybe not everyone at once. Maintaining a balanced life is a delicate thing. We do not want prosperity to drive them into opening a basket manufactory in town, where they might find they have a million Euros in the bank, and then what would become of them? But buying a few baskets couldn't hurt.

The thing that marked off the homesteads of these West Cork settlers—Peter, Robert, and Yvonne—from other migrants who came to find their place or a living in Ireland was their goal to live modestly. Their modest living brought little physical change to the places where they settled. Passersby who saw these places—if they could be seen from the road—would say, Now there's a real, traditional Irish farm or cottage. And they would be right. But they would probably be surprised by who is living there. These people who have come to rural Ireland have changed it the least because what drew them were the qualities of the settled landscape to begin with. They brought with them an idea of Ireland, and their art of living conformed to that aesthetic, giving new life to that idea.

If people are so moved by the idea of a place that they go to live in that idea, then they will be the ones also who are most committed to its preservation. And however the ideas of the artist immigrants may differ according to individual perception, they are likely to coalesce around such goals as resisting the development of condominiums on mountain-sides and commercial strip developments along seashores. In this they will be in step with that strong articulate element of the native Irish who are committed to controlling and channeling commercial development interests. The artisans and artists who have come to get by are not the same new arrivals, native or otherwise, who are building absentee fortress homes.

And it is also true that those who come to make their home in Ireland *as it was* do change the place. For those of this or earlier generations who have left the backroads of Ireland never to return, the picture of the place in their minds will always be the place as it was when they left. In an odd way, those who are drawn to a place because they are more at home there than elsewhere may hope to preserve what they have found by living in it. If that is their goal, they may find themselves chafing against natives who are continuously turning the place into something more useful to their own evolving needs. Or the newcomers may play with the idea of rural Ireland as an experimental theater, one of the many stages that are juxtaposed among the parallel universes that comprise the present state of reality in the world. In this reality the sounds of the Rolling Stones and Muddy Waters running out into the night blend together with the sounds of the rain swelling the muddy waters of the creek that cuts across the steep lane to the potter's cottage. In this reality there is a logic to the fact that fewer EU-subsidized ducks and goats will be growing fat naturally at the weaver's place that is easier to find on the Web than on the road to Kealkil. Nothing about Ireland can or will remain unchanged, and even preservation deliberately undertaken represents a kind of change from the thing as it was before someone decided to preserve it. As we saw in chapter 4 about music, a thing preserved has a different sound from that of the thing simply played in its own time. Immigrants to a simpler and freer life in western Ireland are bound to find wider Europe crowding down the lane or across the open land, even as the immigrants themselves embody that change. Like Peter Potter, those immigrants may well be in the forefront of welcoming the growing diversity and tolerance.

Visitor and native have noted other modest but significant changes brought by the art colonists. In West Cork some small shops stock German and other imported European food. Small towns have outlets for African and Asian foods in shop buildings just around the corner from the main shopping areas. The people behind the counters of the hotel, internet café, and Super-Value stores have names and accents that come from all over the world. And if you ask them where they are from, they are as likely to say "just over the road" or "down the block" as they are to tell you where they were named or where they learned their native language. Their children will certainly tell you that they are from here, that this is their home. Ten years ago an immigrant to Ireland, certainly a settled person of color, was a novelty. Ten years from now the visitor still surprised by Irish ethnic and racial diversity will be the novelty.

As the nation changes, interested people have begun to expect something more of the multidimensional and hard-edged realities of Ireland in stories they hear of the place. Some of the diaspora Irish, in particular, want a more complete picture of Ireland as it is; they want to be updated so they can retain their insider's knowledge that keeps them Irish. The traveled Irish are great consumers of Irish stuff. In the old days it was Belleek, Waterford, and wall calendars. Today it is more likely to be the popular arts — music, theater, and fiction. In recent years we have enjoyed popular writers like Roddy Doyle and Frank McCourt, who play up the grim side of Irish life. They show us the social problems and give us a few laughs as insiders who have grown up Catholic *and* Irish. Maybe some genius could come up with a TV soap opera, something with regular-looking characters bumping up against Ireland's changes and each other. That would offer a virtual homecoming for millions of Irish people all over the world. In that world, at home with TV, maybe there would be tens of millions of Irish, wherever they might live, who would experience a homecoming in television characters struggling to cope with change in Ireland.

THE REAL BALLYKISSANGEL: GOING HOME ON TELEVISION

An interesting aspect of cultural globalization is its capacity to blend together fantasy and reality. As people in different parts of the world learn about one another, they first encounter images of what others look and feel like through the mass media—especially television. For a good number of the world's Irish, the journey home may begin and end there.

The television series *Ballykissangel* was many things: a surprising media success story for producers and cast, a serialized drama depicting romantic and other intrigues in the lives of ordinary-appearing people, a series of vignettes of day-to-day life going on in an imaginary village where characters were facing many issues resembling those faced by people in real towns in contemporary Ireland. It was a useful medium for updating what people outside of Ireland knew of life there, a step away from the fictions of matchmakers and Travelers who drive horse-drawn covered wagons. What Americans might learn of Ireland through watching the series was roughly equivalent to what people in Ireland or other parts of the world might learn of the United States through watching one of its milder daytime soaps. And through the magic imagery of flawed fictional characters moving through the actually lived-in spaces of a little town in Wicklow, viewers gained the illusion of stepping behind closed doors, into the homes and relationships, the inner thoughts and motives, the angst of lives lived at the colliding edge of the Irish village and irresistible globalization.

Because *Bally-K* (as its fans call it) was about lives in a particular village, a place had to be selected as its main setting. This created an interesting cognitive problem for some people—a problem in thinking clearly about what is and is not of this world. Although the series was filmed in many places around County Wicklow and beyond, the fictional Ballykissangel became indelibly associated with the real-life village of

Avoca. Avoca supplied the setting for the opening aerial panorama that began each episode and for the series' main street, the Catholic church (exterior), the local shop, and Fitzgerald's pub. Fantasy and reality were galvanized into one for tens of millions of faithful viewers around the world, just as all the in-between spaces and lives of the village were fused into a single story by the taboo relationship between the mild and wavering young English priest in the church at the top of the road and the irreverent female publican who operated Fitzgerald's at the T-cross at the bottom of the hill.

I decided to spend a couple of days in Avoca to experience firsthand the dimensions of this puzzle piece of the real Ireland. As I crossed the river from the main road that bypasses the village, I found Fitzgerald's facing me. Resist as I might, the impression was seductive, as I parked on the main street and turned to look at my surroundings. I was in a place where I had never set foot, except as a television ethnographer. But as I stood there in Avoca, for the first few minutes, the fictional television presence of Ballykissangel was a nearly irresistible reality. One experiences culture shock when traveling between cultures, but here I had traveled into a fiction, a television fantasy, a cartoon. It was as if some trickster had contrived a stage set and planted it in the path of real world people to see how they would react, to see if they would be able to suspend disbelief. And the cast of characters before me was no help in peeling away reality from fantasy. This was no theater prop, no themed entertainment zone. Everything was eerily normal.

No throngs of foreigners, no tour buses, no guided groups went up and down the streets. That is what I had prepared myself for, the story of a disrupted Avoca with crowds of outsiders choking every public space, with jaded and short-tempered locals giving yet another set of visitors the cold shoulder. Now *that* would have drawn the hard line between fiction and reality. I had come to write about theme park Avoca, with its history of mining, colonial strife, and weaving obliterated by a Disneyfied atmosphere, a dozen *Bally-K* shop fronts turned into gaudy trinket emporiums. Instead there were a few tourists, such as you might find in any picturesque village in Wicklow. But most of the people I encountered were residents going about their business—and many of them initiated casual greetings with strangers. There were Ballykissangel souvenir shops, three or four of them, perhaps one or two more per capita than you might see in another village of this size. The town was more like Blarney, the village I had lived in for a couple of years, than Disneyland, I thought.

In all, the ordinariness of the place was disorienting. I went into Fitzgerald's bar to help clear my thoughts, and found some therapy. Thankfully, the bar staff conformed to my initial prejudices—just this side of surly, clipped, avoiding interaction. There was a mix of outsiders and residents, but most of the patrons in the late afternoon were local people, and the place was full. I sat at the bar. Immediately, the man seated on my left was accosted by a woman with a British accent who announced loudly that she had been born and raised south of Dublin and knew something of the local area from her girlhood. She insisted on knowing the location of Quigley's house—the fictional small-time, wheeler-dealer character well-known to viewers of the TV series. The local patron, a man apparently timid in his approach to life and strangers, had a difficult time getting out the words that would do justice to what he thought of the woman's question—the question of where in this real village where real people like himself had lived all their lives a fictional character lived in his fictional home. For the moment the question stopped him in his tracks, and he hesitatingly admitted that he didn't know the answer to her riddle, that he hadn't thought about it before. The woman was indignant and loud: " . . . And you've lived here all your life and don't know where Quigley's house is? You should be flogged. You should be shot!"

Even the nearly perfectly expressionless bartender, whose otherwise deadpan demeanor had impressed me, seemed a little uncomfortable. He must have grown used to such questions, yet he stared at the woman for a few seconds, then returned to reflectively wiping a beer glass. How should such a question be approached? The TV series had been shot all over the South of Ireland. The setting used for Quigley's house might be anywhere within a fifty-mile radius of Fitzgerald's Pub. As the loud woman moved away, the quiet man beside me looked into his pint. The insistence of the woman who had slipped off the edge of the world and into her television appeared to have pulled him along—he was struggling in the powerful wake of her confusion. They had entered a twilight awareness regarding where they were, and for the moment both the native and the visitor had a difficult time slipping back. I imagined that once he had collected himself, the man at the bar would get plenty of mileage out of retelling the story of another bewildered outsider who had come to look for directions to a pot of television gold. The woman would probably tell her friends back home how benighted some of the locals were, that they knew nothing about even major figures in their own town. I was satisfied with both projections.

I visited Fitzgerald's a few times during my stay in the area. It had an odd atmosphere. The locals who predominated during each visit seemed acclimated to their reclaimed public space, maybe a little quiet. The visitors to the place were very, very quiet, leaning close in their conversations, speaking nearly in whispers. In all, the place had more the atmosphere of a church than a bar. Why not? On the surrounding walls hung the pictures of the departed-from-this-world cast of the no-longer-in-production series, an arrangement reminiscent of the Stations of the Cross, with images of saints and patrons standing in recessed alcoves. The hall was a shrine to a time when larger-than-life beings had and had not inhabited this place, giving it a reality that you had to struggle to avoid, a set of mysteries for believers.

Ballykissangel and Avoca were fused into a single entity in other, more important ways than in the minds of poor confused visitors like myself. The fusion had, during the show's height of popularity, suddenly and violently thrust the village into an international limelight. If the producers of the *Bally-K* series had been surprised at the level of international interest their television series had generated, the people of Avoca had been caught totally off guard. During the first few years the impact was especially convulsive. Traffic, a previously un-thought-of way to refer to cars and farm vehicles passing on the road, often came to a dead stop. Tour buses choked the streets and stopped in every available open space, turning loose hundreds of people at a time, jamming streets, sidewalks, and shops. Some holidaymakers were cheerful and polite; some were not. I was told that at times the customers were so thick in souvenir shops that people could not turn around with their purchases to get to the door and back onto the tour bus. Farmers who needed to make several trips a day through town in the process of cutting and storing silage during optimal spells of fine weather found that hours were added to their day with time wasted on the all-but-impassable single street that ran the length of the village. People who were used to spending a few minutes going from home to work suddenly were "commuters" between the same two points, needing to calculate travel times of the better part of an hour. One shop employee said she was literally driven out of town by the throngs, and had worked her way around the world for a few years until things died down and she thought it was safe to come back.

When she returned to Avoca during the show's reruns, she found business still thriving but at a manageable level. Busloads were largely reduced to a one-at-a-time schedule, as the chance of seeing the show's popular actors on the street came to an end and Avoca became just another stop on touring routes along the East Coast, rather than the main destination point. People got off the bus, came into the shop and the pub, and got back on the bus. They spent their money and left, and that was a good thing. A retired native who had spent decades in the building trades in England had returned to live in Avoca after the TV production had long departed. Yes, things had changed a bit, the town was more lively than when he left, but he had found it otherwise pretty much the same. Cost of living? Well, he didn't need much and was drawing two pensions, one from England and one from Ireland. He was quite comfortable, thanks. The people in the new houses being built all over the place? No, he had no idea what they did for a living, how they could afford the prices, who they were, or where they came from. Luck to them, he had what he needed. He knew and waved to many who passed on the main street. He had left Avoca, and he came back to it. *Ballykissangel* had passed through the town while he was away. What it had left behind he neither saw nor cared about.

Living expenses had risen dramatically here, as in the rest of Ireland, and the *Bally-K* boom added fire locally to the general superheating of Ireland's rising housing costs. A teacher, who was a cousin of the returned world traveler who had fled boomtown Avoca for distant parts, was priced out of the local market recently and found her first house in Arklow, a small seacoast city some miles away. The shop clerk thought that many of the new houses were going to people coming down from Dublin and that their big and ready money was fueling the climbing housing costs. She thought they were drawn here by the *Bally-K* image, the way of life here as it was portrayed on TV. They had come to live in the television place. The Bally-K-ers and Avocans lived side by side.

But mind that she wasn't saying that the popularity of the town and its growth were in any way a bad thing, especially now that the situation had become more manageable day-to-day. The place was "ten times better off" than when she was growing up. Because of the increase in business, more young people were able to stay and work in the town. Some Avocans, those who were just starting their adult lives as the *Bally-K* generation hit, were now doing very well in their own businesses, perhaps owning three or four vans for delivery of their goods or services, and you would never see that before. Yes, prices were sky high for everything, but she said that it was great the way no one was left behind by the village's changing fortunes. There were new opportunities for children: the tourist information office doubled as an instructional technology center, with its six computer workstations easily handling the demand for visitor e-mail and hands-on instruction for public school students.

As I checked my e-mail, two girls, six or seven years old, were being tutored on setting up their own Web pages. The one at the next workstation to me quickly exhausted the stock of personal attributes she thought the world might be interested in knowing about her. At her teacher's prompting she decided to enter information on her cat and her goldfish and the nature of their relationship. This young girl could also avail herself of acting and Irish dancing lessons, if she or her parents wanted them. These amenities were not available to the young woman in the shop while she was growing up in Avoca, and she would have liked having them. If you had a bit of talent and training in theater while the show was in town . . . well, who knows?

Yes, she said, the life of the village had indeed changed, but on balance people were far better off now that Avoca was on the map, even if it was on the map as Ballykissangel, a TV reality that was accommodated at least parenthetically on many of the recently published road maps of Ireland. It takes a minute to register: here are official maps of Ireland that precisely locate a TV town, twinning it to a lesser known place. It will take one just so many miles and just so much time to travel to this location, which has been fit into the paramount reality of the physical world as rendered by that most trusted figure for the traveler, the cartographer. No wonder, if the place was named on maps, that people asked for locations once they were in Ballykissangel that confused the Avocans. The nice young shop woman was saying it was fun while she had been away in Australia, where *Ballykissangel* was very popular, to point out to friends there that the place on TV was the village she "was from."

I asked whether it felt odd to be so far away from home and see your homeplace portrayed as something else, taken over as a fictionalized stage set with outsiders pretending to live in made-up stories there. Yes, it was odd to see it as home and yet not home. But she loved some of the characters on the show. Brendan the schoolteacher: now, wasn't he great? His character was so naturalistic, "real-like," just like someone you might know. And some of them were so nice. The actors came into the shop when she was still working there—before she was driven out—and they seemed just like the people on the show. "Peter, the priest, now what was his name? He was very nice altogether. Yes, I liked him too. But Assumpta, she was not all that well liked locally. Kind of aloof. Now Niamh, she was the best of the lot. She was a great favorite in Avoca." We had done it, slipped off the edge, through the screen, into fantasy.

In the church at the top of the road, the exterior but not the inside of which had been used in the television series, there were names in the visitor's book from all over the world of people who had come to visit the real Ballykissangel. They had come to a familiar place in a kind of homage, *to be there*. The list of visitors, their handwriting as individual as their biographies, as individual as what they had come for and what they had found, was very, very long. Maybe some had come to Avoca, not to Bally-K. Perhaps some had come to Bally-K or Avoca because it was the closest thing to an Irish homeplace they were personally aware of, the most familiar of all the Irish places they knew, if not a place where they knew people, then a place where they knew something of what life in Ireland was like. In all, people had come in such numbers that they virtually defeated the virtual nature of the place, its fictional status. A thing is real if it makes people behave as if it is real.

STAYING AT HOME: CHANGING IN PLACE

Ireland has always been a place where the past struggles with the present, as the island has stood warily facing Europe with its back to the Atlantic and America, in a back-to-back, sort of over-the-shoulder relationship with its more permanently departed bound-for-America emigrants. Families left behind could be more hopeful of news and return visits from those who went to England. To the extent that geography and distance still count for anything in a seamless world economic culture, the West remains the back of the island, with West Cork, Kerry,

Clare, and Connemara still the places that the Ireland Irish of the present day retreat to when they want to get away at home. With the price of land, groceries, and everything else soaring, the western people struggle with a divided heart regarding the coming of changes that appear ever more swift, complete, and irreversible. Here there is the sense that the long-standing ways of living memory are worth retaining, coupled with the need to position oneself on the right side of the social and economic divide brought on by the new prosperity.

In the little towns and villages domestic and international foreigners are seen regularly to spend in a few hours what amounts to a week's wages for the local service worker. It is the ability of outsiders to spend that drives up the local costs of everything and puts a fine point on the dilemma of how to package and capitalize on the world market demand for local culture as a convenient market consumable, without pushing the region further down the path of becoming a folksy theme park. Add to this the actions of the EU that are intended to help the "Irish economy," an abstract concept that boils down to helping certain industries and their particular entrepreneurs, and we have the conditions of externally imposed changes that are hitting the Atlantic coast of Ireland like a tidal wave that has raised some boats while swamping others.

Some miles offshore from the town of Doolin, a town repackaging itself for the world market, are the three Aran Islands. MTV lives here, along with commercial fishermen and farmers trying to scrape a living together. These are the famous rocks where in the past subsistence farmers mixed seaweed and sand with the little existing earth in order to produce enough inches of soil to grow potatoes sufficient to allow people to live close to the margins of survival for another year. Today, for anyone who wants to "get away" from either the economic hustle or the touristic themes of today's Ireland, the Arans remain a very easily reachable choice. Hundreds come every day during the warm months, thousands daily in the peak travel months of July and August. They come to see Ireland as it was before their mothers and fathers were born. They are too late.

I first visited the large island, Inishmore, in 1994. I wish I had come in the late 1970s when I was living in Cork, when, I was told, the place was beginning to make the transition. In 1994 in the main village of Kil Ronan there were a few shops, open to the uncertainties of the weather through large warehouse doors, sweaters piled high on rough shelves, saleswomen wrapped up against the cold and damp. A couple of "beat-ers," old vans or small buses, took visitors to the far side of the island or the ancient semicircular fort of Dun Angus on the southern cliff face. The road over the center of the island went past high stone walls, one-stone-thick, un-mortared, lacey, with light shining through the spaces between the stones. The houses we passed by at the time were modest, mostly cottages, a few bungalows, some two-story houses in poor re-pair. I hiked around Dun Angus, an indistinct pile of stones, silted in and overgrown. The site was accessible across an open field of burren, where you made your own way, following a couple of rough signs di-recting you to the ancient center. The nationally sponsored archeologi-cal dig to improve and fully expose the walls was in full swing then. On the way to restoring what they could of the 2,500-year-old site, they discovered that the place was set on the bones of a structure that was considerably older.

When I visited again in 2003, Dun Angus was prospering as a sight-seeing destination, restored to what was thought to have been its origi-nal dimensions with new stone: it had the look of a modern construction site. The site was accessible through a new interpretive center that col-lected €4 from each visitor on the way through the building that formed the courtyard with the new gift shop and restaurant. The ancient come-to-life Dun Angus, attuned to the expectations and pocketbook of the international traveler, was a metaphor for the island.

A shuttle bus driver thanked his lucky stars out loud for the restora-tion of the magic place that brought tourists by the thousands to the nine-mile-long island that, as far as he could see, had little else to offer. The revenues had improved local fortunes, both private and public, the latter evidenced by the new senior citizen complex. The driver showed that he was not very happy we were only going as far as the site with him, since we planned to hike back along the roads; he was *only* collect-ing €5 each from my partner and me for the one-way ten-minute ride. He would be getting ten from all the other round-trippers on his packed, recent model bus.

As we walked back toward Kil Ronan, we passed a number of new residential building sites. A decade earlier I had asked locals about whether outsiders would buy land here for summer retreats and was assured that they could not—at any rate, they did not. I thought my question was regarded suspiciously, and I was assured at the time that no one would sell to an outsider. After making our way back to Kil Ronan, I asked an idle pony cart driver about all the housing development we had seen underway on the island that day. We were standing across from the old stone barn where, on my last trip, saleswomen bundled against the damp wind sold Aran sweaters and wool in the open building. Now workers were putting finishing touches on the new facade that enclosed the new shops in the old building, shielded from the sea by large arched windows. Inside, the stock hung on chrome racks, and stylish young women catered to the international customers who crowded in. My companion commented that the prices seemed very high, even compared to the prices in major mainland towns.

The trap driver was adamant as he expressed his feeling about all the new development, but the logic of his narrative seemed fragmented by the contradictions that framed his life. He said that the new home building was all for native island people. No one was interested in buying property or building on the island. Once you leave the island, he said, good riddance to it. Keep going, and don't look back. There is nothing here. I asked whether the young people were doing that, and he said, yes, they were, most of them, but a few stayed on. Yes, they were doing all right. Then he blurted, "Everybody says, 'Keep the Germans out; don't let them buy,' but how do you do that, when the money's the same?" Then, with a sharp glance in my direction, he continued on the original path—no, no one wanted to buy out here anyway. He said it as if it were a local mantra: no one will cross the water to build a summer place or a home; they'll stick to the mainland. He was certain of it.

Where did the locals get the money for the building? The EU gave grants to fishermen to buy the big boats that could stay out for fourteen days. Yes, the fish stocks were going down, and it made no sense to fund more European fishermen, but there was the issue of fairness in international competition with others in the EU. They were all fishing the same waters, and the fishermen qualified for the grants and made loads of money on the new boats in the past ten years. Some of them were funding the new tour buses; with the buildup of tourism and the Dun Angus restoration and all came change. It was a shame to see the culture and the local ways go down. And I should see the place in August, crawling with people—you're not able to move. He hates August. But that's your bread and butter? I asked. So it is, he said bitterly, and then quickly changed his demeanor with the approach of a large family party asking to see if they all could fit into his cart. "Of course you can; of course you can," he said, and jammed them all in, with a young child perched high on a kind of backpack on his father's back, sticking outside of the cart. I had wanted to ask a few more questions to clarify some of what he said about the new development, nobody from outside wanting to buy on the island, and the problem of "keeping the Germans" from buying, but business is business. We gestured goodbye for the time being.

I raised the question about outsiders buying property with another cart driver across the square. No one wants to buy out here, came the chanted reply. And if they did? He shot a look at me from his otherwise straight-ahead (to where I wasn't standing) stare. No one does, he said with finality.

His cross and dismissive nature may have made me more persistent than usual. "Say someone made an offer on a piece of land, a foreigner who wanted to put up a house, what then?" He shifted himself only a little, was not about to waste another look in my direction — someone who didn't understand a simple statement, maybe someone who wanted to buy a piece of land himself.

"Land is passed on from father to son to son here," he said slowly and deliberately. "That's the only way it changes hands. It stays in the family generation after generation. That's the way it is." He didn't say, "And good-day to ye," but he was done. Just one more question.

"And if a fellow wanted to sell, I mean, there's no law, right? What would happen to him?"

He said his neighbors would see to it that he didn't sell. He would be given a hard time.

I let it go. So Germans or anyone else buying land on the islands wasn't really a problem: that was the story, and they were sticking to it. If time stood still, and a few miles of water between a string of picturesque islands and a mainland being gobbled up by purpose-built holiday attractions, tourist accommodations, and summer homes remained an effective barrier in a global economy, then the world would leave the Arans as they are today. I had heard the same story when I asked about foreign ownership ten years earlier. But as the first driver had said, the "culture" of the place was being "spoiled" already. It is harder for a spoiled culture to hold its values intact than a whole one. On the other hand, who knows what power there is in a local culture that is determined to make a stand to protect itself.

There are ways to find out who is buying property and where they are buying it. But my work has been about the stories people tell about themselves, about their view of the world. Ireland is changing, has changed. There are no more outposts anywhere in the world. The Aran Islands are a close-in suburb within the European metropolis, now that Ireland itself has become a bustling commercial neighborhood within the single global marketplace, that exquisitely efficient masterpiece of international exchange. To be sure, costs are involved in the changes that are coming and those that have come. But the changes have also brought a new prosperity and freedom. Will any future generation of Irish youth ever again have reason to seek their fortune abroad? And what will be the nature of the home that holds them? Will the meaning of home thin out, coming to refer to an address rather than a mesh of social ties to people in place? In the new language of home, a sense of local involvement may be optional. Why should this aspect of life be any different for Irish natives, compared with the lives people live in other prospering places, now that the island has at last drifted into the main current of the affairs of the world?

Societies that have long been at the center of the rationalizing world absorbed the kinds of social changes we have been exploring ages ago. In those places conventional wisdom has learned to minimize the cost of what was left behind, emphasizing the liberating consequences of affluence. In the case of Ireland, a single generation links past to future through living memory; its members can talk about how different their world has become. These people make up the last generation to measure the nature of current change through personal experience. It includes aging farmers throughout Ireland. Today's farmers can still tell stories of how it was in their own fathers' time. What stories will their children tell?

This is also the first generation of people to immigrate to Ireland in numbers large enough to be a felt presence. They are the first and last generation to be able to talk about what it was like to introduce genuine cultural pluralism to the native Irish. Their children will also write an important chapter of change. Will the New Irish become a minority, a target of prejudice and discrimination, or is there something about coming late to the feast that will allow the native Irish to outsmart the rest of us?

The stories of change have a fleeting life, a single season — how was it, that time when the world arrived with blinding speed? Here we have sampled what people have to say about their experiences and concerns, as they paused to catch their breath for a minute. Assembled here as they are, these stories may provide something of an answer to the question "What was it like?" The stories in this book have been a gift to me, to all of us, given freely, even eagerly. They were given by strangers whom I accosted as they went about their business, many of whom became friends as we shared our personal tales. Thanks, again, to the people in this book for what you have told us about yourselves, for what I learned about myself, and for what you have told us about what it has been like to be living in this time, for telling change in Ireland.

Bibliography

2006 Index of Economic Freedom. 2006. Washington, D.C.: Heritage Foundation and the Wall Street Journal.

Aalen, F. H. A. 1963. "A Review of Recent Irish Population Trends." *Population Studies* 17 (July): 73–78.

Allen, Kieran. 2000. *The Celtic Tiger: The Myth of Social Partnership in Ireland.* Manchester: Manchester University Press.

Arensberg, Conrad. [1937] 1968. *The Irish Countryman: An Anthropological Study.* Garden City, N.Y.: Natural History Press.

Barry, Dan. 1997. "From Poets to Pubs, Irish Imports Are in Demand." *New York Times,* March 17, 1997.

Bernstein, Nina. 2004. "Back Home in Ireland: Greener Pastures." *New York Times,* November 10, 2004.

Binchy, Maeve. [1990] 1991. *Circle of Friends.* New York: Dell.

Bottigheimer, Karl S. 1982. *Ireland and the Irish: A Short History.* New York: Columbia University Press.

Busteed, M. A., and R. I. Hodgson. 1996. "Irish Migrant Responses to Urban Life in Early Nineteenth Century Manchester." *The Geographical Journal* 162 (20): 139–53.

Byrne, Anne. 2000. "Luxury Goods Dearer Here Than in the US." *Irish Times,* November 27, 2000.

Cantillon, Sara, Carmel Corrigan, Peadar Kirby, and Joan O'Flynn, eds. 2001. *Rich and Poor: Perspectives on Tackling Inequality in Ireland.* Report Commissioned by the Combat Poverty Agency. Dublin: Oak Tree Press.

Carswell, Simon. 1999. "Luxury Goods Firm To Sell Latin Chic to Irish: Udaras Helps Set Up Italian Leather Goods Factory in Dingle Peninsula." *Irish Times*, October 15, 1999.

Cassidy, Colman. 2002. "State Now Near Top of Euro Zone Prices League." *Irish Times*, June 29, 2002.

Central Statistics Office Ireland. 2000. *Principal Statistics for 2000*. http://www.cso.ie/principalstats.

———. 2003. *Population 1901–2002*. http://www.cso.ie/statistics/Population 1901-2002.htm.

Coogan, Tim Pat. 2003. *Ireland in the Twentieth Century*. London: Hutchinson.

Coyle, Dominic. 2002. "Property Price Rise is First In Six Months." *Irish Times*, March 22, 2002.

Danaher, Kevin. 1966. *Irish Country Folk*. Cork: Mercier.

de Paor, Liam. 1986. *The Peoples of Ireland: From Prehistory to Modern Times*. London: Hutchinson; Notre Dame, Ind.: University of Notre Dame Press.

Dezell, Maureen. 2000. *Irish America Coming into Clover: The Evolution of a People and a Culture*. New York: Doubleday.

Dolan, Jay P. 1972. "Immigrants in the City: New York's Irish and German Catholics." *Church History* 41 (September): 354–68.

Doyle, David Noel. 2006. "The Remaking of Irish America." In *Making the Irish American: History and Heritage of the Irish in the United States*, ed. J. J. Lee and Marion R. Casey, 213–51. New York: New York University Press.

Doyle, Roddy. 1987. *The Commitments*. London: Secker & Warburg.

Fanning, Bryan. 2002. *Racism and Social Change in the Republic of Ireland*. Manchester: Manchester University Press.

Feehily, Patricia. 2003. "When the Milking Is Nearly Done." *Limerick Leader*, February 1, 2003.

Handlin, Oscar. 1951. *The Uprooted*. Boston: Little, Brown.

Harrison, Frank Llewelyn. 1988. *Irish Traditional Music: Fossil or Resource?* Cork: Irish Traditional Music Society, University College Cork.

Hoge, Warren. 2000. "Money, Jobs, Big Cars: How's an Irishman to Cope?" *New York Times*, July 17, 2000.

Holmquist, Kate. 2000. "Loser Chic: The Best Thing Since the Celtic Tiger." *Irish Times*, July 25, 2000.

Humphreys, Joe. 2002. "With Prices On the Rise, Consumers Need to Become More Conscious of What Products Cost." *Irish Times*, June 22, 2002.

Jordan, Kieran. 2002. "Riverdance Revolutionizes Irish Dance, Inspires New Generation of Dancers." *Boston Irish Reporter*, July 2002.

Kenny, Kevin. 2003. *New Directions in Irish-American History.* Madison: University of Wisconsin Press.

———. 2006. "Race, Violence, and Anti-Irish Sentiment in the Nineteenth Century." In *Making the Irish American: History and Heritage of the Irish in the United States,* ed. J. J. Lee and Marion R. Casey, 364–78. New York: New York University Press.

Kerry Group. 2003. *Kerry Group Annual Report and Accounts 2003.* Dublin: Irish Dairy Board.

Kinsella, Jim, Susan Wilson, Floor de Jong, and Henk Renting. 2000. "Pluriactivity as a Livelihood Strategy in Irish Farm Households and Its Role in Rural Development." *Sociologia Ruralis* 40:481–96.

Kuhling, Carmen, and Kieran Keohane. 2002. "Case Studies in the Localization of the Global." In *Ireland Unbound: A Turn of the Century Chronicle,* ed. Mary P. Corcoran and Michel Peillon, 103–18. Dublin: Institute of Public Administration.

Madhavan, Cauvery. 2001. *Paddy Indian.* London: Black Amber Books.

———. 2003. *The Uncoupling.* London: Black Amber Books.

Marston, Sallie A. 1988. "Neighborhood and Politics: Irish Ethnicity in Nineteenth Century Lowell, Massachusetts." *Annals of the Association of American Geographers* 78:414–32.

McCann, Anthony. 2001. "All That Is Not Given Is Lost: Irish Traditional Music, Copyright, and Common Property." *Ethnomusicology* 45:89–106.

McCarthy, Marie. 1999. *Passing It On: The Transmission of Music in Irish Culture.* Cork: Cork University Press.

McCourt, Frank. 1996. *Angela's Ashes.* New York: Scribner.

Murphy, Jeremiah. 1998. *When Youth Was Mine: A Memoir of Kerry 1902–1925.* Mentor Press: Dublin.

Murphy, Seamus. 1950. *Stone Mad.* Belfast: Blackstaff Press.

Muthiah, S. "Three Authors from Madras." *The Hindu: India's National Newspaper* (online). February 17, 2003.

Myers, Kevin. 1998. Irishman's Diary. *Irish Times,* January 16, 1998.

———. 2000a. Irishman's Diary. *Irish Times,* September 27, 2000.

———. 2000b. Irishman's Diary. *Irish Times,* November 25, 2000.

National Consultative Committee on Racism and Interculturalism. 2004. *Reported Incidents Relating to Racism: May 2004 to October 2004.* Dublin: NCCRI.

O'Casey, Sean. [1957] 1994. "Playwright in Exile." In *The Green Crow: Selected Writings.* London: Virgin Publishing.

Ó Conghaile, Pól. 2001. "Defending the Faith: Islam in Ireland, Post-September 11th." *Irish American Post,* November 2001.

O'Crohan, Tomás. 1986. *Island Cross-Talk: Pages from a Blasket Diary.* Trans. Tim Enright. Oxford: Oxford University Press.

O'Dea, Clare. 2001. "Rents Soar As Supply Squeeze Bites." *Irish Times,* August 3, 2001.

O'Doherty, Caroline. 2002. "Car Prices Higher Here Despite EC Move." *Irish Times,* February 6, 2002.

O Rócháin, Muiris. 1989. Liner notes to *The Russell Family.* Ossian Publications.

O'Toole, Fintan. 1996. *The Ex Isle of Erin.* Dublin: New Island.

———. 1997. *The Lie of the Land.* London: Verso.

Riding, Alan. 1997. "The Arts Find Fertile Ground in a Flourishing Ireland." *New York Times,* December 21, 1997.

Ruane, Medb. 2000. "Celtic Tiger Fosters Greed and Poverty in Housing." *Irish Times,* September 15, 2000.

Soper, Kerry. 2005. "From Swarthy Ape to Sympathetic Everyman and Subversive Trickster: The Development of Irish Caricature in American Comic Strips between 1890 and 1920." *Journal of American Studies* (August): 257–96.

Sweeney, Paul. 1998. *The Celtic Tiger: Ireland's Economic Miracle Explained.* Dublin: Oak Tree Press.

Twohig, Patrick J. 1986–2002. *Chronicus* (diary). 2 volumes.

———. 1991. *The Dark Secret of Bealnablath.* Ballincollig, Cork: Tower Books.

———. 2001. *A Brief Catechism of the Catholic Church.* Ballincollig, Cork: Tower Books.

Ui Ógain, Rionach. 1995. "Traditional Music and Irish Cultural History." *Irish Musical Studies* 3:77–100.

United Nations. 2004. *United Nations 2004 Human Development Report.* New York: UN Human Development Reports Office.

Walter, Bronwen. 1985. "Ethnicity and Irish Residential Distribution." *Transactions of the Institute of British Geographers* (New Series) 11:131–46.

Wren, Maev-Ann. 2001. "Why Is Government Against Falling House Prices?" *Irish Times,* April 3, 2001.